Marguerite Duras Revisited

Twayne's World Authors Series
French Literature

David O'Connell, Editor
Georgia State University

TWAS 840

MARGUERITE DURAS
Photograph by John Foley

Marguerite Duras Revisited

Marilyn R. Schuster

Smith College

Twayne Publishers•New York
Maxwell Macmillan Canada•Toronto
Maxwell Macmillan International•New York Oxford Singapore Sydney

Marguerite Duras Revisited
Marilyn R. Schuster

Copyright © 1993 by Twayne Publishers
All rights reserved.

Twayne Publishers
Macmillan Publishing Company
866 Third Avenue
New York, New York 10022

Maxwell Macmillan Canada, Inc.
1200 Eglinton Avenue East
Suite 200
Don Mills, Ontario M3C 3N1

Library of Congress Cataloging-in-Publication Data

Schuster, Marilyn R.
    Marguerite Duras revisited / by Marilyn R. Schuster
        p. cm. — (Twayne's world authors series ; TWAS 840. French literature)
    Includes bibliographical references (p.) and index.
    ISBN 0-8057-8298-2
    1. Duras, Marguerite—Criticism and interpretation. I. Title. II. Series: Twayne's
world authors series ; TWAS 840. III. Series: Twayne's world authors series. French
literature.
PQ2607.U8245Z857 1993
843'.912—dc20   93-9411
                                                                          CIP

10 9 8 7 6 5 4 3 2 1

Printed in the United States of America

For Susan

Contents

Preface

The whole colony. The whole rotten refuse heap of the colonies, it's me. It's obvious. I was born of that. I was born of that and I write.

In this volume I revisit Marguerite Duras in many senses of the term. Alfred Cismaru first visited Marguerite Duras in the Twayne series in 1971. For this new Twayne volume, both the site and the visitor have changed. Since the first volume, Marguerite Duras has published more than twenty major works, written and directed nearly as many films, participated in more interviews than she probably should have, and produced articles, essays, and other occasional pieces too numerous to count. Her early works, often retold in later texts, look different in this new, richer context. In 1971 the bibliography of Duras's work was relatively slim. Duras said in 1974 that although her books were read abroad she thought there was practically a blackout in France; she thought of herself as a clandestine writer.[1]

This could hardly be said today. A proliferation of readings of Duras, special issues of literary magazines, and debates in France have turned Duras into a national monument in popular culture, not just literary circles. She is revered by some, reviled by others, but in any case essential to the landscape of contemporary French culture. Duras's work is well known in North America and England as well. In preparing this volume I compiled a bibliography of more than 350 titles in French and English on Duras's work; more than a third of these have appeared since 1985. The popular success of *The Lover* in 1984 accounts for some of this attention, after which many of her works have been translated or rereleased in translation. But the intense attention she has received goes beyond the remarkable success of one slim volume. Her narratives speak desire and destruction, the psyche and power in a relentless, mesmerizing style that fascinates her readers and provokes intense reactions. In recent years Parisian reviewers have divided themselves into "Durasophiles" and "Durasophobes"; no one is indifferent. Duras both confirms and challenges the deepest erotic impulses shaped by her culture and shared by most of her readers.

The Duras we read in English, however, is rather different from the French "Duras." Aside from scholars, American readers have focused on two or three texts and have not paid much attention to the full context of her work. Because she frequently reworks images, names, themes, and narrative structures, a failure to account for the full context of her writing leads to incomplete readings of any single text in a more serious way than with other writers. One might even say that it has led to a partial blackout of her work among American readers.

To revisit suggests having traveled through other places since a first exposure; having been other places, the visitor sees in a new way. Theoretical debates on both sides of the Atlantic have transformed our ways of reading. Interpretive strategies and postmodernist insights from deconstruction, psychoanalysis, feminism (both French and Anglo-American), and reader theory in particular raise new questions about Duras's work. Some of the chief architects of these theoretical approaches (Foucault, Cixous, Kristeva, and Lacan, for example) have given us their own readings of Duras. Duras has frequently condemned theory and has recently suggested that the work *about* her writing is often more difficult than the writing itself.[2] Nonetheless, we read differently now than we did twenty years ago, and a revisiting of Duras must take that into account.

Even though Duras has sometimes been characterized as a writer who stands outside literary movements and schools, from the vantage point of the 1990s her fictions anticipate, reflect, and shape the major literary problems of the past fifty years. She explored realism (though in an ironic mode) in her early novels, experimented with the dissolution of fictional conventions with the new novel in the late fifties and sixties, made films in the seventies, and engaged in the seduction of autobiography in the eighties. She both signs and inscribes "Duras" in disconcerting ways: In her stories she incorporates events from her life; in her autobiographical texts she uses stories to construct her life, in each case enticing or distancing the reader.

Duras elicits a special interest at this moment in literary history because she borrows from her bicultural upbringing and her experience as a woman during a time when Western European, male dominance has undergone serious scrutiny. In written texts, theater, films, and interviews she tests the generic borderlines, undermines the (false) cultural pairings, and explores (or empties) the psychic and textual spaces that have fascinated French and American readers in this postmodern, postcolonial period. And yet, her work is also characterized by a seeming sameness, an obsessive repetition—retelling the same story, reusing names, images, words, and dream fragments that echo from one text to another, slightly changed with each new context but hauntingly familiar. Many useful, legitimate frameworks have been used to read Duras. Absence and alienation, the body, nothingness, silence, love, desire, sorrow, forgetting, and destruction (among other recurring obsessions) have all been seen as structuring Duras's writing.[3] Some readers have chosen instead to organize her works by periods or cycles into realist novels, quest or travel novels, detective stories, the cycle begun by *The Ravishing of Lol Stein*.[4] Her more recent texts form an autobiographical cycle in which Duras represents herself explicitly, or implicitly, through a storyteller whose profile coincides with aspects of her persona. This cycle includes, for example, *The Lover, The War: A Memoir, Emily L., The North China Lover, Yann Andréa Steiner*, and many of the essays and articles collected in *Summer '80* and *Practicalities* as well as interviews beginning with *Les Parleuses* in 1974.

Sharon Willis, in her excellent book on Duras and writing on the body, has noted that "in their refusal of textual boundaries—their intertextual recall and perpetual rewriting—the texts from the 1960s to the present resemble more one long narrative than a series" (Willis, 3). I would suggest that even her earlier texts from the 1940s are part of this fluid, sometimes dizzying narrative stream. My goal in this book is to provide for the reader of Duras in English a sense of the full range of her expression, from the earliest novels to recent autobiographical texts, from written narratives to film experiments.

I argue that a woman's story is always at the center of Duras's long and varied narrative. The drama of Duras's work, taken as a whole, is her struggle to find the means to tell a woman's story. Borrowing from theory developed on both sides of the Atlantic, I propose a feminist reading of Duras. From her earliest novels, Duras represents woman as a split subject who is defined by powerful male figures but obliquely resistant to those definitions; she is an object of desire and bearer of life but disruptive of order and bearer of death as well. Duras represents woman as fragmented in her early works; she enacts or performs a split feminine subject through narrative strategies in her later works.

To propose a feminist reading, however, is not to suggest that Duras is a feminist writer. She resists efforts to reduce her writing to an argument in service of any politics.[5] More important, I argue that while she exposes the workings of an ideology of gender, power, and desire in which woman is "other" to man, she is also complicit with it. She unsettles the dominant ideology of Western European culture but continues to use its language; the speaker has changed, but the story remains intact.

Recent approaches to literature that incorporate the insights of cultural, queer, and postcolonial studies also enable us to see that figures of the homosexual, the colonial subject, and the Jew in Duras's writing are ideologically comparable to the figure of woman in her work. Just as she is complicit with an ideology of gender in which woman is "other," she participates in what Edward Said has defined as "Orientalism."[6] Said, looking at representations of the "Orient" in the social sciences and in writers such as Flaubert, shows that "European culture gained in strength and identity by setting itself off against the Orient as a sort of surrogate and even underground self" (Said, 3). His work, and work that has built on it since, maintains that the "Oriental" (and, by extension, other subjects who are not white, Western, European, Christian, and heterosexual) is represented as "other," in opposition to a self that depends on that "otherness" for its own stability. The "Oriental," as a cultural (and political) product of the West, reveals more about the workings of the dominant ideology than about its ostensible subject.

The epigraph to this preface[7] articulates the contradictory relation Duras maintains with French culture. At once formed and repulsed by the colonial system she was born into, her project is to write it, to express and expose it. This colonial context and her ambivalence toward it shape the woman's story she tells and retells. The force of Duras's writing depends, in part, on the simultaneous exposure and tacit maintenance of an ideology that represents "woman," the homosexual, the colonial subject, and the Jew as "other."

In the Introduction, I situate Duras's work in the context of current critical debates, particularly feminist literary theory as it has been elaborated in North America. I also examine the representation of woman that Duras begins to articulate in her earliest fictions and suggest how it sets terms that help interpret her later work. Chapter One discusses, briefly, the events of her life and the historical, cultural, and family context within which she writes. In the remaining chapters I discuss representative texts and films that demonstrate changing narrative strategies, especially the ways Duras represents "woman" throughout her work. I do not discuss her theater, with a few exceptions, because the problems of representation and interpretation in her plays are quite distinct from the problems raised by her prose and films. Chapter Two considers the novels and short stories of the 1940s and 1950s as parodies of realism, expressing her ambivalent relation to literary conventions. Chapter Three looks at the novels of the sixties, particularly the cycle of texts generated by *The Ravishing of Lol Stein*, in which she uses a male narrator to tell a woman's story. The movement toward a minimalist style in the sixties ended in an impasse that led Duras to abandon writing for filmmaking in the seventies. Chapter Four looks at the new narrative strategies she develops through making films. In Chapter Five, I look at Duras's return to writing in the eighties, at the erotic and autobiographical texts that turn her into a literary monument and a source of scandal in the current French literary scene, and at texts about writing that interrogate literature itself. Finally, in the Conclusion, I ask questions about the reception Duras's work has had in France and in the United States and about what our readings of her tell us about her work and about ourselves.

Acknowledgments

My debts, both intellectual and personal, as I complete this book are multiple and deeply felt. The many scholars interpreting the work of Marguerite Duras in France and the United States and the diverse and often tumultuous community of feminists working on theory and practice in North America have enriched and challenged my thinking at every step of the way. Several "Durassians" ("philes," "phobes," and in between) were especially generous with their time and resources—in particular, Deborah Glassman, Bernard Alazet, Vicki Mistacco, Catherine Portuges, Barbara Bray, and Aliette Armel. The staff at P.O.L. publishers kindly allowed me to use their archives on the reception of Duras's work in France. I am deeply indebted to the many colleagues at Smith College whose own work and whose critiques of mine have enriched my life for over twenty years, especially the Smith feminist theory group (Martha Ackelsberg, Leyla Ezdinli, Betsey Harries, Ann R. Jones, Jo Lee, Deborah Linderman, Ranu Samantrai, Cynthia Smith, Ruth Solie, Vicky Spelman, Nancy Sternbach, Susan Van Dyne) and other colleagues in the Women's Studies program.

My students at Smith have given me much to think about, and several have put in long hours to help me uncover the rapidly growing bibliography on Duras: Nancy Hunter, Katherine Linton, and Anna-Marie Russo. David O'Connell, the series editor, and Carol Chin at Twayne have been patient and helpful over the years. The Smith Committee on Faculty Compensation and Development provided funding that allowed me to travel to Paris to consult with Durassian scholars and view many of Duras's films.

Above all, I want to acknowledge in a public way my collaborator in work and in life, Susan Van Dyne, who read every word of every draft and who reminds me daily that we teach and write because we believe in it and because we enjoy it.

Permissions to quote from the English translations were granted by the following:
Editions Gallimard for *The Ravishing of Lol Stein.* Copyright 1964 by Editions Gallimard; Reprinted by permission of Georges Borchardt, Inc.

John Calder Publishers, Ltd., for "The Boa," from *Whole Days in the Trees*. Copyright 1954 by Editions Gallimard; translation copyright 1984 by John Calder Publishers Ltd.

The New Press for *The North China Lover*. Translation copyright 1992 by The New Press.

Random House, Inc. for *The Lover*, translated by Barbara Bray; translation copyright 1985 by Random House, Inc. and William Collins Sons & Co. Ltd. *Emily L.*, translated by Barbara Bray; translation copyright 1989 by Random House, Inc.; reprinted by permission of Pantheon Books, a division of Random House, Inc.

From *The Poems of Emily Dickinson*, Thomas H. Johnson, ed., Cambridge, Mass.: The Belknap Press of Harvard University Press, copyright 1951, 1955, 1979, 1983 by the President and Fellows of Harvard College. Reprinted by permission of the publishers and the Trustees of Amherst College.

Note on Translations

Most of Duras's major works have been translated into English. I quote published translations unless otherwise noted. For works that have been translated I have given publication information in the bibliography and in the first note referring to the work. I also include publication information for the French edition. In subsequent references within the text I indicate the page numbers for each edition, with the English translation first. For example, for *The Sea Wall* (*Un Barrage contre le Pacifique*), after the initial reference I indicate page numbers in parentheses after each citation, such as: (*SW*, 203; *B*, 221). For works that have not been translated I supply translations and give page references to the French edition.

Abbreviations of Titles

L'Amant: *A*; *The Lover*: *L*
L'Amant de la Chine du Nord: *AC*; *The North China Lover*: *NL*
L'Amante anglaise: *AA*; *L'Amante anglaise* (same in English): *AM*
L'Amour: *LA* (no translation)
Un Barrage contre le Pacifique: *B*; *The Sea Wall*: *SW*
Le Camion suivi de Entretien avec Michelle Porte: *C* (no translation)
La Douleur: *D*; *The War: A Memoir*: *W*
Emily L.: *E*; *Emily L.* (same in English): *EL*
Hiroshima mon amour: *H*; *Hiroshima mon amour* (same in English): *HM*
L'Homme assis dans le couloir: *HA*; *The Seated Man in the Passage*: *M*
L'Homme atlantique: *HAt* (no translation)
Des Journées entières dans les arbres: *J*; *Whole Days in the Trees*: *WD*
La Maladie de la mort: *MM*; *The Malady of Death*: *MD*
Le Marin de Gibraltar: *MG*; *The Sailor from Gibraltar*: *SG*
Nathalie Granger suivi de la Femme du Gange: *NG* (no translation)
Navire Night: *NN* (no translation)
Outside: Papiers d'un jour: *O*; *Outside: Selected Writings*: *OS*
La Pluie d'été: *PE*; *Summer Rain*: *S*
Le Ravissement de Lol. V. Stein: *LVS*; *The Ravishing of Lol Stein*: *LS*
Le Square: *S*; *Moderato Cantabile*: *MC*; *Dix heures et demi du soir en été*: *DH*; all
    found in *Four Novels by Marguerite Duras*: *FN*
Le Vice-Consul: *LVC*; *The Vice-Consul*: *VC*
La Vie matérielle: *VM*; *Practicalities*: *P*
La Vie tranquille: *VT* (no translation)
Yann Andréa Steiner: *Y* (no translation)
Yeux bleus cheveux noirs: *YB*; *Blue Eyes Black Hair*: *BE*
Les Yeux verts: *YV*; *Green Eyes*: *GE*

Chronology

1914   Marguerite Donnadieu born 4 April in Gia-Dinh, near Saigon, the daughter of Henri Donnadieu and Marie Legrand; has two older brothers, Pierre and Paulo, called "the little brother."

1918   Father appointed to post in Phnom Penh but takes ill and returns to France, where he dies a short time later.

ca.1919–1921   Marie Donnadieu takes her three children to Lot-et-Garonne to settle the estate of her husband.

1922   Marguerite sees a woman named Elizabeth Striedter, the inspiration of "Anne-Marie Stretter."

1924   Marie Donnadieu appointed to teach in a school for indigenous children at Sadek, then to Vinh-Long on the Mekong River; she purchases property near the Siamese border, hoping to farm, but the land proves unarable.

1926   Marguerite experiences a nervous crisis and shortly after leaves for Saigon to study.

1930   Meets the "Chinese lover."

ca. 1932   Returns to France with her family (though her mother and Paulo soon return to Indochina). Studies law and political science in Paris.

1939   Marries Robert Antelme.

1941   Her first manuscript, *La Famille Tameran*, turned down by Gallimard.

1942   Marguerite and Robert Antelme move to rue St-Benoît in the Latin Quarter. In May, she loses a child at birth. In summer, she meets Dionys Mascolo. Her brother Paulo dies in Saigon of bronchial pneumonia.

1943   Takes name Marguerite Duras when her first book, *Les Impudents*, is published. Enters Resistance, Mitterrand's group.

1944   *La Vie tranquille* published by Gallimard. Robert
       Antelme arrested and deported to Dachau. Marguerite
       joins Communist Party.

1945   Antelme returns to Paris, near death.

1946   Marguerite divorces Antelme.

1947   Has a son, Jean Mascolo, with Dionys Mascolo.

1950   Publishes *Un Barrage contre le Pacifique* (*The Sea Wall*).
       Leaves the Communist Party.

1952   *Le Marin de Gibraltar* (*The Sailor from Gibraltar*).

1953   *Les Petits Chevaux de Tarquinia.*

1955   Publishes *Le Square* (*The Square*) and *Des Journées entières
       dans les arbres* (*Whole Days in the Trees*), a collection of
       stories including "The Boa," "Madame Dodin," "The
       Building Site," and the title story.

1955–1960 Engages in political activity to protest the war in
           Algeria.

1958   *Moderato Cantabile* becomes a best-seller; Marguerite
       buys a house at Neauphle-le-Château, west of Paris.

1959   Writes scenario for *Hiroshima mon amour* and partici-
       pates in the film's production.

1960   *Les Viaducs de Seine-et-Oise*; *Dix heures et demie du soir en
       été* (*10:30 on a Summer Night*).

1961   *Une Aussi longue absence.*

1962   *L'Après-midi de M. Andesmas* (*The Afternoon of Mr.
       Andesmas*).

1964   *Le Ravissement de Lol. V. Stein* (*The Ravishing of Lol Stein*).

1965   Has first success in theater with production of *Des
       Journées entières dans les arbres*, Madeleine Renaud play-
       ing the lead; publishes *Le Vice-Consul* (*The Vice Consul*).

1966   *La Musica* (film).

1967   *L'Amante anglaise* (novel).

1968   *L'Amante anglaise* (theater).

1968   Participates in "events" of May in support of student
       strikers.

1969   Makes film *Détruire dit-elle* (*Destroy, She Said*).

1970   *Abahn, Sabana, David.*

1971   *Jaune le soleil* (film); *L'Amour.*

1972   Makes *La Femme du Gange* and *Nathalie Granger* (films).

1974   *Les Parleuses* (*Woman to Woman*), interviews with Xavière Gauthier; *India Song* (film).

1976   *Son Nom de Venise* (film).

1977   *Le Camion* (*The Truck*) (film); *L'Eden-cinéma.*

1979   Makes films *Le Navire Night, Césarée, Les Mains négatives,* and *Aurélia Steiner* (two short subjects with the same title).

1980   Hospitalized in January; Yann Andréa moves in with her in July; Marguerite publishes *L'Eté 80*; *Les Yeux verts*; *Vera Baxter*; and *L'Homme assis dans le couloir* (*The Man Sitting in the Corridor*).

1980–1981   Participates in colloquium in Montreal, published as *Marguerite Duras à Montréal*).

1981   Publishes *Agatha ou les lectures illimitées* and *Outside: Papiers d'un jour* (*Outside: Selected Writings*). Makes film *L'Homme atlantique*, published as a text in 1982.

1982   Makes *Dialogo di Roma* for Italian television; her play *Savannah Bay* produced. Enters the American Hospital at Neuilly in October for alcohol detoxification program, leaves in November (Yann Andréa chronicles her treatment in *M.D.*). Dictates the text of *La Maladie de la mort* (*The Malady of Death*) to Andréa.

1984   Videocassette edition of Duras's films published by Ministry of Culture. She makes film *Les Enfants* and in September publishes *L'Amant* (*The Lover*). Does television interview with Bernard Pivot on "Apostrophes," 28 September. Receives the Prix Goncourt 12 November.

1985   Hospitalized 17 April for short stay; writes article on Christine V. for *Libération* 17 July; does first interview with François Mitterrand on 24 July (published in *L'Autre Journal* as first of four in February 1986); publishes *La Douleur* (*The War: A Memoir*).

1986   *Les Yeux bleus cheveux noirs* (*Blue Eyes, Black Hair*); *La Pute de la côte normande.*

1987   *Emily L.*; *La Vie matérielle* (*Practicalities*).

1988   Does four hour interview with Luce Perrot on television in June and July. Goes into a coma in October that lasts five months, stays in the American Hospital until June 1989, and has a tracheotomy that leaves her with a breathing device in her throat.

1990   *Pluie d'été* (*Summer Rain*). Robert Antelme dies in October.

1991   *L'Amant de la Chine du Nord* (*The North China Lover*). Does television interview with Bernard Rapp for "Caractères" on 5 July.

1992   *Yann Andréa Steiner* published.

Introduction

Perhaps, before everything else, before being Duras, I am—simply—a woman.

Interview with Susan Husserl-Kapit

Like Duras reading herself in the epigraph to this chapter,[1] readers are often tempted to define an origin, a single, basic "truth" that takes precedence and explains—simply—everything in her work. But like the terms of this statement, what appears at first to be clarifying masks a vaster complexity. "Duras," after all, is an assumed name, taken when Marguerite Donnadieu (Madame Robert Antelme) published her first novel. Is the Duras referred to in this statement the girl born in Indochina in 1914 or the writer created in Paris in 1943? When Duras made this statement in 1975, one could no longer speak simply of *a woman*. French theorists were exploring the repression of the feminine and the possibility of *écriture féminine*; Anglo-American feminists, following Simone de Beauvoir in *The Second Sex*, rejected the idea that one is born a woman and were theorizing the cultural construction of gender. To speak of *woman* in the 1990s is an even less simple task. Many literary critics question the primacy of sexual difference or the possibility of a stable identity, asserting that the very concept of a separate, consistent "self" is a product of Western ideology and a discourse of dominance.

Duras, "Woman," and Women

Yet, like all myths of origin, Duras's statement of identity may have heuristic value, provided we remember that each term—in its abstraction and ambiguity—can lead in many directions. This book focuses on the woman's story that is always at the center of Duras's lifelong narrative. In revisiting Duras, I examine how *a woman's story* gets told at different moments and in different modes. Who tells it? Who is the "woman" inscribed in the text? Who is the presumed reader or spectator? How do "women" in their historical and cultural particularity complicate a "woman's" story?

What do I mean by *woman* here? *Woman* in the singular is the most vexed term in feminist theory today, especially in the United States. It is pivotal in the debates about essentialism that have stymied and stimulated the development of theory in literature and philosophy. The singular conjures an essentialist position. Diana Fuss has defined an essentialist position as a "belief in the real, true essence of things, the invariable and fixed properties which define . . . a given entity. In feminist theory, the idea that men and women . . . are identified as such on the basis of transhistorical, eternal, immutable essences."[2] American feminists have been highly critical of essentialist assumptions because they obscure historical and cultural differences. American feminists, mindful of the ways that the meaning of "woman" changes when inflected—as it always is—by race, ethnicity, historical moment, sexuality, age, class, and other markers of specific cultural positions, have resisted efforts to define woman in the abstract or to assume an eternal feminine. There is nothing singular or natural about "woman," the anti-essentialists would say; gender is a social and cultural construction whose meaning varies according to one's position within the culture.

A strict antiessentialist position, however, prevents us from accounting for the ways in which an essentialist definition of "woman" itself has functioned historically to determine the social construction of "woman" at specific historical moments in the service of the dominant class, race, and gender. Fuss argues that it is the deployment of essentialism that should interest feminist theorists rather than a wholesale condemnation of any position deemed to be essentialist. Her argument reminds feminists of one of our theoretical points of departure, at least in the United States: the politics of gender. How do representations of women and definitions of gender relations support or subvert larger power structures?

The constructionist position is not without other problems, particularly for the reader of women's texts. The social or cultural determinism on which the constructionist position is based makes discussion of female resistance to ideology and agency within it problematic at best. To what degree can a writer contest or reconfigure the construction of gender that has shaped her and the language she uses? One resolution to the question of agency for constructionists is to identify the gaps and contradictions within the culture that provide positions from which to critique. Those who are not entirely served by the assumptions of the culture, who stand somewhat outside the privileged power positions of the culture may begin to articulate resistance.

Judith Butler has proposed another approach to the problem of agency and the social construction of gender that is especially useful for literary critics. Rather than assume that identity (the gendered self) exists before action, that identity is to be discovered through its expression (social or literary), Butler suggests that gender is performative: "The distinction between expression and performance is crucial. If gender attributes and acts, the various ways in which a body shows or produces its cultural signification, are performative, then there is no preexisting identity by which an act or attribute might be measured."[3]

Butler notes that social sanction and cultural taboo regulate acceptable performances of gender and that the myths of true or essential masculinity and femininity conceal the "performative character" of gender. The culturally validated and policed performances of masculinity and femininity assume heterosexuality as the natural expression of desire. She asks: "How does language itself produce the fictive construction of 'sex' that supports . . . various regimes of power? Within a language of presumptive heterosexuality, what sorts of continuities are assumed to exist among sex, gender, and desire? . . . What kinds of cultural practices produce subversive discontinuities and dissonance among sex, gender, and desire and call into question their alleged relations" (Butler, xi)?

Discussions of essentialism and constructionism depend on a prior understanding of the relations between ideology and culture, ideology and language, culture and convention. Janet Todd in *Feminist Literary History* has identified ideology as one of the few terms to enter into both French and American feminist criticism "while retaining some residue of common significance."[4] The common significance is largely rooted in Louis Althusser's definition of ideology as "the imaginary relationship of individuals to their real conditions of existence."[5] Althusser's definition locates all subjects within ideology rather than assuming that ideology is a set of principles that one knowingly accepts or rejects.[6] As Janet Todd says, ideology "is not so much a clearly *false* representation of some truth as the truth itself as we know it, for we are all in ideology, and the various representative systems, such as the political, the religious or the mythical, are reflections of actual relations in which people live" (Todd, 85). Language in general and literary language in particular are representative systems articulating the ideology of the culture they express.

Literary conventions (established tropes or figures, patterns of plot, genres) are one means through which ideology is expressed. Because they are familiar, conventions are often transparent to the reader, they seem to provide an adequate expression of experience rather than a highly determined mediation between the writer and reader. Rachel Blau

DuPlessis summarizes the operation of literary conventions by saying "Any literary convention . . . as an instrument that claims to depict experience, also interprets it. No convention is neutral, purely mimetic, or purely aesthetic."[7]

In my discussion of Duras, I use the term *woman* in the singular in two ways: as an ideological and discursive product and position. First, *woman* in the singular designates a literary convention, a trope or figure of woman that has so dominated Western literature that it seems natural rather than a product of ideology. I am borrowing a formulation developed by Teresa de Lauretis: "By 'woman' I mean a fictional construct, a distillate from diverse but congruent discourses dominant in Western cultures." Specifically, as de Lauretis goes on to say, "*woman*, the other-from-man (nature and Mother, site of sexuality and masculine desire, sign and object of men's social exchange) is the term that designates at once the vanishing point of our culture's fictions of itself and the condition of the discourses in which the fictions are represented."[8] Many contemporary women writers contest the conventional figure of woman—woman as Other, gap, absence, silence, object of male desire. Monique Wittig, for example, rejects the word *woman* because it is contaminated by (misogynist) meanings; she maintains that *woman* is a product of masculine language. Duras seems, rather, to adopt the conventional figure of woman even while recognizing that it is a masculine construction, arbitrary and inadequate rather than transparently expressive of a natural, immutable reality.

The originality of Duras's use of the dominant figure of woman lies in how she positions the woman subject in her narrative, or, in Butler's terms, how she "performs" woman. My second sense of *woman* in the singular depends on Linda Alcoff's formulation of woman as positionality. Building on de Lauretis, she maintains that "the concept of woman is a relational term identifiable only within a (constantly moving) context; . . . the position that women find themselves in can be actively utilized (rather than transcended) as a location for the construction of meaning . . . rather than simply a place where a meaning can be *discovered* (the meaning of femaleness)."[9] Alcoff's formulation suggests that women are not merely subject to the cultural construction of *woman* but are also active subjects within their cultural context, capable of constructing meaning, within limits, and not just passive objects (sexual or cultural). Meanings are made, not discovered, but made within the limits of the (changing) context in which the writer is located. Her argument is compatible with Butler's idea of gender as performative. By performing "woman" differently, women writers might contest the construction of gender that has shaped them as women and as writers. Women, in other words, can complicate the woman question. Women can rewrite *woman*; by writing within and against the dominant figure of woman, contemporary women writers define and question the limits of its meaning. The plural *women*, in de Lauretis, Alcoff, and other feminist theory, is taken to mean historical subjects (Duras) in contrast to a cultural construction (a woman), to return to the epigraph to this chapter. Duras constantly interrogates the meanings of *woman* by telling a woman's story. She uses the dominant figure of woman, creating a female subject who is antagonistic to dominant ideology without being wholly oppositional. Rachel Blau DuPlessis, in her analysis of the oppositional stance of many twentieth-century English and American women writers toward the social and cultural construction of gender they inherited, shows that their opposition is made possible by their marginality in relation to the dominant culture. Subordinated within the ideology of their culture through gender, they are also, often, marginalized by race, class, sexuality, or colonial status. A woman writer might, however, seek "conformity and inclusion" as a personal, psychosocial defense rather than develop a critique as a political stance (DuPlessis, 33).

Duras is both culturally privileged and marginalized in her personal history. As a white, French girl in Indochina, she is aligned with the colonizer; as the daughter of a poor schoolteacher, who was widowed when Duras was young, she is marginalized by class. Returning to France at eighteen to continue her studies and lead her adult life, she is a "Creole," both inside and outside French cultural identity. In most of her writings she appears to maintain both the contradictory positions that DuPlessis identifies. She conforms to the dominant definition of woman and she critiques it.

Duras's work is of special interest to contemporary readers of both French and feminism because she is located in the gap between essentialism and constructionism. She exposes and examines the constructed character of *woman*, showing how the construction is articulated, by whom and in whose interest. She also writes, however, as if that construction expressed an essential truth, a transcendent rather than a contingent meaning of *woman*. She writes, in other words, as if the construction of woman she exposes were an immutable reality of women's lives.

The figure of woman that dominates Duras's work is remarkably consistent from her earliest writings to her most recent: other-from-man, object of male desire whose own desire is defined by men, absence, mother or lover, bearer of life, bearer of death, mad witness to a society that has formed her, insider and outsider. She uses, in Butler's terms, a language of "presumptive heterosexuality."

Duras moves from a representation of woman as a subject within narrative to a performance of woman through a feminine subject speaking a woman's story. In most of the works of the fifties and sixties a woman's story is mediated by male representation: A male narrator tells a woman's story, or a male character urges a woman to tell her story in his terms. Her film experiments in the seventies enabled Duras to develop an authorial and narrative voice in the feminine. The divisions within the representation of woman in the early works and the split female subject in later works are linked to an understanding of feminine sexuality as lack, dependent on male discovery, generative but potentially destructive. Although the first novels are less successful narratives than her later texts are, the representations of woman that Duras elaborates in them set terms that continue to inform her more recent work. *La Vie tranquille* (*The Tranquil Life*), published in 1944 and never translated, presents with special clarity what might be termed a Durassian "mirror stage" that forms the feminine "I."

The Tranquil Life: Reflections on Becoming a Woman

In an often-quoted commentary on *The Ravishing of Lol Stein*, Jacques Lacan stated that "it turns out that Marguerite Duras knows, without me, what I teach."[10] *The Tranquil Life*, written twenty years before *The Ravishing of Lol Stein*, centers on a mirror scene that incorporates important aspects of Lacan's mirror stage. Lacan's mirror stage concerns the eighteen-month-old child when he perceives himself as a seemingly autonomous subject and enters into the symbolic order of language. Duras's mirror scene in this novel centers on a young woman (here she is twenty-five, but in later works the eighteen-year-old woman will dominate) as she perceives herself as alien, or "other," before entering the social order and adult sexuality.

The Tranquil Life begins just after a bloody fight between a man and his nephew (Nicolas) in which both are deeply wounded. The uncle dies several days later. Nicolas's victory is sexual as well as physical—his uncle had had an affair with his wife and had been a tyrannical presence in their household for countless years. Nicolas's sister, Francine, is the

is feminine in French, the feminine pronouns in
image underscore the sexual metaphor and its
story with her sexuality. In the partially effaced
ipates the incomplete name of "Lol" for "Lola" in
ut more important, the "true story" or "true lack
he orange crate here will be taken up in the "hole
" that Jacques Hold will imagine as capable of
V. Stein.

st section of the novel, Francine returns home
a Lazarus-like return to life after three days of
ealth and, apparently, her mental equilibrium.
for her and their marriage is arranged, bringing
xual reintegration and creating the appearance of
ader knows, however, that this tranquillity is pre-
identity has been arbitrarily assumed. When she
f woman-as-other, it is a self-conscious act; she
structions of female sexuality. Both insider and
y split female subject can imagine no alternative
woman she discovers in her solitude, but she
ruction.

man she has become, will haunt Duras's work.
an illusion, apparently integrated into the social
sruptive of it, searching for the story that would
or express her, she will take on many other forms

teller of this tale, and she describes the opening scene in highly sexualized language, expressing Nicolas's manhood and her own muted incestuous desire. While the novel opens with Nicolas's seemingly victorious manhood, it is Francine's solitary rite of passage to womanhood that shapes the novel. The three parts of *The Tranquil Life* correspond to the three stages in Francine's becoming a woman: her obscure physical awakening, the solitary discovery of subjectivity, and her apparent reintegration into family and marriage. Francine had denounced her uncle to Nicolas, thus bringing about the fight that leads to death at the opening of the book. At the end of the first part, Nicolas's body is found, his suicide provoked by guilt and failure in love.

In this context of violence and death, Francine begins to become aware of her body through physical sensations aroused by her brother, her infant nephew, and her newly found lover, Tiène. For example, her sleeping nephew tries to suckle her: "The noise he made while trying to suck my breast, so delicate, made me discover that I had a body, still young under thick layers of ancient fatigue. I felt it shudder with pleasures so new, so fresh that I laughed by myself."[11] When Tiène caresses her, she becomes more fully aware of her body and the pleasures it can feel and arouse. Her nascent awareness of her body is thus mediated and defined by the child and her lover, awakening her as potential mother and mistress.

If, in the first part, Francine slowly discovers her physical self through others, in the second part she confronts herself alone at a seaside hotel. In *The Tranquil Life*, as in later novels by Duras, to be "en vacances," is to enter a vacant state, absent from the familiar. Alone in her room, Francine confronts the mirror in two dramatic scenes. First: "There, in my room, it's me. One would think that she no longer knows that it's about her. She sees herself in the wardrobe mirror" (*VT*, 121). The pronoun shift from "I" to "she" and the insertion of an observing "one" dramatize the split self that Francine is experiencing. In Lacan's account of the mirror stage, the child's subjectivity emerges when he discovers his image. The mirror image creates the joyful sensation of a coherent, recognizable identity. But the self discovered in the mirror image is a fiction, and a fiction that splits identity in two even as it creates the illusion of wholeness and coherence. Jacqueline Rose summarizes Lacan as follows:

> The mirror image is central to Lacan's account of subjectivity, because its apparent smoothness and totality is a myth. The image in which we first recognise ourselves is a *misrecognition*. . . . The "I" with which we speak

stands for our identity as subjects in language, but it is the least stable entity in language, since its meaning is purely a function of the moment of utterance. . . . For Lacan, the subject is . . . constituted in language *as* this division or splitting.[12]

Kaja Silverman further develops the implications of Lacan's mirror stage by stressing that the child's initial perception of self "is induced through a culturally mediated image which remains irreducibly external, and which consequently implants in the child a sense of otherness at the very moment that identity is glimpsed. . . . Subjectivity is thus from the very outset dependent upon the recognition of a distance separating the self from other."[13] Unlike the effect on Lacan's child who experiences a joyful moment of recognition (albeit illusory) when he encounters his image, Francine's (adult, female) mirror stage dismantles the myth of a coherent self. She experiences the distance separating her self as observer from her self as observed. Francine's experience of the mirror image is exactly opposite to the child's as described by Lacan. The Lacanian child experiences a sense of wholeness as he gains access to language, though the sensation is based on a fiction. Francine experiences a fragmentation of self as she uncovers the fiction of the mirror image; her split subjectivity is expressed through the use of both the first and third-person pronouns in the language of the narrative.

Duras goes on in a second, more elaborated mirror scene to spell out how the image that Francine encounters is culturally mediated and to link it to female sexuality. Her second night in the hotel, she no longer recognizes the woman in the mirror. She tries to eliminate her by closing the wardrobe so that the mirror is no longer in her field of vision. But the image proliferates in her mind, both "fraternal," as she puts it, and "foreign," and finally she appropriates as her identity the most familiar image of herself. The self she chooses to become is shown to be both arbitrary and inadequate, but it is there, ready-made. The "other" that Francine takes on as her identity is recognizable to her because it is how she has been seen (by her brother, among others); this "self," though it does not quite fit, is an available construction of the female. "Who was I, whom had I taken for me until then? Even my name didn't reassure me. I was unable to place myself in the image I had just come upon. I floated around her, very close, but between us there was a sort of impossibility of bringing us back together" (*VT*, 122–23).

Slowly she recounts her own story to herself, recreates memories in an effort to assume by an act of will and of language a past she had lived

Chapter One
A Telling Life

One never knows the story before it is written.

Marguerite Duras, *Yann Andréa Steiner*

The precarious identity that Francine constructs in *The Tranquil Life* is shored up by stories she tells herself and enacts for others. She becomes the subject she tells, taking her place in society but keeping for herself the unspeakable knowledge that the woman she has become is a performance, an effect of language. Anyone trying to recover an authentic narrative of Marguerite Duras's life is faced with a dilemma similar to that experienced by the reader of Francine: stories told in interviews, fictions, plays, and films create an infinite regression. The subject constantly refers back to itself as stories are built on other stories, retold in slightly changed settings, revised as time passes.

Although there is an abundance of material about her life, it is difficult to know the woman.[1] Duras has said repeatedly that dates and the kind of facts biographers seek to verify are of no concern to her. What matters is the story of the unconscious, of what lives beneath the surface of "objective" data. For many of the events in her life, however, especially concerning her childhood in Indochina, she is the only remaining witness. No two "chronologies" of her life given in biographies, interviews, or special issues of literary magazines are exactly alike. For example, in her autobiographical works she often talks about Paulo, the "little brother" she loved so intensely. Some, taking "little" to mean "younger," give 1917 as his date of birth—three years after Duras's. Elsewhere she has said that he was "little" in relation to their other brother, Pierre, whom she dreaded physically and psychologically, but that she was the youngest of the three children. In this scenario, Paulo was born in 1912, two years before his sister.

A similar problem arises when we try to determine when Paulo died. In *The Lover* and in *The War: A Memoir*, Duras says that he died of bronchitis in Saigon in 1942 during the Japanese Occupation because he couldn't get proper medication. But she also says that he was twenty-seven when he died. If he had been twenty-seven, he would have been

1

born in 1914 or 1915, about the same time as Duras herself. It seems safe to say that the age she ascribes to him at death has a meaning that is more significant to her than historical accuracy. In her fiction, age twenty-seven comes to represent a moment of irreparable loss. The characters who most closely resemble her in her fiction identify very closely with the "little" brother. By giving him her age at his death she shows that a part of her has died. In *The Lover*, at the moment when the young girl separates forever from her older, Chinese lover, he is twenty-seven. Throughout her work, radical separation from a loved man creates an internal absence for the woman who goes on, an absence that becomes the space of the imagination and desire and writing.

It is difficult to know many verifiable details of Duras's life for another reason. Since 1984, when *The Lover* brought her intense public attention, journalists, critics, and would-be biographers have tended to read her fictions as if they were unmediated representations of her life. As we shall see in chapters 5 and 6, she has colluded with this tendency even while mocking it. A recent biography is a telling example. In *Duras*, Alain Vircondelet moves back and forth between texts (fiction, interviews, documents, other peoples' accounts) without making any distinctions and often without indicating the source of quoted material. The book becomes a personal meditation inspired by Duras's works and life, riffs that rework Durassian themes, telling more about the biographer than his subject.

Whether out of discretion or self-defense, Duras has also been silent about some aspects of her life. She usually will not name her lovers, she rarely discusses friendships, and except when his professional life has joined hers, she has rarely talked about her son, Jean Mascolo. There are other moments she refers to only obliquely, if at all. Given all these limitations, it is, nonetheless, possible to reconstruct a partial picture of Duras's life, which is interesting to us, finally, because of her work.

A Colonial Childhood

Marguerite Duras was born Marguerite Donnadieu on 4 April 1914 in Gia-Dinh, a suburb of Saigon. Her mother (née Marie Legrand) had gone to French Indochina in 1905 to teach indigenous children—a low-status position in the hierarchy of colonial life. She was the daughter of farmers from Pas-de-Calais in northern France and, according to Duras, her peasant temperament was closer to the Indochinese peasants than to the French colonists with whom she had to interact. Marie Legrand met Henri Donnadieu, a math teacher, in Indochina. He had come from southwest France—the department of Lot-et-Garonne, near the Dordogne region. Marguerite Donnadieu had two brothers, both of whom were probably older than she. In 1918 her father, Henri Donnadieu, was named to a post in Phnom Penh. He contracted amoebic dysentery shortly after the family moved to Cambodia and returned alone to France for treatment. He died a short time later, in France. In accounts she has given of her childhood since *The Lover* was published in 1984, Duras has always emphasized her Creole origins ("I'm Creole. I was born over there," she said on television that year[2]), that she is a child of the colonies who grew up speaking Vietnamese as fluently as French, that she knew only the light clothes of the tropics, the forests where her brother hunted panthers, and that she ate only Asian food, finding apples and beef strange and unappealing. Sometime after her husband died, however, Marie Donnadieu took her children back to his home in southwest France for the two years it took to sell his property and settle the estate. Duras has referred briefly to this period at least twice (Porte, 16, and Lamy, 57). The dark, brooding rural setting in southwest France that characterizes her first two published novels is informed by these two difficult years from her early childhood.

The family returned to Cambodia in 1920 or 1921. Duras's mother took a position at Sadek and then in Vinh-Long on the Mekong River. Duras has said, repeatedly, that when she was about eight years old she saw a woman named Elisabeth Striedter, the wife of a colonial administrator, who would become the model for Anne-Marie Stretter in the Lol V. Stein cycle of texts and films. She says she learned that a young man had killed himself because of his love for Elisabeth Striedter, who was a married woman with two daughters around the same age as Marguerite. In 1977, Duras received an invitation from Odile Le Roy, the granddaughter of Elisabeth Striedter, to hear her grandmother speak in her retirement home outside Paris. Duras did not go but after the event received a note from Striedter saying that Duras was right not to contact her: "Through the young woman that I was, your imagination created a fictional image whose charm comes, exactly, from that mysterious anonymity that should be preserved."[3] A year later, Duras found Elisabeth Striedter's obituary in the newspaper.

Sometime between 1924 and 1926, Duras's mother took her savings to the colonial authorities to purchase a "concession," or farming property, in rural Prey-Nop in the Kampot province of Cambodia near the Siamese border. Naive about the workings of the colonial bureaucracy, Marie Donnadieu was unaware that good land could be purchased only with considerable bribes. After moving to their bungalow in Prey-Nop and planting rice, the family discovered that the China Sea inundated their land for six months of every year. After trying unsuccessfully to construct dikes to hold back the tides, the mother returned with her children to Vinh-Long, though she kept the worthless Prey-Nop property for a number of years. This episode marked Duras profoundly and would be told and retold in *The Sea Wall, Eden Cinéma, The Lover,* and *The North China Lover.*

About the same time as the injustice her mother was suffering at the hands of colonial authorities, Marguerite was undergoing a nervous crisis linked to puberty. She often refers with indignant intensity to the suffering her mother endured because of a capricious, corrupt exercise of political power. Sometimes she links her personal drama, a traumatic experience of menarche—seemingly endless blood issuing from her body over a period of months—to those events.

A short time after the family returned to Vinh-Long, Marguerite went to Saigon to study. In many of the interviews she gave after *The Lover* was published, Duras said that around 1930 she met the Chinese man who would become her lover. In *The Lover,* and again in 1991 in *L'Amant de la Chine du nord (The North China Lover),* Duras makes a special point of not naming the lover, maintaining his anonymity. In an interview in the summer of 1992, however, she talked about the last time she spoke to him, on the telephone in Paris: "He didn't even say 'It's Thuylê.' He only said: 'It's me.'"[4] Having learned of his death, she was free to name him. She was also embattled with the director of the film of *The Lover,* which at the time she gave the interview was a hit in Paris; naming the Chinese lover gave her a chance to reassert her authority as sole witness and to reconfirm the historical accuracy of the story.

In 1932, when she was eighteen, Marguerite returned to France for good on a ship that traveled west following the Indian coast, then north to the Suez Canal and the Mediterranean. Again, Duras's own writings are contradictory about the date of her return to France. She often says she returned when she was eighteen; sometimes she specifies 1932. But a short piece she included in *La Vie matérielle (Practicalities),* published in 1987, would suggest otherwise.[5] In "The train from Bordeaux," Duras says that when she was sixteen, in 1930, *after* the Chinese lover and her return to France from Saigon, she took a night train from Bordeaux to Paris with her family. While her family slept, she and an anonymous stranger had sex; he left the train in the darkness, before it reached Paris: "When I opened my eyes in Paris his seat was empty" (*P,* 75; *VM,* 85).

"The train from Bordeaux" recounts in an autobiographical mode the same story of an anonymous lover in a night train that will mark the "mother" in *Summer Rain*, published in 1990. In this instance, as in so many others, correspondences between these two texts (*Practicalities* and *Summer Rain*) are probably more significant than any possible (unverifiable) correspondence between Duras's life and her text, "The train from Bordeaux."

What is certain, though, is that Duras left Indochina definitively about 1932 and that the experience of growing up in the colonies—privileged by race and national origin but marginalized by class and gender—would profoundly mark her work. In a conversation with Elia Kazan in 1980, she said: "I never could and I never will return to my native land. . . . I don't feel French" (*GE*, 157; *YV*, 200).

Marguerite Donnadieu becomes Marguerite Duras

Marguerite's mother and "little" brother returned to Saigon almost immediately. Her older brother stayed in France, where their mother would join him in 1949. In Paris, Marguerite studied law and political science while exploring intellectual and cultural life, particularly the theater. In 1937 she got a job at the Colonial Ministry. Three years later, she co-authored a book (as Marguerite Donnadieu) called *L'Empire français* (*The French Empire*) with Philippe Roques. Responding to recent criticisms that it is a reactionary argument in favor of French imperialism, she has said: "That's false, it's just a description of French possessions at that time. . . . It's perhaps as boring as a book by Roland Barthes because the imagination plays no role in it at all" (Ezine, 55).

During her student years, Marguerite met Robert Antelme, who was also a law student. They married in 1939 and were able, through their friends Betty and Ramon Fernandez, to get an apartment on the rue Saint-Benoît in the sixth arrondissement, where Duras continues to live today. In 1942, the same year she learned of her "little" brother's death in Saigon, Duras lost a child at birth in part because a doctor couldn't get to her in time owing to the Occupation. It was only in 1976 that she publicly mourned the loss of her first child at birth in an article for the feminist periodical *Sorcières*.[6]

The apartment on the rue Saint-Benoît has often been the scene of political activity—when Duras participated in the Resistance during the war, when she and Antelme were active in the Communist Party, and later during the events of May 1968, when Duras sympathized with student protesters. The exact history of her political affiliations is not always easy to trace, in part because she has often resisted aligning herself with a party line of any sort. In his recent biography of Duras, Alain Vircondelet says that after Duras left the Colonial Ministry when Pétain came to power in 1940, she worked for the "Cercle de la librairie," which recommended what manuscripts could be published using the limited, rationed paper available to publishers. It was not until 1943 that she, Antelme, and a new friend, Dionys Mascolo, joined the resistance network established by François Mitterrand a year earlier.

On 1 June 1944, Robert Antelme was arrested and deported by the Gestapo for his involvement in the Resistance. Duras recounts the long wait for his return from Dachau a year later in *The War: A Memoir*, published in 1985. While Antelme was gone, Duras joined the Communist Party. In *The War: A Memoir* she dismisses the seriousness of her commitment to the party by saying that it was an effort to find a political solution to a personal problem, intimating that it provided a sense of connection in a time of anguish and confusion. She has often said that she is sympathetic with the ideals of communism but finds the French party lacking. In 1950, after a dispute with Jacques and Colette Martinet, who were trying to control the direction of the party cell to which Duras, Antelme, and Mascolo belonged, Duras left the party. In her letter of resignation she said: "I remain a communist, profoundly, organically. I've belonged for six years. . . . My confidence in the Party is intact. I am even sure that with time the Party will reject the Martinets. . . . I think that, in reality, the Martinets were mistaken about their vocation. They shouldn't have joined the P.C. [the Parti Communiste] but the fire department (where, in addition to the prestige conferred by a uniform, they might have been able to take an occasional, salutary shower), or the priesthood where they would have been amused by the delights of the confessional" (Vircondelet, 168–70).

When Antelme returned in 1945, discovered near death at Dachau by Mitterrand and returned to Paris by Mascolo, Duras nursed him back to health. She had already decided, however, to end their marriage because she wanted to have a child with Dionys Mascolo. She divorced Antelme in 1946; they remained friends and worked on several projects together. She had a son, Jean, with Mascolo the next year. Her personal relationship with Mascolo ended ten years later, although they, too, continued to collaborate on many projects.

In the midst of all the personal and political upheaval of the 1940s, Marguerite Donnadieu became Marguerite Duras when she published her first novel with Plon in 1943: *Les Impudents*. Though Gallimard had rejected the manuscript (as *La Famille Tameran*), their reader, Raymond Queneau, had expressed interest in it. As *Les Impudents* was being published, Duras was working on her second novel, *The Tranquil Life*, which Gallimard published in 1944. After the war she enjoyed her first, major critical success with the publication in 1950 of *Un Barrage contre le Pacifique* (*The Sea Wall*). Unlike her first two novels, *The Sea Wall* draws on the Indochinese landscape of her childhood. The book nearly won the Goncourt Prize, which Duras received, finally, thirty-four years later for *The Lover*, which rewrites the earlier novel in many respects. Duras has said on numerous occasions that she did not win the Goncourt in 1950 because they did not want to give the prize to a woman or a Communist.

A curious gap separates Duras's personal experience in these early years and her writing. In recent years, Duras has frequently and emphatically identified with the suffering of the Jews in the Holocaust, writing in the first person, for example, through Aurélia Steiner, a Jewish character whose parents are killed in the camps. The question of Jewish identity and suffering, however, did not enter her work in the wake of World War II, but only after the events of May 1968. Many people have maintained that Duras, like most of her contemporaries, did not know the full horror of the concentration camps until after April 1945, when the survivors, including her husband, returned as witnesses. But even *The War: A Memoir* is a text of the eighties rather than a postwar work.

Janine Ricouart, in a recent study of violence in the works of Duras, has astutely observed that the image of the Jew first appeared in Duras's writing in *Un Homme est venu me voir*, a play from 1968, and *Abahn Sabana David* in 1970.[7] When de Gaulle tried to discredit the student revolt of 1968 by calling the leader, Daniel Cohn-Bendit, "a German Jew," the students and their sympathizers shouted back "We are all German Jews" to proclaim their solidarity and to expose the anti-Semitism of the Gaullist regime. Ricouart maintains that this political slogan provided an image of alliance with the marginalized that Duras adopted in her work. As Ricouart says, Duras uses the image of the Jew as a "symbol of all difference" (Ricouart, 13). In other words, the image of the Jew entered Duras's work as an abstraction, meant to stand for otherness. In chapter 4, we will see that this appropriation of the image of the Jew poses some problems. By constituting the Jew as "other" (as she will also do with colonized peoples, homosexuals, women, and children), Duras abstracts Jewish experience; she replaces the historical experience of Jews with the image of the Jew. While she professes sympathy, the singular abstraction she creates tends to obliterate the diversity of lived experience, including resistance to being reduced to the "Other."

In the fifties, Duras established her reputation as a writer to be watched and continued her political activity. In *Le Square*, published in 1955, Duras uses a new, minimalist style that met with mixed reviews but that would permanently change her approach to narrative. *Moderato Cantabile* in 1958 sparked an even more mixed critical response, but clearly set the terms for her work to come. Claude Roy, a friend of Duras, praised *Moderato Cantabile* in *Libération* on 1 March 1958, calling it "Madame Bovary rewritten by Bela Bartok."[8] Not all critics were as enthusiastic. *Moderato Cantabile* did, however, give her some measure of financial security, and she bought an old house in Neauphle-le-Château, which she later used in the film *Nathalie Granger*. In her conversations with Michelle Porte in 1977, Duras talked about the importance of place to her, particularly this place, this eighteenth-century house inhabited by many generations of women who left no written trace of their existence.

During the fifties Duras started to write regularly for the popular and political press—a practice that continues today with her occasional pieces for the leftist paper *Libération*. A frequent contributor to *France-Observateur*, Duras wrote on film and popular culture as well as on political issues. She also contributed to *Vogue* and, later, during the women's movement, to the feminist journal *Sorcières*. In 1955 Duras and her friends joined other French intellectuals to express solidarity with Algerians as the French government waged war to keep its colony. Three years later, Dionys Mascolo and Jean Schuster established a journal called *Le 14 juillet* to provide a more varied forum for leftist political writing. In 1958 she took her co-workers at *France-Observateur* to task for criticizing the formation of *Le 14 juillet* (*O*, 86–87). She defends the need for a diversity of views and is characteristically critical of political journals that impose a single editorial voice or vision (*O*, 86–87). Duras's activism concerning Algeria and, later, during the events of 1968, make her silence about the war in Indochina before Dien Bien Phu in 1954 even more striking.

Duras's writing, while often compared to that of the "new novelists" like Alain Robbe-Grillet and Nathalie Sarraute, who also published at the Editions de Minuit (which published *Moderato Cantabile*), is less and less easy to categorize by genre or movement. In the late fifties and early sixties, Duras made two discoveries that would have a long-term effect on her writing. First, she adapted some of her works, such as *The Square*, for the theater and then wrote directly for the stage. Second, she wrote the scenario for Alain Resnais's film *Hiroshima, mon amour* in 1959 and participated in the production. The experience was a financial disaster for Duras, who took a flat fee instead of a percentage, but it brought her to the attention of a much larger public and introduced her to filmmaking. Other filmmakers adapted Duras's earlier texts to the cinema with mixed results. In 1957, René Clément made a film based on *The Sea Wall*; Peter Brook adapted *Moderato Cantabile* in 1960 with Jeanne Moreau in the lead role; Tony Richardson chose Moreau again for the lead in his adaptation of *The Sailor from Gibraltar* in 1967. Duras has been very dismissive of these film adaptations while recognizing that some of them were financially beneficial to her. The film of *Moderato Cantabile*, for example, allowed her to buy an apartment at the Roches Noires in Trouville on the coast of Normandy, which she has used as a setting for some of her own films and many of her texts of the eighties.

As a result of her success with *Moderato Cantabile*, Duras was invited to serve on the jury for the Médicis prize in 1960, taking her place as an arbiter of quality in contemporary fiction. She was partly responsible for Monique Wittig's prize for *The Opoponax* in 1964. By the end of the sixties, Duras had established herself as an important novelist and playwright to some, an obscure and difficult writer to others; while she was as often critical of friends on the left as she was of the government, she was known as a sympathizer with leftist, anti-Gaullist political causes.

1970 to the Present

As chapter 4 will show, Duras turned to filmmaking in the 1970s and while she developed a small but faithful following among serious students of cinema, she was less and less available to many of her readers. She continued both her journalistic and political activities. She contributed to the feminist journal *Sorcières* and signed the "Manifesto of the 343," in *Le Nouvel observateur* in April 1971. This was one of the first big, public acts of the French women's movement. A manifesto demanding free and legal access to contraception and abortion was signed by 343 women, many of them very well known, who declared that they had had abortions—thus testing the French law criminalizing abortion.

In 1974, Duras participated in a lengthy set of taped interviews with the feminist Xavière Gauthier that were transcribed and published as *Les Parleuses* (*Woman to Woman*). In some ways this interview, in which Duras explores her thoughts about everything from desire to politics, is a prototype of the many interviews Duras would do on French television and radio and for the press in the late eighties, after the publication of *The Lover*. Her relation to feminism, like her relation to other political movements, is at once sympathetic and distant. She signed the manifesto and has spoken out on many occasions in support of women's legal and political issues. At the same time, her understanding of what constitutes women's experience is in many ways deeply conservative. For example, she has emphatically equated fully realized womanhood with motherhood. In 1981, in an interview with Suzanne Lamy, Duras said unequivocally: "I know that if one doesn't have a child, one has lost half the world. . . . The function of maternity is irreplaceable. Homosexuality will never know maternity. That's its immeasurable poverty" (Lamy 66).

Like the image of the Jew, however, the image of the child is often an abstraction in Duras's fictions and films, assuming the role of the "other." *Nathalie Granger* embodies an outlaw violence, Ernesto in *Summer Rain* is a sort of idiot savant, assuming in his character a radical knowledge that is disruptive of established systems and, ultimately, of God. Other children, such as the child in *Moderato Cantabile*, seem to function as signs to mark the maternity of the primary, female characters, the better to signal their transgression as desiring female subjects, adulterers.

Her life and her work change dramatically in the eighties because of Yann Andréa and *The Lover*. Yann Andréa, a young homosexual student from Caen, wrote several admiring letters to Duras in 1979. In *Practicalities* she says: "The affair . . . started when I was sixty-five, with Y.A., who's a homosexual. That's probably the most unexpected thing that's happened to me in the latter part of my life—the most terrifying and the most important" (*P*, 69; *VM*, 79). In another piece in *Practicalities* she says that she met Yann, thirty-five years her junior, at a screening of *India Song* in Caen. He wrote her several letters, which she did not answer. Then, after being hospitalized in January 1980, she wrote Yann about the drinking and blackouts that sometimes landed her in the hospital. In July 1980 he called to ask her if he could come to her at Roches Noires: "He left his home and his job. And he stayed" (*P*, 128; *VM*, 143).[9] She rewrites the story of their encounter in *Yann Andréa*

Steiner, which takes up again elements of both *Practicalities* and *L'Eté 80*.
In the title, *Yann Andréa Steiner*, Duras merges his identity with Aurélia
Steiner, incorporating him into her work in a name that blurs gender
while conferring Jewish identity.

As the story of her encounter with Andréa illustrates, Duras's long-
standing problem with alcohol—and smoking—caught up with her in
the 1980s. She has been hospitalized numerous times. Her harrowing
detoxification treatment for alcoholism at the American Hospital in
Neuilly in October and November 1982 is documented in great detail in
Yann Andréa's book *M.D.* In October 1988 she was again hospitalized at
Neuilly and, for reasons the doctors could not determine, went into a
coma that lasted for five months. She stayed in the hospital until June
1989; a tracheotomy has left her with a breathing apparatus in her
throat. In the television interview for "Caractères" that she did in July
1991, her voice is altered by the metal tube, barely disguised by a scarf.

When Duras published *The Lover* in 1984, she returned to the
Indochinese landscape that she had abandoned after "The Boa," in 1954.
Written in the first person, the book was read almost exclusively as autobiography at a time when many writers, such as Sarraute and Robbe-
Grillet, were also turning to that mode. The tremendous commercial
and critical success of *The Lover* turned Duras, who had been a relatively
private person, into a media star. She has been asked for her opinions on
everything and has been criticized for speaking about issues she understands only superficially.

She created a sensation in France when she wrote an article for
Libération on 17 July 1985, about a case known as the "affaire
Grégory."[10] The article, characterized by the editor of *Libération* as a
writer's fantasy about a crime, concerns Christine Villemin (whom Duras
calls Christine V. in the article), accused of murdering her child, whose
body was found in 1984. Fascinated by the case—as she had been by a
newspaper story about the murder that inspired *L'Amante anglaise* in the
sixties—Duras tried unsuccessfully to meet Villemin, and traveled to the
rather desolate town in Vologne where she lived. In her article, she
argues that Villemin murdered her child but that she is not guilty. Duras
claims to recognize in Villemin's absent gaze (seen in a photograph) the
madness induced by an abusive marriage and the emptiness of provincial
life. She calls the crime "sublime." Duras's fascination with woman as
bearer of life and of death is played out again using the figure of
Christine Villemin.

The *Libération* article caused an immediate, angry reaction in France. Many were astounded that Duras declared the woman a murderer, when the accused denied having committed the crime, at a moment when the case was still being heard. Some women protested that Duras was unforgivably arrogant to speak in the name of all women in her article, assuming a feminist authority and reducing women's experience to an abstraction they did not recognize. The phrase Duras used in the article to characterize Villemin ("sublime, forcément sublime") has been parodied countless times since to ridicule Duras and her style.

Duras's life and writing have been marked by other sensational quarrels in the last few years as well. Her falling out with Claude Berri and Jacques Annaud (the producer and director of the film adaptation of *The Lover*) will be discussed in chapter 5. While preparing her 1991 novel, *The North China Lover*, Duras ended her long-standing friendship and collaboration with Jérôme Lindon, her editor at the Editions de Minuit, and returned to the Editions Gallimard.

The boundaries between Duras's life and her work have been increasingly blurred in recent years. Considering the place of writing in her life, and the reworkings of her life in her writing, it would, perhaps, be wise to consider the statement she made to a friend in 1985 and to look to her texts rather than to her life to measure the meaning of Duras: "True writers have no life at all. . . . My books are truer than myself."[11]

Chapter Two

Coming of Age Stories: Defining the Woman and the Writer

The Tranquil Life, discussed in the Introduction, recounts the coming of age of a (divided) female subjectivity through the character of Francine. Most of Duras's works of the early fifties are stories of female coming of age. As in *The Tranquil Life*, Duras writes within or against available terms for feminine subjectivity, sexuality and textuality, testing available meanings of "woman," "writer," and "fiction." As I look at early coming of age stories by Duras in which gender shapes terms for both writing and reading, I will draw on American feminist critics, particularly as they have used reader theory. American feminist literary critics have examined the meanings of "woman," "writer," and "fiction" by focusing on gynocritical texts, texts written by women, and by looking at their own practice as readers.

For the most part, French feminist theory has been more concerned with the "feminine" as an effect of language rather than with the material conditions of women's lives. French feminist readings have tended, therefore, to focus on "écriture féminine" (feminine writing) or the repression of the "feminine" in both male and female writers. As Elaine Marks, Domna Stanton, and Nancy Miller have pointed out, however, it does matter, for the time being at least, who signed the texts we read.[1] Most feminist critics who have read Duras's texts have used French theoretical models and have sought to show that she provides a model for "écriture féminine" or that she inscribes an antifeminist, though feminine, position in her work.[2] According to most of the readings of Duras rooted in French theoretical models, the feminine is repressed in discourse, is inarticulate, and therefore disrupts or destablilizes (masculine) language at moments of silence or disjuncture. The Lol V. Stein cycle, particularly the formulation of a "hole word" or "absence word" to express Lol's subjectivity, has preoccupied many of these critics.

American critics have shown that the voices of women writers are articulated through a negotiation between their experience of the dominant myths and stories of their culture and their subversive experience of

13

forbidden, suppressed, or repressed texts: other women's writing, their reading of men's texts, their own desire. The inflection of gender with race, ethnicity, sexuality, and class is central to American feminist critics, growing out of an awareness of the multicultural character of American literatures. As Teresa de Lauretis has observed, the writings of American feminists of color have been particularly useful in unveiling the complicity of feminism with a gender ideology that maintains a single view of "woman" that obscures the ways race, ethnicity, and sexuality complicate gender. The relation of gender ideology to other forms of cultural oppression (racism, anti-Semitism, heterosexism, and colonialism, for example) has become a central concern of U.S. feminist theory, particularly as it intersects with ethnic studies, gay and lesbian studies, and postcolonial studies.[3] The more contextual bias of American feminist theory—with its attention to the interrelations of forms of oppression—is of particular use in interpreting Duras's work because of the cultural complexity of her upbringing and her relation to literary conventions.

Duras explores gender in her early work by focusing on female characters who come to self-awareness and by interrogating the narrative position of women in these texts. In *The Sea Wall* (1950), Suzanne is the center of narrative consciousness, but the third-person narrator is removed from the text. Through Suzanne, Duras explores coming of age as a poor, white, French woman in colonial Indochina. In "The Boa" (1954), an older female narrator explores her younger self in a sexual coming of age. *The Sailor from Gibraltar* (1952) represents a literary coming of age for Duras in which she parodies realist fiction. In *The Sailor from Gibraltar* Duras represents the narrator in the text as a man, a device that dominates in her work through the Lol V. Stein cycle. If we consider the gender of the reader in looking at *The Sailor from Gibraltar*, another set of meanings emerges, providing an important interpretive strategy for reading her later works.

Throughout these coming of age stories Duras shifts her relation to social and literary conventions as she struggles to tell stories of desire through the eyes and bodies of women.

Coming of Age in Indochina

Most American readers know Marguerite Duras primarily through *The Lover* (1984) and, therefore, as a French woman who grew up in Indochina. Very few of Duras's works, however, represent the landscapes of her childhood directly. Colonialism and the colonial mentality permeate most of her work, but are displaced onto an imaginary Indian landscape or small provincial cities in France. *The Sea Wall* (1950), the first of her novels to win a substantial popular and critical success, *Eden-Cinema* (1977), a play based on *The Sea Wall*, and "The Boa" (1954), a short story, are the only texts before *The Lover* that Duras situates in Indochina. *The Lover* itself is, in many ways, a retelling of *The Sea Wall*.

The Sea Wall: Colonial Fictions. *The Sea Wall* can be read as a countertext to colonial fictions, a story told to unmask the lies invented by colonial authorities to lure unwitting victims and to maintain control. Narrated in the third person, it is told from the point of view of Suzanne, privileged by race and nationality but marginalized because of sex and class.

Briefly, *The Sea Wall* tells the story of a mother (never named) and her children: Joseph, who is twenty, and Suzanne, seventeen. Widowed when the children were very young, the mother supports them by playing the piano to accompany silent films at the Eden Cinema. She saves her money and, after ten years, buys rights to a concession—land to be farmed and, ultimately, owned by French settlers—from colonial authorities. She learns too late that good concessions go only to those willing to bribe the authorities. Her land is inundated yearly by the Pacific Ocean, making it impossible to cultivate.

She devises a scheme to build sea walls to hold back the tides and enlists the help of the peasants who also inhabit this remote land—500 kilometers from the city. Tiny crabs eat away at the structures and the sea walls give way with the first tide. The mother refuses to let go of the mad hope that she can overcome both the authorities and the elements. She becomes increasingly sick and mad until she dies at the end of the novel. Resistance, in the mother's story, is shown to be pointless, so the children dream of escape: from the mother, whom they love, and from the poverty of the concession, which they hate. Each imagines a lover who would take them away: Joseph would rescue a stranded (rich) woman, Suzanne would be rescued by a rich man. Eventually the son of a wealthy planter, Monsieur Jo, takes an interest in Suzanne. As his race is never specified, the reader is supposed to understand that he is white. In many ways, however, he resembles the Chinese lover in *The Lover* and, like him, is seen as repulsive and unacceptable by the girl's brother. A legitimate union between them is deemed impossible by Monsieur Jo's father because of class, just as in *The Lover*, marriage is rejected by the Chinese lover's father because of race.

Joseph is ultimately taken in by a rich woman and escapes to the city. At the end of the novel he returns for the mother's burial, incites the peasants to insurrection against the colonial agents, and goes back to the city. Suzanne also leaves, but her fate is less clear. Jean Agosti, another settler slightly better off than the mother, has taken her as a lover, but she chooses to leave him in order to escape the sterility and poverty of that remote land. There is no closure at the end of the book, only stories in suspension and the vague promise of revolt.

Like so many of Duras's novels, *The Sea Wall* is about fictions and desire. It was a fiction that lured the mother to the colonies in the first place. As young schoolteachers in northern France, the mother and her husband saw colonial recruitment posters inviting them to make their fortune in exotic lands like those they had read about in the romantic works of Pierre Loti: "'Enlist in the Colonial Army!' said some. And others: 'Young People, a Fortune awaits you in the Colonies!' The picture usually showed a Colonial couple, dressed in white, sitting in rocking-chairs under banana trees while natives busied themselves around them."[4] As teachers in schools for the Indochinese, rather than for white children of the ruling class, however, they do not belong to the class represented by the poster. Further marginalized and impoverished by widowhood, the mother has deeper connections to the "natives" than she has to the leisured class of white colonials.

The posters and popular literature that promote romantic exoticism represent fictions of leisure and privilege that disguise the truth of exploitation underlying colonial dominance. The mother is a naive reader of these fictions, unable to discern the fiction as a fabrication, mistaking it for a transparent representation of the truth. Finally, it drives her mad. Suzanne and Joseph, more canny readers of the fictions that entrapped their mother, create a fiction of escape. They are both readers and creators of stories that can be read, literally, as escape fiction. Though their fictions, like the recruitment poster, are nourished by conventional clichés, Joseph and Suzanne retain a certain degree of narrative control. They are both readers and narrators of stories that combine cultural expectations and personal dreams. The differences between Joseph's stories and Suzanne's reveal the differences between what it means to be a man and what it means to be a woman in their social circumstances, particularly the differences in how each experiences sexuality and desire.

The first example of Joseph as a storyteller occurs in the second chapter when the mother, Joseph, and Suzanne go to the canteen in Ram, the village nearest their concession. It is the evening of their first encounter with Monsieur Jo. For Joseph, the conditions of life on the concession have become intolerable. Everything they touch seems to fall to ruin: his ancient car, an old horse that has just died, the sea walls the mother has tried to build. Joseph turns the pain and poverty of their existence into a series of jokes by inventing a hyperbolic narrative that progresses from bad to worse, along the lines of "if you thought that was bad, wait until you hear this." He gains control of the room through his stories, creating a huge joke ("la grande rigolade"). It is through his narrative that we first learn the story of the sea walls, either a tragedy or a joke depending on the day, adds the narrator. To tell a story confers power—over the meaning of events and over those who listen or read.

Joseph's central story in the book is the story of his escape from the mother and the concession. At first it is a gap in the narrative because, as readers, we are limited to Suzanne's consciousness, and she can only note his absence for over a week during a trip to the big city the children make with their mother. Later, he tells Suzanne the story in terms that are self-consciously narrative. After a prologue that begins "I went to the movies" (*SW*, 203; *B*, 221), he leads into the heart of the story: "Here begins the most extraordinary night of my life."[5]

In many ways, the cinema is to the children what romantic literature and the recruitment poster were to their parents: idealized images that shape their dreams, perhaps trapping them in an illusion that is always beyond reach. But the cinema, as represented in this book, is a zone one can move in and out of, a darkened space in which desire circulates freely. Like music, alcohol, drugs, and madness, the cinema creates a zone of semiconsciousness that acts as a buffer against harsh realities while nourishing desire. Both Joseph and Suzanne go to the movies hoping to lose themselves, hoping to be washed over by the screen images, but also hoping to find dream lovers. They grew up beneath the flickering screen as their mother played the piano at the Eden-Cinema. But the mother was denied the escape provided by cinema: She could not see the screen from where she sat.

The story of desire and escape that Joseph tells begins, significantly, at the movies, the privileged scene of fantasy, where he had gone to pick up a new woman. His familiar lover, Carmen, a sometime prostitute who helps run the hotel where they always stay in the city, is too familiar, unable to stimulate fantasy and desire. He says he had "grown sick and tired of Carmen, it was almost like sleeping with a sister when I slept with her" (*SW*, 203; *B*, 221). The story Joseph tells to Suzanne is punctuated by remarks to the effect that she must tell this to "Ma," she must remember this story so that she will remember him. He wants the story, in other words, to remain behind, to stand in for him when he is gone.

The story he tells centers on a beautiful and wealthy woman, Lina, who sits next to him at the movies, with her husband, asleep, on the other side. She flirts with Joseph and their exchange becomes more fascinating than the story on the screen. After the movie, she and her husband take Joseph drinking. Joseph's desire is intensified by alcohol, music, and dance. At one point, Joseph dances with another woman. When he returns to Lina, she says: "When I saw you dancing with that girl, I called out to you, but you didn't hear" (*SW*, 213; *B*, 233). This triangle of desire (a woman observing her lover transfer his desire to another woman, watching her own exclusion, speaking and yet unheard) prefigures in important ways the central obsession of the Lol V. Stein cycle written fifteen years later. The husband eventually passes out and Lina and Joseph make love in her expensive car. They then spend eight uninterrupted days and nights at a hotel.

Joseph tells Suzanne his story just before Lina comes to the concession to take him back to the city with her. As she listens to Joseph, Suzanne becomes his apprentice in storytelling and in life: "Suzanne did not get the full significance of Joseph's words, but she listened to them religiously, as to a hymn of virility and truth. Thinking them over she perceived with emotion that she herself felt able to conduct her life as Joseph said she must. She saw, then, that what she admired in Joseph was also in herself" (*SW*, 224–25; *B*, 246). To Suzanne, Joseph speaks in "the Master's voice," the slogan on the side of his favorite victrola, another instrument of escape and dreams.

Once she listens to his stories, her own story incorporates his terms, revealing the effect of her apprenticeship to his authority. Suzanne's story follows a trajectory that is almost the inverse of Joseph's. He sleeps with Carmen, among others, a woman of his class, and tires of her because she seems like "a sister." He then realizes a fantasy love, discovering Lina in the movies and finding a way out of misery through her attention. Suzanne first meets Monsieur Jo, who appears to be the dream lover she had imagined would take her away. But Joseph does not like him, and she realizes that he will never marry her so she loses interest in him. After Joseph's departure, she agrees to sleep with Agosti. She is attracted to him to the degree that he begins to resemble her brother.

Suzanne learns from Monsieur Jo the power of her body as an object of desire and exchange. He offers her a gift if she will let him watch her in the shower. Later he offers her a diamond if she will spend several days in the city with him. She refuses, but he gives her a diamond ring anyway. When the mother, Joseph, and Suzanne go to the city to sell the ring, Joseph meets Lina. Indirectly, Suzanne's body has brought Joseph to his dream lover. The topography of the city reproduces the class and race hierarchies of the colony. The *haut quartier*, or upper district, is the protected quarter belonging to rich whites who circulate in luxurious cars. Throughout the novel, cars inspire envy and desire or frustration. For example, Monsieur Jo's limousine, a Léon Bollée, is an emblem of wealth and power, a car belonging to dreams or the cinema, promising escape. Joseph's Citroen is ridiculous, part of his "great joke." Other districts belong to the indigenous people who travel by tram. The mother and her children stay at a hotel in a transient district where salesmen and sailors circulate. Suzanne, dressed and tutored by Carmen in how to use her femininity, goes to the upper district but feels the unpitying looks of the rich whites. She cannot have access to this district on her own as Joseph can. The only place in which she can escape the judgment of their gaze is the cinema, where she rediscovers the free circulation of desire, sharing touches with anonymous men, experiencing the cinema as a "palpitating gloom" ("obscurité féconde") (*SW*, 178; *B*, 192).

By chance, Monsieur Jo finds Suzanne one day in the city and his car supplants the cinema as a scene of fantasy and desire. In the protection of the Léon Bollée, she rediscovers the power of her body and sees the upper district differently: Moving through the streets and the bright lights, she experiences the city as if it were a film. Monsieur Jo touches her breasts and tells her they are beautiful: "The thing had been said very softly. But it had been said. For the first time . . . above the terrifying city, Suzanne saw her breasts, saw the erection of her breasts higher than anything that stood up in the city. Her breasts, then, would be justified. She smiled" (*SW*, 180; *B*, 195). Only through a man's gaze—even an unacceptable man—does Suzanne feel the power of her body.

After Joseph tells her the story of his extraordinary affair, Suzanne agrees to sleep with a man. Agosti, who begins to remind Suzanne of Joseph by his laugh and gestures, comes to get her, not in a Léon Bollée but in a modest Renault; he takes her to a clearing in a forest on his plantation and makes love to her. She would have preferred his hotel room at Ram with the shutters closed, she thinks: "it would have been a little like the violent darkness of the cinema."[6] Like Joseph and Lina, they then spend eight days and nights at the hotel room, but this time the mother has her last crisis. Suzanne returns to watch her die. Suzanne's love story imitates Joseph's in certain respects: It enables separation from the mother and a way out of the concession and all it represents. The ending of her story is far less certain, however. She says she is leaving, but to what is left unresolved. Agosti is not a way out, as Lina is, because he belongs to the same remote community as Suzanne. Suzanne, then, borrows Joseph's story to try to create her own. But the transfer to a woman's story is not entirely satisfactory and the differences between them are striking. Joseph, for example, loses erotic interest when a woman begins to remind him of "a sister." For Suzanne a man becomes desirable when he begins to resemble her brother. Joseph circulates freely in the city; Suzanne is constrained unless she is with a man. Joseph gets his fantasy lover and leaves more ordinary lovers behind; Suzanne rejects her fantasy lover and gets Agosti, then no one, in his place. The contrasts between the two stories confirm stereotypes about gender and the asymmetrical experience of gender for men and women in their particular cultural context.

The novel also presents a series of women's stories that further compel Suzanne to listen to Joseph and try to "conduct her life as Joseph said she must" (*SW*, 225; *B*, 246). The models of womanhood available to Suzanne include the mad mother (isolated, angry, and powerless), the peasants (reduced to reproductive machines), and Lina (unavailable to Suzanne as a model because of class). Suzanne expresses deep ambivalence, both desire and distrust, toward Carmen, who is valued because Joseph sleeps with her and who tries to be a mentor to Suzanne in the ways of femininity. Even as Carmen teaches her how to use her body, Suzanne imagines herself in Joseph's place, watching her. In this gesture she learns the desire of the female body through the male gaze and then represses her appropriation of the male gaze, fearful, perhaps, of being in that position as desire circulates:

> Suzanne knew that it was in this room that Joseph had slept with Carmen. When Carmen undressed in front of her, she thought of it every time. And every time that made one more difference—not with Carmen, but with Joseph. . . . Suzanne itemized her every evening, and every evening her difference from Joseph was accentuated. Suzanne had undressed in front of Carmen only once. Then, Carmen had taken her into her arms. . . . It was that same evening that Carmen asked her to bring her the first man she picked up. Suzanne promised. But never again did she undress in front of Carmen. (*SW*, 162; *B*, 174)

At the end of the novel, though, Suzanne's story is unfinished.

In a note to the play *Eden Cinema*, based on *The Sea Wall* and written more than twenty years later, Duras makes it very clear that she does not want closure at the end of this novel. In 1957, René Clément made a film based on *The Sea Wall* in which he rewrote the ending. Rather than have the children leave the concession after the mother's death, Clément has them stay on, as Duras says in her note, "like American pioneers in the Middle West, 'to continue their parents' work.'"[7] In Duras's view, this was an "irremediable betrayal" of the meaning of the novel. The children should leave the colony and the story should end with the violence and potential rebellion unresolved; the parents' work, in the context of the corruption and exploitation represented by the colony, was a travesty. In the play, Duras has the mother rather than Joseph incite violence. Her "work" is not to settle the colony but to unsettle it.

Suzanne derives her sense of the terms and power of femininity and fiction from Joseph and, to a degree, from Monsieur Jo. The pleasure she experiences with Agosti is possible once she sees Joseph's features projected on his body. Suzanne and Joseph both seek escape in the zone of semiconsciousness produced by alcohol, drugs, music, and the cinema. The threshold between reality and the zone of semiconsciousness is permeable in *The Sea Wall*, but clearly marked. Desire discovered in the fantasies of semiconsciousness maintains the erotic in everyday reality. "The Boa" and *The Sailor from Gibraltar* offer further explorations of female sexuality and the meanings of fiction.

"The Boa": A Cautionary Tale. In 1954, Duras published four short stories under the title *Des Journées entières dans les arbres (Whole Days in the Trees)*.[8] Just as *The Tranquil Life* tells a story of female subjectivity, one of the stories in this volume, "The Boa," presents a story of female sexuality. Although the story is told in the first person, both temporal and geographic distance between the adult narrator and her younger self is carefully established at the beginning: "This happened in a large city in a French colony, around 1928" (*WD*, 71; *J*, 99). The use of an impersonal, reflexive construction ("cela se passait") reinforces the distancing of the narrator and is the first mark of split female subjectivity in this text, in which the woman tries to read her own adolescence. In the story, the adult narrator situates her thirteen-year-old self between two spectacles that provided the only terms available to her to understand her awakening sexuality.

The narrator describes her younger self as a poor student at Mademoiselle Barbet's boarding school for girls. The other girls have friends in town, and every Sunday their developing minds and bodies are nourished by endless adventures: cinema, teas, drives in the country, afternoons at the pool or tennis courts. The narrator, however, has no such social life and spends all her time with the seventy-five-year-old spinster, Mlle Barbet. Mlle Barbet provides the girl with the two spectacles that mark her coming of age. Every Sunday she takes her to the zoo, where, with other fascinated onlookers, they watch a boa constrictor consume a live chicken. If they arrive too late, they contemplate the boa napping on "a bed of chicken feathers" (WD, 72; J, 100). They remain transfixed because "there was nothing more to see, but we knew what had happened a moment before, and each of us stood before the boa, deep in thought" (WD, 72; J, 100–101).

The other spectacle is provided by Mlle Barbet herself, with the girl as an unwilling witness. In a routine as certain as the boa's, Mlle Barbet calls the girl into her room. Under the pretext of showing the girl her fine lingerie, Mlle Barbet exhibits her seminude body. The old woman had never shown her body to anyone before and would never show it to anyone else because of her advanced age. She instructs the girl that beautiful lingerie is important in life, a lesson she learned too late.

The narrator adds that Mlle Barbet's body exudes a terrible odor that permeates the entire boarding school; she had noticed the odor before, but could not locate it before seeing the woman's exposed body. The old woman sighs during their secret sessions, saying "I have wasted my life. . . . He never came" (WD, 74; J, 105). The girl is induced by her own impoverished circumstances to tell the woman that she has a full life, that she is rich and has beautiful lingerie: The rest is unimportant.

This Sunday double feature, repeated weekly for two years, is developed in great detail by the narrator, who spends most of the story linking, contrasting, and interpreting the two spectacles because they illuminate the only two avenues through which the young girl could imagine her future. The narrator insists that one weekly event without the other would have led to other effects. If, for example, she had witnessed only the boa's devouring of the chicken, she might have seen in the boa the force of evil and in his victim, goodness and innocence; she might have understood the world as an eternal struggle between these two forces revealing the presence of God. Or, she could have been led to rebel (WD, 73; J, 102). She could have internalized the weekly lesson at the zoo, that is, as a morality tale, a story of good and evil leading to conformity or rebellion.

The spectacle of Mlle Barbet alone might have led the girl to understand social inequities and the "multiple forms of oppression" that result. Coupled with the zoo experience, the second spectacle shifts the meanings of both because of the terrifying glimpse of aging female flesh, undiscovered by the male gaze and imprisoned in its own virginity. Together, the two events become not a morality tale of good and evil, of inequity and injustice, but a cautionary tale of female sexuality. The terms the narrator uses to reconstruct each event and the conclusions she draws articulate a specific construction of the female body and hetero-sexuality. Within the terms of the story—shown especially in the contrast between the young narrator and her school friends—she seems to suggest that this is an anomalous construction. At the same time, fatalistic language and implications of social determinism suggest that this is a distilled experience of female sexuality rather than an anomalous one. In any case, the highly individualized definition of female sexuality elaborated in this text will be generalized in other texts by Duras, passing imperceptibly from one woman's story to the story of "woman." For that reason, as well as the fact that this is one of the few texts with explicit autobiographical references situated in Indochina and written before *The Lover*, "The Boa" merits close consideration.

From the start, the narrator insists that she is an involuntary, yet complicit, solitary voyeur of Mlle Barbet. The girl undergoes this weekly drama and keeps Mlle Barbet's secret in exchange for Mlle Barbet's silence about her mother's poverty. The girl is in the school because her mother thinks that it is the only way she will meet a husband and thus find a way out of poverty and marginalization in the strictly ordered society of the colony.

The girl shares her mother's belief that Mlle Barbet is better suited to help her find a husband, even though the old woman's "secular virginity" exudes the odor of death that permeates the school (*WD*, 74; *J*, 105). The narrator specifies that Mlle Barbet is consumed by lack, by "the lack of the man who never came" (*WD*, 74; *J*, 105). Each week, after leaving the old woman, the girl returns to her room, looks at her own body in the mirror, and admires her white breasts. In a gesture that superimposes the boa and female sexuality, she says that her breasts provide the only source of pleasure for her in the entire house: "Outside the house there was the boa, here there were my breasts" (*WD*, 76; *J*, 107).[9] Feeling trapped in the school, the girl goes out on the balcony to attract the attention of passing soldiers.

The spectacles of the old woman and of the snake involve consumption and violence valued in opposite ways. Mlle Barbet is consumed by lack, and the private viewing of her enclosed, undiscovered sexuality inspires disgust and dread. The boa consumes his prey, and his public act is characterized as a sacred crime inspiring horror and respect. The boa itself is described in hyperbolic, highly sexualized terms: "Curled into himself, black . . . in admirable form—a plump roundness, tender, muscular, a column of black marble . . . with shudders of contained power, the boa devoured this chicken in the course of a single process of digestion . . . transubstantiation accomplished with the sacred calm of ritual. In this formidable, inner silence, chicken became serpent" (*WD*, 72; *J*, 101). This spectacle in the open daylight attracts spectators who are fascinated, entranced by the vital beauty and violence of the beast. In sharp contrast, the narrator calls Mlle Barbet's secret "hidden" and "nocturnal."

The narrator does not read the formative stories of her youth as a simple contrast between powerful male and sterile female sexuality, two stories of devouring desire—one the passionate devouring of an innocent, the other the passionless devouring of the self by a hypocritical innocence. In her work on reader theory, Jean Kennard talks about the shaping role of both gender and sexuality in the recognition and interpretation of literary conventions.[10] She shows how new meanings can be assigned to conventions to subvert their apparent or traditional sense. The narrator of "The Boa" can be read as a woman thinking back on the cultural texts available to her to understand and revalue her sexuality through a complex negotiation between her needs and the stories available. Duras accomplishes this negotiation by mapping a story of female sexuality onto the spectacle of the boa constrictor so that *both* stories recount possibilities for female sexuality. Female sexuality is redeemed by the power of the phallus in the first story, condemned by its own inadequacy in the second.

To map a story of female sexuality onto the story of the boa, the narrator must negotiate a complex series of substitutions and displacements. Her narrative sleights of hand recall the convoluted associations and displacements of a Freudian map of female sexuality—one that privileges the penis and defines woman by lack. The slippage that results from this imperfect, if ingenious, mapping compounds the division within the woman/girl's experience of the female body marked thematically by the two spectacles.

In an increasingly intense meditation on the links between the spectacle of the boa and of Mlle Barbet, the narrator expresses the despair she felt as a girl: unable to flee the closed world of Mlle Barbet, "nocturnal monster," unable to join the fertile world revealed by the boa, "monster of the day." In a passage presented as a waking fantasy, she imagines the world represented by the boa. She fantasizes a green paradise, a scene where "innumerable carnal exchanges were achieved by one organism devouring, assimilating, coupling with another in processes that were at once orgiastic and calm" (*WD*, 78; *J*, 110). The contrast of this paradise with the prison of Mlle Barbet leads her to define two types of horror. One horror—hidden vices, shameful secrets, hypocrisy, concealed disease—inspires a deep aversion. The other—the horror of assassins, crime, the outlaw—inspires admiration. The boa is the "perfect image" of this second kind of horror that elicits respect. In a series of substitutions she expresses contempt for those who would condemn certain species such as "cold, silent snakes . . . cruel, hypocritical cats." She establishes one category of human being that could be considered among these privileged outlaws: the prostitute. She parenthetically links assassins and prostitutes, imagining both in "the jungle of great capital cities, hunting their prey which they then consumed with the impudence and imperiousness of fatalistic temperaments" (*WD*, 79; *J*, 112). She thus establishes a train of associations that shifts the story from the masculine figure of the snake to the male assassin/outlaw to the feminine figure of the prostitute, from the jungle to the city.

The transfer of value from the snake to the prostitute also takes place at a deeper, linguistic level. The boa consumes a chicken, put in the masculine in the French: "un poulet." A common word for prostitute in French, which is implied though not invoked in the story, is the feminine form of chicken: "une poule." The prostitute figure in the story, like the chicken that is ingested by the boa and becomes one with his flesh, is absorbed into the values of the phallic figure of the snake. Another substitution and transfer of values is hinted at more explicitly in the story. The same soldiers who walk under her balcony are also spectators at the zoo. She would attract their gaze, fascinate them, in the same way as the boa, substituting herself for the great serpent in her fantasy.

At the moment that she transfers values from the male figures to the female, the image of Mlle Barbet erupts into her fantasy as a reminder of the body she is fleeing. She tells herself that if she does not marry, at least the brothel would provide an escape for her. This leads her to a fantasy of the brothel: "a sort of temple of defloration where, in all purity . . . young girls in my state, to whom marriage was not accorded, would go to have their bodies discovered by unknown men, men who belonged to the selfsame species" (*WD*, 79; *J*, 112). The brothel, painted green, recalls the zoo garden as well as the tamarind trees that shade her balcony, where she tries to attract the gaze of passing soldiers. She imagines this as a silent place, marked by a sacred anonymity; girls would wear masks in order to enter. Anonymity pays homage to "the absolute lack of 'personality' of the boa, ideal bearer that he was of the naked, virginal mask" (WD, 79; J, 113).[11] The ritual initiation and anonymity shift this from the story of one girl to the story of woman, from a specific sexual awakening to a model of female sexuality. She imagines cabins in which one could "cleanse oneself of one's virginity, to have the solitude removed from one's body" (WD, 80; J, 113).

The oscillation between the brothel fantasy and the memory of her despair on the balcony, between the snake and the prostitute, situates her as both spectator and participant in an initiation where phallic sexuality is worshiped and woman is freed of the isolation and lack of her body. She invokes another, earlier childhood memory as "corroboration" of this way of seeing the world. One day her brother asked her to show him her sex. When she refused, he said "girls could die from not using it, and that hiding it suffocated you and made you seriously ill" (WD, 80; J, 113). The spectacle of Mlle Barbet's body seems to confirm her brother's dire prediction. Her brother's voice, like the "fraternal image" that Francine sees in the mirror in The Tranquil Life and the voice of "virility and truth" that Suzanne hears in Joseph's stories, is the voice of male authority. In an image that recalls Suzanne's pleasure in Monsieur Jo's gaze, the narrator generalizes the power of male authority by saying, as she remembers Mlle Barbet's decaying body: "From the moment a breast had served a man, even by merely allowing him to see it, to take note of its shape, its roundness, its firmness—from the moment a breast was able to nourish the seed of a man's desire, it was saved from withering from disuse" (WD, 80; J, 114).

While admitting the terror of being consumed that the boa inspired, the narrator appropriates that story to imagine the female body and female sexuality redeemed by the male gaze and desire. In "The Boa," female heterosexuality defined by the phallus is intrinsically linked to a loathing of the female body. The key transition in her fantasy chain of images that allows the narrator to transform the story of the boa into the story of the prostitute and, hence, into a model for female sexuality, is the glorification of crime and the figure of the outlaw. And yet, I would argue, Duras has not written a story of outlaw female sexuality. Her representation of female sexuality is outlaw only in its flamboyant display and excess, without the pretense of monogamy. Far from being deviant, the construction of desire and the deployment of erotic power in this representation remains conventional. Rather than disrupt sexual and social order in this narrative, she imagines a way for woman to fit into the dominant construction of heterosexuality that privileges the phallus and demeans the woman's body.

The early works of Duras are often characterized as realist fiction. *The Sea Wall* and "The Boa" seem to fit that assessment, particularly in narrative structure and the descriptive details of the Indochinese landscape and colonial milieu. The center of interest in these texts, however, is the source and power of stories themselves, the shaping force of fiction. In *The Sea Wall*, the zone of semiconsciousness induced by drugs, alcohol, music, and movies, and sustained in madness, provides escape from the unbearable "real." Fantasy and fiction are cultivated in the zone of semiconsciousness and allow for the free circulation of desire. Fictions confer power. Joseph's stories give him the power to redefine the catastrophes of their life and to capture an audience. His stories also provide a means for Suzanne to understand and define herself.

In "The Boa," the narrator looks to formative stories to understand her sexuality. Most of the narrative is focused on fantasy, on imagination and interpretation, rather than on realist representations. There is a potential tension in these works between the conventions of realism and Duras's explicit attention to fiction and its power to shape meaning. The illusion of an unmediated representation of reality that realist fiction tries to maintain is undermined when the artifice of fiction and the power of interpretation become important thematic concerns. In *The Sailor from Gibraltar*, Duras effects a literary coming of age, exploring her ambivalent relation to the predominantly male models of fiction that had formed her. Rather than disguise the fictionality of the novel to create the illusion of "reality," she exaggerates the fictionality to create a parody of contemporary realism as represented by Hemingway and the American novel.

The Sailor from Gibraltar: A Literary Coming of Age

Duras maintains clear distinctions between the zone of semiconsciousness and consciousness in *The Sea Wall* and between experience and fantasy in "The Boa."[12] In neither of these works does Duras undermine or question the status of the conventional fictional character; overall, the narration is "realist," though narrative self-consciousness about the making of fictions creates an internal tension. Realist conventions begin to dissolve in *The Sailor from Gibraltar*. The zone of semiconsciousness comes to the foreground of the narrative and the artifice of the fiction becomes more pronounced both thematically and structurally. Even so, this is a novel that Duras has characterized as "anchored in the real."[13]

Unlike Suzanne or the girl in "The Boa," Anna, the central female character of *The Sailor from Gibraltar*, does not wait passively to be discovered by an idealized, male lover. She sails the world on a yacht named *Gibraltar* in search of a sailor she claims to have once rescued and loved. The narrator of the novel is a young man who was brought up in the colonies but is now bored by the routine of his job at the Colonial Ministry and by his dull mistress. Like Ishmael in the opening chapter of *Moby Dick*, he takes to the sea when there is "nothing in particular to interest me on shore." In the intense heat of a vacation on the Italian coast, the narrator of *The Sailor from Gibraltar* breaks with his past in order to follow the rich woman on the yacht *Gibraltar*.

"Make something up, anything. . . . But you must talk to me."[14] When the narrator says this to Anna early in their voyage together, he sets terms that will characterize this novel and much of Duras's fiction through the 1960s: a man seeking to tell a woman's story, to prod her to tell her own story; a woman, compliant or withholding, who uses the male interlocutor to claim the story she dreads and desires. Sandra Gilbert and Susan Gubar, recognizing the patriarchal construction of the feminine psyche, have examined the ways in which women writers suffer an "anxiety of authorship." It could be argued that Duras exhibits an "anxiety of authority" in her early texts: Who has the authority to define women's subjectivity, sexuality, and fictions? Whose voice will articulate these meanings?

Many of Duras's works are retold tales. Although it could be argued that all storytelling is a reworking of other tales, in Duras's work the retelling itself is a central concern. *The Sailor from Gibraltar*, often dismissed as imitative of the American novel, actually represents a dismantling of a type of American novel and, with it, of certain expectations of meaning. To borrow a term from Judith Fetterley, Duras in this book is a "resisting reader" of the American novel as defined by Hemingway. She resists the conventions of the American novel and the values they convey because they were shaped by male writers to serve masculine dominance.[15] *The Sailor from Gibraltar* establishes a model for retold tales; closure is precluded in favor of infinite repetition because of the nature of desire, which can never be fulfilled and must constantly be imagined.

The Sailor from Gibraltar undermines the American novel by retelling a Hemingway story. References to the American novel and to

Hemingway are playful and parodic from the start. Early in their relationship, the narrator tells Anna that he intends to write an American novel about her one day.

> "One day," I said, "I'll write an American novel about you."
> "Why American?"
> "Because of the whiskies. That's what Americans drink. Go on."
> (*SG*, 149; *MG*, 142)

Much later, in an African episode that parodies and rewrites Hemingway's *The Snows of Kilimanjaro*, Anna says:

> "In your American novel, will you say anything about kudus? As Mr. Hemingway has already written about them, mightn't it be considered in bad taste?"
> "If it wasn't for Mr. Hemingway," I said, "we shouldn't be talking about them at all. Do you think it would be better to lie and say we were talking about something else?"
> "No," she said. "It's better to tell the truth and hope for the best."
> (*SG*, 305; *MG*, 282)

These passages undermine the conventions of realism even while appealing to them; Duras self-consciously assumes an ironic stance toward Hemingway. The passages about Hemingway and the American novel demonstrate that what appears to be the subject of the story is merely a pretext to say something else. The implications of the author's ironic stance surface when we compare *The Sailor from Gibraltar* with the narrative conventions and assumptions about meaning that Hemingway develops in *The Snows of Kilimanjaro*.

In the Hemingway story, the central character, Harry, in a characteristically resentful, dependent relationship with a rich woman, is dying from gangrene while stranded during a hunt in Africa. Much of the text consists of the stories that he tells himself he would have written if he had not met with this fatal accident. The stories are drawn from his experience but require a mature voice to be told. If he had been able to tell them, the story suggests, his life would have had a meaning which death is now denying him. At first he considers entrusting them to his woman companion, but she has never learned dictation and so cannot be used as a compliant vehicle for his narration.

Thematically, the stories are left untold because Harry dies, but structurally they are transmitted to the reader by the invisible author/narrator who has a privileged access to the character that the woman companion does not. The story is constructed around an extended para-leipsis: The author says he is not saying what is being said. As such, it is a rhetorical triumph over the silencing of death. The special bond between the hero, the invisible narrator, and the presumed male (or unresisting female) reader maintains the fiction of the transcendent and redemptive power of literature even though on a thematic level the story seems to tell of its defeat.[16] The companion—identified as "the woman," "a woman," "the rich bitch"—is left only with the writer's corpse, his corpus being beyond her skills and comprehension. Although the Hemingway story affects cynicism, it maintains a romantic, not to say fetishistic, concept of literature within a realist setting. It also shows story-telling to be men's work. The woman companion has learned how to shoot, but she cannot be entrusted with stories.

Although outfitted with all the props of a quest novel in the realist mode, *The Sailor from Gibraltar* is, rather, like the maritime atlas Anna claims to know by heart: "It was the atlas of a topsy-turvy universe, a negative of the world" (*SG*, 147; *MG*, 140). The author does not pretend to offer us an unmediated reflection of experience. The universe we are in is self-consciously fictional, and the character's ironic stance toward literary precursors signals that conventional modes of interpretation are inadequate. As the novel progresses, the apparent object of the quest—the sailor—takes on multiple identities, all exaggerations of novelistic heroes: a great lover, a criminal (the assassin of Nelson Nelson, American millionaire), and an African folk hero, among others. Messages from around the world put Anna and the narrator on his trail and inspire new stories about his identity and whereabouts. The result is that the fictional circuits become overloaded and burn out. By overdetermining the central character, the author underscores his nonexistence.

At the end of the novel, Anna and the narrator consume kudu together after an adventure in Africa, with Anna adding that the narrator must tell how they ate kudu in his American novel. When they return to port, the yacht, like the overloaded fictions of this novel, is smoking, in ruins after a fire: "Only the bar and the upper deck had escaped" (*SG*, 318; *MG*, 293). Anna says, "One thirty-six metre yacht the fewer. . . . That'll lighten your American novel, won't it" (*SG*, 318; *MG*, 293)?

Whereas in the Hemingway story the hero's death gives birth to fictions that eclipse the woman but give meaning to the hero through the narrator, in Duras's novel the absence of a hero engenders fictions that shape the story of Anna. The making of the narrative is still man's work because the novel takes form through the words of the male narrator. But in seeming to tell the stories of the sailor, he tells the story of Anna. The absence of the hero makes possible her fictional presence; the narrator will tell Anna's story only so long as the quest for the sailor continues. In order for the story to continue, the fiction of the sailor must be maintained; in order for it to be maintained, there must be no sailor, only his impossibility.

The impossibility of the sailor and the discontinuity between Anna and the sailor is the point of departure for the narrative. In *The Sailor from Gibraltar*, Duras dismantles conventional character and demonstrates that it is through its absence that the female subject's story can begin to be articulated.

The Duras novel, in other words, reverses the terms of the Hemingway story. While the sequence of fantastic stories seems on a thematic level to uphold a romantic concept of literature, structurally the novel undoes the myth of transcendent and redemptive meaning that Hemingway's story promotes. The character of the narrator in *The Sailor from Gibraltar* undermines the illusion of meaning maintained by Hemingway even further. In *The Snows of Kilimanjaro* the passing on of Harry's literary legacy is possible only through the lucid, presumably masculine bond between the omniscient narrator, the central character, whom he knows like a second self, and the reader. The gender of both the narrator and the reader are assumed because "the woman" has been dismissed as an unworthy listener. In *The Sailor from Gibraltar*, Duras signals the fictional and masculine nature of the narrator by representing him as a character; but in *The Sailor from Gibraltar*, Anna remains an enigma to the narrator, never entirely knowable.

The narrator of *The Snows of Kilimanjaro*, and the reader through him, have direct access to the central character's meaning. The narrator of *The Sailor from Gibraltar*, and the reader through him, have access to Anna's shifting stories about an absent central character. There is, therefore, not only dissolution of the hero figure in *The Sailor from Gibraltar* but dissolution of the male bond that facilitated interpretation. The "rich bitch" is no longer a resented accessory to the tale; she is the center—but at *her* center is the absent hero.

The reader is forced to collude with the absence that defines both Anna and the story. For the woman reading as a woman, this presents a special dilemma.[17] Like the other Durassian heroines we have looked at, Anna is twice defined by men—the absent sailor, the present narrator—but these male figures are created by the woman author in order both to name Anna and to demonstrate that she cannot be known. The woman reader may feel like a voyeur in the Hemingway tale: As a reader she is privy to the narrator's assigning of meaning, as a woman she is excluded as an inadequate vessel for narration. In the Duras novel the woman reader must accede to the male narrator's incomplete story of Anna. The rhetorical illusion of a lucid, masculine bond is not replaced by the illusion of a feminine bond. To unveil the gender of the conventional narrative undoes the terms that allow it to function.

Duras's work does not present a feminization of narrative in the sense of rewriting Hemingway in the feminine or creating a triumphant female speaking subject. The repeated reconstructions of a woman subject's story in *The Sailor from Gibraltar* are built around absence and incomprehension. The rhetoric of discontinuity thus established in *The Sailor from Gibraltar* parallels the representations of female subjectivity in *The Tranquil Life* and female heterosexuality in "The Boa," which are constructed through substitutions and displacements. The rhetoric of the discontinuity of female subjectivity that emerges from these texts undermines the terms of meaning and habits of interpretation of the conventional (male) narrative. Duras places at the center of her text the figure of woman as absence; through that specifically female alienation she undoes the lie of transcendent, redemptive meaning and the illusions of masculine lucidity that constructed that absence in the first place.

Whether the story is about woman as subject, sexual being, or storyteller, in these tales of coming of age, male mediation is required. In the late fifties and the sixties, Duras explores the explosive tension created by a feminine subject requiring male mediation—a tension at once generative and destructive—in two ways. She writes stories—usually constructed as mysteries—centered on an interrogation of desire in which a male character interrogates a female character, continuing the injunction of the narrator in *The Sailor from Gibraltar* to "Make some thing up, anything. . . . But you must talk to me" (*SG*, 159; *MG*, 151). Or she represents a male narrator within the text to tell, or invent, the story of the woman at its center. From a rhetoric of discontinuity she creates interrogations of desire leading toward a narrative of silence.

Chapter Three

Criminals of Love: From Interrogations of Desire to a Narrative of Silence

> "How about the difference between what I know and what I say—what will you do about that?"
> "That's the part of the book the reader has to supply for himself. It exists in any book."
>
> Marguerite Duras, *L'Amante anglaise*

As a smaller, unnamed yacht replaces the burned out *Gibraltar* at the end of *The Sailor from Gibraltar*, Anna, the narrator, and a diminished crew have a radio receiver installed and set sail for new waters. They have untied narrative practice from its realist moorings, replacing it with a more modest but as yet unnamed vessel. Where it will lead is uncertain. The last sentence of the novel, "But I can't talk about it yet" (*SG*, 318), both recalls and rewrites Ishmael's epilogue to *Moby Dick*: quoting Job, he says, "And I only am escaped to tell thee." After the ship went down with the rest of the crew, Ishmael, the chosen one, is saved to tell the story that gives narrative life to Captain Ahab's pursuit of the great white whale. The nameless narrator of *The Sailor from Gibraltar* cannot yet imagine how to talk after the conventions of the realist novel have been dismantled.

Engendering Narratives

Duras's parody of Authorship in *The Sailor from Gibraltar*, the substitution of changing meanings for an underlying fixed meaning and the open-endedness of the multiple texts that constitute the novel, anticipate Roland Barthes' 1968 essay "The Death of the Author."[1] Duras has vehemently distanced herself from literary theory and theorists, particularly Barthes. Nonetheless, the narrative practices she develops after *The Sailor from Gibraltar* mirror (sometimes in advance) the critical debates about the status of the Author (dead or alive) and the place of the writer (outside or inside the text, in control of meaning or a product of discourse) articulated by French theorists, primarily Barthes, Michel Foucault, Jacques Derrida, and Jacques Lacan. The French theorists, especially as inflected through feminist critical debates and reading practices in the United States, provide a useful means of reading Duras's narrative experiments of the late fifties and sixties.

Nancy Miller, in an essay that reads Roland Barthes alongside Adrienne Rich, delineates a contested space between (French) postmodernism and (American) feminism that aptly describes, I think, the narrative region Duras negotiates in the sixties until she reaches an impasse of silence.[2] In "The Death of the Author," Barthes replaces the concept of Author, standing behind his works and determining their meaning, with *writing*, a textuality in which the writer is merely a "scriptor" (Barthes, 145). With the death of the Author comes the death of the Critic, replaced by the reader, the new locus of meaning: "a text is made of multiple writings, drawn from many cultures and entering into mutual relations of dialogue, parody, contestation, but there is one place where this multiplicity is focused and that place is the reader, not, as was hitherto said, the author" (Barthes, 148). Because the Author was part of a humanist system that sacralized the "personal," that made of the Author a monument behind the text, Barthes is careful to specify that the reader is not personal: "the reader is without history, biography, psychology; he is simply that *someone* who holds together in a single field all the traces by which the written text is constituted" (Barthes, 148).

Nancy Miller argues that "[t]he postmodernist decision that the Author is Dead and the subject along with him does not . . . necessarily hold for women, and prematurely forecloses the question of agency for them" (Miller, 106). Feminists might have found grounds for an alliance with the postmodernist dismantling of the work of art as a male-authored monument, Miller argues, but the destabilizing of this authority took with it "discussion of any writing identity in favor of a (new) monolith of anonymous textuality" (Miller, 104). Just as postmodernist theorists argue for a model of anonymous textuality, (American) feminists have argued for the need to situate and contextualize practices of writing and reading, to account more fully for the "history, biology, psychology" of both writer and reader.

In *The Sailor from Gibraltar*, Duras signals her separation from the humanist tradition that worshiped the Author behind the work. The ending suggests, however, that as a woman writing, particularly a woman who would write a woman's story, she is in search of new means for inscribing a female writing subject. In the novels of the late fifties

and sixties, Duras experiments with several types of narrative voices—
from anonymous frame narrators to gendered narrators represented
within the text. She "stages the drama of the writing subject," in Miller's
phrase, in the space between postmodern anonymity and feminist specificity and in the process enlarges the "part of the book the reader has to
supply," as the interrogator in *L'Amante anglaise* states in the epigraph to
this chapter.[3] If, as feminists using reader theory have suggested, we
consider the gender of the reader, the part of the book the reader sup-
plies might take on different meanings. What I am proposing is the
hypothesis of reading as a woman that Jonathan Culler in *On
Deconstruction* calls the second moment of feminist criticism.[4] How does
reading as a woman situate the reader in contrast to reading as a man?
What does the hypothesis of reading as a woman show us about the
making of meaning in these texts? What sorts of collusion, complicity,
distance, or denial are demanded of the woman reader?

Most of Duras's works prior to this period, as *The Sea Wall* illustrates,
are third-person narratives, with occasional eruptions of the first person,
in which narrative point of view is associated with a central female character. *The Sailor from Gibraltar* is the first extended narrative using the
first person in the masculine; it establishes in rudimentary form two types
of narrative structures that will shape Duras's fiction through the sixties.
One narrative mode, which I call interrogations of desire, involves the
performance of a text in the making in which masculine and feminine
voices alternate. This mode is illustrated in the dialogues between the
narrator and Anna: He interrogates her, using a pretext (the story of the
sailor from Gibraltar) in order to create her story (or their story).

The other type of narrative mode figures a narrating male character
telling the story of a woman who is first an object of his desire and then
the subject of his narrative.[5] In some texts the reader is strictly bound to
the perspective of the male narrator/character. In others there are hints
of a frame narrator's voice. For example, before the story of Anna and
the yacht, the narrator tells his own story in an extended frame. While
the frame narrator tends to fade into the character of the narrator in *The
Sailor from Gibraltar*, a narrating presence distinct from the character can
be detected setting the scene, establishing context, and specifying tone.
In these ways, the frame narrative serves to inscribe the writer's subjectivity in the text, to answer the question: Who is writing this text?

A narrator, like the masculine, first-person narrator of Anna's story,
who is represented in a text is localized—attached to a pronoun and a
point of view; gender, class, race, and age positions are either explicitly

or tacitly marked. The same might be said, of course, for a reader or interlocutor represented in the text. The frame narrator in Duras's early works, including *The Sailor from Gibraltar*, is abstract, anonymous, loosely linked to a character's consciousness, but not given a gender, class, race, or other specified cultural position. To the extent that the frame narrator stands in for the writer, one could argue that suppressing these markers is one way in which Duras disguises or displaces the female narrating subject in a tradition where the narrative voice has conventionally been masculine.

In most of the works of the decade following *The Sailor from Gibraltar*, the "writing subject" is inscribed through a split narrative voice, either through a male/female interrogation of desire or through a male character/narrator in varying degrees of tension with an abstract frame narrator. In the interrogations of desire, Duras frequently uses the genre of the detective story or mystery to frame the narrative. *The Square* (1955), *Moderato Cantabile* (1958), and the cycle of *L'Amante anglaise* (*Les Viaducs de Seine-et-Oise*, 1960; the novel *L'Amante anglaise*, 1967; and the 1968 play of that title), as well as the scenario for *Hiroshima mon amour* (1960), are built around interrogations of desire. *10:30 on a Summer Night* presents an interesting variation on the male/female interrogation of desire. In this mystery story focused on crimes of passion and betrayal, a split narrative voice is inscribed within a woman character who interrogates crime and desire. In the interrogations of desire, the rhetoric of discontinuity noted in *The Sailor from Gibraltar* gives way to a rhetoric of reinscription, using one (incomplete) story to tell another. This, in turn, leads to disarticulation—the collapse of common logic, mute resistance to communication.

The other narrative mode is developed in the Lol V. Stein cycle (*The Ravishing of Lol Stein*, 1964; *The Vice-Consul*, 1965; and, to some extent, *L'Amour*, 1971), where the frame narrator is anonymous and a male narrator is a character in the text. In these texts, reinscription and repetition create a closed loop, with the story endlessly reflecting back on itself. Ultimately these novels represent a narrative of absence, marked by inarticulate cries, songs in a language inaccessible to the average Western reader, and the "hole word" of Lol's story that has generated a great deal of critical commentary. *L'Amour*, with its geometrically abstract narrative, moves further in the direction of postmodern anonymity of the writing subject. With *L'Amour*, however, Duras reaches a creative impasse that will be broken only through new narrative discoveries provided by filmmaking.

Interrogations of Desire

New Narrative Voices: *The Square* **and** *Moderato Cantabile.*
Narrative form changes dramatically in *The Square* (1955). Unlike the
early novels, which were marked by narrative display and profusion—
Joseph's "huge joke" ("la grande rigolade") in *The Sea Wall* in which one
disaster story led to even sadder tales, or the proliferation of stories in
exotic settings about the sailor in *The Sailor from Gibraltar*, for example—Duras now turns to nearly Racinian unities of time and action;
excess is tightly contained. Duras also splits the narrative voice in a new
way. The frame narrator is minimized, and remains abstract, removed
from the text and expressed only through sparse descriptions. The main
narrative consists of a conversation between a maid caring for a child and
a traveling salesman sitting in a park for several hours one afternoon.

Each of the three sections of the text begins with the same sentence in
the anonymous frame narrator's voice: "The child came over quietly
from the far side of the Square and stood before the girl."[6] Each time,
the sentence is followed by the child's expression of a need that echoes in
its simplicity the last words of Christ on the cross: "I'm hungry," in the
first chapter; "I'm thirsty," in the second; "I'm tired," to open the last
chapter. The repetition and religious reference (rare in Duras's writing)
give a ritual simplicity and intensity to the frame of the book.

The elements of later interrogations of desire are in place: a man and
a woman, strangers at the start, in a public place, questioning each other
about meaning and desire. Each character tells a story and interprets the
other's story: selecting, valuing, or denying what he or she is hearing,
incorporating it into his or her own story or distancing from it. The
reader, faced with these patterns of storytelling and interpretation, tries
to understand their meaning in the starkly sketched context provided by
the writer.

The main difference between *The Square* and the later texts is that the
man and the woman are narrative equals, and violence is contained.
Although the man initiates the conversation, the woman asks as many
questions as he does. Neither controls or directs meaning more than the
other; they are alternately transparent and opaque to each other. The
maid, dissatisfied with the meaningless anonymity of her existence, waits
"to be chosen" by a man, to marry and therefore change her life. Hers is
not a benign or indifferent passivity. She loathes her present state but
refuses any attempts to improve it. She has murderous fantasies; her
capacity for rage and destruction is held in check only by the belief that

violence would not change anything or, worse, would falsely suggest that an intolerable condition could be improved.

The two stories, hers and the salesman's, are separate narrative strands, remaining distinct until the suggestion, at the end, that he may enter into her story by coming to the weekly ball she attends, where she waits to be chosen by a man who would change her life. Through their conversational exchanges, particularly her observations about him, the salesman has an insight about his own character that may give him the courage to take that step, a courage he observed in her but found lacking in himself.

In *Moderato Cantabile*, class differences compound gender differences, intensifying both desire and violence. A crime of passion, partially witnessed, becomes a model for the narrative a working-class man and bourgeois woman invent. The frame narrator in *Moderato Cantabile* is anonymous, loosely associated with the woman's consciousness. Toward the end of the novel the frame narrator assumes a more fully developed voice and function than the frame narrator had in *The Square*. But for the most part, the dominant narrative voices in *Moderato Cantabile* are the man and the woman, telling their own stories and inventing the novel we are reading.

The story in *Moderato Cantabile* is set in motion by a violent crime: A man kills his lover in a café. Anne Desbaresdes, brought to the neighborhood by her son's piano lessons, partially witnesses the crime, like Chauvin, an unemployed worker who frequents the café. Their efforts to complete what they have witnessed by reconstructing the crime make up the narrative of the novel. Once they have reconstructed—or invented—the story of the crime, they become the characters they have created, they make the story of the crime their own. Theirs is not a shooting but a social crime realized through narrative; it is no less violent for being bloodless.

In a preface she wrote for a school edition of *Moderato Cantabile*, Duras says that the crime at the beginning of the novel is a "model crime" that allows Anne Desbaresdes and Chauvin to live an adulterous love affair and to arrive immediately at the final stage: death.[7] Chauvin and Anne never know anything more than they do at the moment of the crime. Chauvin says, "I tried to find out something more. But I couldn't" (*FN*, 79; *MC*, 54). They construct their narrative in the space between what they know and what they desire. Anne initiates the story they create and Chauvin elaborates or deepens what she invents to make her speak more. Even more aggressively than the narrator in *The Sailor from Gibraltar*, Chauvin constantly goads Anne: "Talk to me. . . . Go on."

As in *The Square*, three narrative lines emerge in *Moderato Cantabile*: the story of each character and the story of the couple they form. Each character's story is associated with distinct motifs and themes that merge in the novel's climax, more dramatically than they do in *The Square*. Anne, as object of Chauvin's desire and subject of the narrative that becomes *Moderato Cantabile*, has a more fully developed story. Presented as the wife of the most powerful man in this provincial, seaside city, she seems from the beginning to be at odds with her role and without a history of her own. Her child, and her responsibility for him, are the surest sign of her class and gender identity as bourgeois mother. The child also provides the excuse for her to go into this working-class neighborhood— for his piano lessons and then as a pretext for afternoon walks to the café to pursue daily conversations with Chauvin.

The revolt against the ruling powers suggested at the end of *The Sea Wall* is internalized in *Moderato Cantabile*, represented as a split between Anne and other women characters and as a division within Anne herself. Sharon Willis has noted that in the detective genre particularly, "an obsession with the law and its transgression must be related to an inscription of desire in narrative" (Willis, 139). She goes on to show that "woman embodies the law; the maternal body is the site of the law's inscription. Woman is therefore the embodiment of the law, as well as its subject" (Willis, 140). At the beginning of *Moderato Cantabile* the piano teacher and the café proprietor (both women) act as guardians of social order, an order on which the rich bourgeoisie is founded. During the child's piano lesson in the first chapter, Anne admires her son's resistance, his refusal to conform to the discipline his teacher tries to impose. Later, seeing the ambivalence of the mother, the teacher suggests that Anne stop coming with her son. Similarly, the café proprietor who at the start welcomes the respectable Anne Desbaresdes into her café begins to regard her with the same disapproval she expressed when she talked about the victim of the crime, who, like the woman Anne is becoming, was a married woman and a drunkard.

Chauvin, whose story is told only as it intersects with Anne's, is an unemployed worker who had worked in Monsieur Desbaresdes' factory. He reminds her that he had met her at a reception in her house; a magnolia flower—emblematic of desire in the novel—was pinned between her breasts. Because of their relative class status, he knew the influential name she carried, but he remained an anonymous worker in the line. During their third conversation in the café he names himself, completing the introduction of that day: "Last June—in a few days it will be a year ago—you were standing facing him on the steps, ready to receive us, the workers from the foundries. Above your breasts, which were half bare, there was a white magnolia. My name is Chauvin" (*FN*, 88; *MC*, 77). Chauvin's is the story of the circulation of desire. He walks the streets, circles Anne's house, imagines her life behind the great fence, through the bedroom window. As they construct their story, he tells Anne's as he has witnessed it, from a distance, in his fantasies of desire.

Having named himself, Chauvin reminds Anne of the anonymity at the core of her social persona. She is one of a series of "Madame Desbaresdes" who have lived for generations in this big, impersonal house, who have died there haunted by the sound of the wind in the hedges. Anne's story and the story of the murder intertwine; sometimes Anne talks about the murder in order to deflect Chauvin's intense reconstruction of her own life. At other moments she weaves the story of her life together with the story of the murder. She identifies with the victim, for example, by comparing the victim's cry in death with her own cry when she gave birth to her child. As the narrative Anne and Chauvin construct progresses and as it gives verbal reality to their adulterous collaboration, the child will be taken away from her and her cry will merge with the victim's cry.

The cheap wine Anne becomes addicted to in her daily conversations with Chauvin is poisonous. It allows her to continue inventing, with Chauvin, a love story that can only end, like the model crime on which it is based, in death—the death of the social person she had performed until then. The performative nature of her role is stressed in the penultimate chapter, told in the voice of the frame narrator moving from Anne's perspective inside her house to Chauvin's outside. When she arrives late to a dinner party at her own house, she is drunk from the café wine and she can no longer play her assigned role. At the beginning of this passage she tries to play over any incongruity: "A fixed smile makes her face acceptable" (*FN*, 107; *MC*, 127). Her performance, however, is seriously marred; even her husband fails to recognize her: "A man, facing a woman, looks at her as though he does not recognize her. Her breasts are half exposed. She hastily adjusts her dress. A drooping flower lies between them. . . . Her lips are pale. Tonight she forgot to make herself up" (*FN*, 106, 107; *MC*, 126, 128).

Gradually she recognizes her incongruity in this otherwise "perfect ritual." She is no longer playing to this audience, to the man who barely recognizes her when she arrived, but to Chauvin who paces outside the house, looking up at her window, imagining her performance and remembering the reception at which he met her in a different role. At the dinner party, the guests are represented without faces and through fragments of conversation that reveal a social milieu in which the individual is suppressed: "Little by little the chorus of conversation grows louder and, with considerable effort and ingenuity, some sort of society emerges. . . . And little by little a conversation builds that is partisan in its generalities but neutral in its details. It will be a successful party" (*FN*, 108; *MC*, 129).[8] Anne, ejected by this society, goes up to her child's room:

> From the big bay window of the long corridor of her life she will look at the boulevard below. The man will already have left. She will go into the child's room, and lie down on the floor. . .paying no attention to the magnolia crushed to pieces between her breasts. And to the inviolable rhythm of her child's breathing she will vomit forth the strange nourishment that had been forced upon her. (*FN*, 112; *MC*, 140)

After this evening, responsibility for her child is taken away from her.

The next time she returns to the café she is alone. She has come to finish the story of the crime that she and Chauvin have made into her own. "'I wish you were dead,' Chauvin said. 'I am,' Anne Desbaresdes said" (*FN*, 118; *MC*, 155). Fiction in *Moderato Cantabile* becomes an instrument of desire and death. Anne does not tell this story with Chauvin's help in order to understand or to escape the horror of the person she had become but to kill her, to live as fully as she can the story of fatal passion that she discovers when she witnesses the crime. The dislocation of a fictional character, the absent sailor, suggested in *The Sailor from Gibraltar*, becomes the disintegration of a character who invents and embraces her own destruction. She kills off the bourgeois mother and wife she had performed, but there is no role available for her to assume other than the destroyed woman. As Erica Eisinger has pointed out, Anne moves from witness to detective to victim in this variant of the detective story.[9] Chauvin is a narrator-accomplice throughout in this social murder/suicide.

Changing Stories: The Reader's Place in *L'Amante anglaise*. In *Moderato Cantabile*, Anne and Chauvin retell a partially witnessed story in order to invent their own. With *L'Amante anglaise*, Duras retells at least three times a crime story she says she saw reported in the newspaper. The differences in the retellings significantly alter the answers to three questions: Whose story is being told? Who is telling it? What relationship is established with the reader, particularly if she is a woman?

The newspaper account that Duras reconstructs as the story of origin for her own tale describes the discovery of severed parts of a woman's body found on trains throughout France. All the trains had passed under one viaduct in the department of Seine-et-Oise, which led the police to the murderers: an ordinary retired couple. The victim was a deaf-mute cousin who had kept house for them for twenty-seven years. With each retelling, Duras gives greater attention to the story of the wife and at the same time inhibits the reader's access to her story through the creation of a narrator-interrogator. With each telling the distance between what the central character knows and what she says, the part of the book the reader must supply, becomes increasingly the central concern of the work.

In the play, *Les Viaducs de Seine-et-Oise*, Duras's first version, the reader-spectator learns directly from the couple in the first act that they are the murderers; the second, final act becomes a joint public confession leading to their arrest. The crime is a folie à deux in which Claire, the wife, had a more responsible role. Her husband seeks to understand their act through her, and as they talk and listen to each other they arrive at some sort of understanding. The brutal violence of the crime is portrayed as the logical outcome of provincial routine, a desperate gesture to create an extraordinary moment in the ordinary dullness of aging. The horror of the crime—reinforced by characters who act as a chorus—is that its authors are not anonymous monsters stalking an innocent town; rather, it is the town, the boredom of dailiness that produces monsters.

Seven years later, Duras takes up the story again in the novel *L'Amante anglaise* (the translator kept the French title because of the multiple puns related to Claire's confusion about language that cannot be rendered simply in English; it means at once "the English [woman] lover," "the mint plant in mud," "the English [woman] lover in mud," and "the English mint plant"). In the novel, Claire alone is the murderer; her husband is not an accomplice or even a witness, having slept through the event. The narrative now begins after Claire's arrest and trial, and she has become the explicit center of interest. The narrator is a man who intends to write a book about the crime. He tells his interlocutors that they are free to answer the questions or not, as they wish. The novel turns around these persistent questions: Who is Claire Lannes, and what does her act mean? In three interrogations—of a café owner, of Claire's husband, and then of Claire—the reader is brought gradually closer to Claire and closer to the enigma of her act. The interrogator's function—like that of the narrator in *The Sailor from Gibraltar* and Chauvin in *Moderato Cantabile*—is to make Claire talk, to learn her story first from witnesses and then to prod her to tell him her version, to explain the meaning of the act that now defines her as a murderer. But unlike the earlier interrogators, this one has an adversarial relationship with Claire. In both the novel and the play by the same title that

Duras published the following year, the subject, the narrator, and the reader are bound by conflicting self-interests. The subject wants to withhold certain information in order to keep hold of her interlocutor. The interrogator is no longer a mediator promising meaning, as Chauvin does Anne; in fact his powerlessness in the face of the withholding subject makes him more aggressive. The reader wants to understand, to find a means of interpreting Claire's story, a means the interrogator is not able to supply.

With the shift in focus from the couple to Claire and with the addition of the interrogator have come other significant changes in the story. First, unlike Anne in *Moderato Cantabile*, Claire is given a history that is both discontinuous with her married life and central to her self-definition. Two added stories situate Claire in her past and present. As a girl she was devout, but a passionate affair with a policeman from her home town, "l'agent de Cahors," replaced God as the object of her desire and her means of self-definition. When the policeman betrayed her, there was nothing left of her identity but its discontinuous history. Through her husband's testimony we learn that she had tried to commit suicide. When that failed, in a pattern that parallels Lol V. Stein's, she married, left Cahors—scene of her youth and her love—and led an ordered, unremarkable married life. The other story that situates her concerns her daily routine and the spaces she occupied. The figure of her deaf-mute cousin, according to Claire, loomed disproportionately large in the house. Enacting her feelings of exclusion, Claire obsessively tried to erase all traces of herself in the house and chose to sit on a garden bench next to her English mint plant. The mint, a purgative, represents for her the opposite of the heavy cuisine her cousin prepared daily. The mint was also a pretext for letters she wrote to garden columns in the paper. Both her cousin and her husband represent routines and blocked communication she silently rejects. Her cousin cannot hear her and her husband will not listen. His testimony reveals contempt for her barely literate attempts to write letters to the paper.

In contrast, Claire talks about the multiple insights she had on her bench—bringing together her past, her thoughts about the world, things she has read. She has a story but lacks the means to tell it. In one progressively inchoate monologue, Claire spews out bits and pieces of the concepts she wishes she could articulate. Duras refuses to use the interrogator to make Claire's story accessible. The monologue remains inarticulate, connections are garbled, meaning is blocked. She says, finally, "I wasn't intelligent enough for the intelligence that was in me, and I wouldn't have been able to express it" (*AM*, 102; *AA*, 163).

The most significant change in this version is the crime itself. The generalized alienation of *Les Viaducs de Seine-et-Oise* is replaced by a specifically feminine alienation. Claire's dismantling of her cousin's body is an attempt to articulate herself: In that violent act of rupture she brings together the disjointed parts of her history. She inscribes two words on parts of the body: "Alphonso" and "Cahors." Alphonso was the one man who sensed meaning in her words when her husband refused to; Cahors was the town of her lover and her coming of age. What has been an incidental, grisly detail in the first version (the victim's head was not found) becomes a willed act of concealment in the later versions. Claire refuses to tell where she hid the head because if she gives up this knowledge, the interrogator will cease listening to her. By refusing communication, by withholding that intelligence, maintaining that absence, she has control over a continuing narrative. He cannot pretend to have access to her whole story and, therefore, cannot interpret it for her or for the reader. The absence (of the sailor) that motivated Anna's story in *The Sailor from Gibraltar* now becomes a consciously chosen strategy on the part of the woman-subject. This heightens the antagonism between the narrator and the subject and shifts the narrative power (if only by default) from the narrator to the subject.

Marcelle Marini has argued that when Claire murders her cousin she rebels against a construction of the feminine that risked subsuming her: her cousin's obstinate optimism in the face of brutish routine, an objectified deaf-mute presence in a world she can maintain but not define. For Marini, Claire's act breaks that objectification, creates a break in daily routine through which she can create a story, a history. Like many other feminist critics in search of a speaking female subject, a female-gendered narrative voice, Marini sees in Claire's act of violence the birth of a female subject who can speak for herself.[10]

At first glance, the third version of the story—the play *L'Amante anglaise*, written a year after the novel—would seem to bear out Marini's reading. In the play all characters have been eliminated except for Claire. But the continued presence of the interrogator creates an obstacle to the interpretation of Claire's story that Marini proposes. The reader (or spectator) has access to Claire's story only through the interrogator's mediation. Again her primary means of control is concealment—withholding the information about the head, maintaining the enigma. Claire's power is in delineating that part of the story which the reader must supply: the difference between what she knows and what she will say. The interrogator seeks to close the gap, to create a closed text with a fixed meaning, foreclosing the reader's interpretive role. Claire's refusal to close the gap invites the reader to collaborate. The reader in colluding with her ruse recognizes that nothing would be learned if she revealed the secret; what is meaningful is the nonrevelation. If the head were recovered the corpse would be complete, but the narrative corpus would be suppressed. Just as the nonexistence of the Gibraltar sailor was the impetus for fiction in the earlier novel and created a pretext for Anna's story, the concealment of the apparent resolution of the crime allows Claire's story to continue. At the end of the novel she says, "If I were you I'd listen. Listen" (*AM*, 122; *AA*, 195). She implores the reader to hear what she is actually saying rather than to maintain the illusion that what she is withholding would explain her.

Duras challenges the "reader" of *L'Amante anglaise* to assume an active role in making meaning, but the woman reader of *L'Amante anglaise* is faced with a dilemma. The interrogator keeps searching for the right question that would yield the answer he seeks—resolution, explanation, closure. The reader has access to Claire's story through the interrogator but can see that there is no right question: Resolution would merely end the story, not give it meaning. The meaning is already there—in Claire's efforts to purge herself of an existence that oppresses her and to keep intact the passion and anger of her memory of the policeman from Cahors. A woman subject's power is not in what she says but in her silence. Meaning is situated in the gap between her words and her refusal to speak, a split she protects within her own subjectivity. In these texts the female speaking subject requires the active participation of the reader and rejects closure. Claire's story, like Anna's, centers on absence: the betrayal of a lover, the purging of the debris of daily living. But in this novel, violence that was contained in *The Square* and internalized in *Moderato Cantabile* is acted out by the woman subject in the killing of her cousin, another woman. Paradoxically, in *L'Amante anglaise*, Claire does not eradicate her victim and with her a certain construction of the feminine, she becomes her. Her only power at the end is to be mute, to refuse to speak certain words. She expels her monologue in the same way she rejected her cousin's undigested, overrich stew. The woman reader as reader is told to listen; as woman, Claire's example tells her to keep silent.

Hiroshima mon amour, like *Moderato Cantabile* and *L'Amante anglaise*, is an interrogation of desire (a man interrogating a woman, abetted by alcohol, in a series of cafés) with even higher stakes: War has replaced the crime of passion, violence is cataclysmic, nuclear. The story the

Frenchwoman had withheld until questioned by the Japanese man is her own (like Claire's) rather than borrowed from another woman (like that of Anne Desbaresdes). Unlike Anne, the Frenchwoman has an affair with her interlocutor; unlike Claire, she hands over her secret. Through a series of substitutions and performances, the Japanese man and the Frenchwoman create their own story through the remembrance and invention of their different histories. Duras shows that possession of the woman's story is more intimate than sexual possession. I will discuss the film and its relation to *Moderato Cantabile* in the next chapter because, even though it was a collaborative project with Alain Resnais, it is useful to consider the scenario in the context of Duras's own filmmaking.

Midsummer Nightmare: The Fantasmatic Scene in *10:30 on a Summer Night*. In *10:30 on a Summer Night*, Duras returns to earlier narrative strategies to stage an interrogation of desire internalized within a woman's subjectivity. As Carol Murphy argues in a persuasive article about thematic and textual violence in this novel, "Duras aims at portraying the 'unknown' element of a troubled consciousness and this mysterious perturbation becomes the center of the text."[11]

Like *Moderato Cantabile*, *10:30 on a Summer Night* begins with a conversation between a man and woman in a café about a crime of passion that has taken place in a small town. No one knows exactly what happened, why, or when, except that Rodrigo Paestra discovered his nineteen-year-old wife (a stranger to the town) with his best friend and shot them both. The woman in the café is Maria, traveling through Spain with her husband, Pierre, their little daughter Judith, and Claire, a friend who, Maria suspects, may be having an affair with Pierre. A violent storm traps them in this village for twenty-four hours. During that time Maria finds Rodrigo Paestra and leads him to safety in a field outside of town; before she can return to help him escape he commits suicide. During the same night she believes she witnesses Pierre's betrayal with Claire. The stories become entwined in her thoughts, already troubled by jealousy, alcohol, and exhaustion. Like Anne, she uses the fragments she knows of Rodrigo's story to fuel her own.

To tell this story, Duras combines narrative strategies from earlier novels. As in *The Tranquil Life*, she situates a third-person narrative voice within the subjectivity of a female character. The first-person pronoun breaks through at several moments when Maria experiences betrayal, signaling a split within her consciousness. In the most important scene in the novel (10:30 on this summer night), Maria, scanning the rooftops of the village from a hotel balcony, believes she sees at the same time Rodrigo cowering in a blanket on a rooftop and Claire and Pierre in an embrace on another balcony. The storm and darkness obscure her vision; the light is "livid." She witnesses Pierre's betrayal by imagining herself in his place: "Was it on her eyes, behind the screen formed by the dark sky, that he had kissed her? How could one know. Your eyes were the color of your fear in the afternoon, the color of the rain at that very moment. Claire, your eyes, I could hardly see them, how could I have noticed it before, your eyes must be gray" (*FN*, 138; *DH*, 47–48).

The language surrounding this moment of (voyeuristic) vision, which may be real or imagined, casts doubt on Maria's ability to *see*, though she clearly *perceives* betrayal. The couple is described, repeatedly, as a "single, blinding shape." The lightning creates shadows and unpredictable flashes of light. She keeps trying to imagine what they are doing and saying what they "must" have done. To "see" the lovers more clearly she imagines herself in Claire's place as well as Pierre's:

> A new phase of the storm was coming up that was going to separate them and prevent Maria from seeing them.
> As he did it, so did she, bringing her hands to her lonely breasts, then her hands fell and, useless, grasped the balcony. (*FN*, 138; *DH*, 48)

The narration is steeped in language that casts doubt on the reality of Maria's vision. The couple creates a "*blinding* shape"; auxiliary verbs suggest that Maria is filling in unseen details ("your eyes *must* be grey")[12]; simple assertions are set in a context of movement and uncertainty: "She could see them fully outlined against the *moving* sky" (*FN*, 138; *DH*, 47; emphasis mine). These qualifiers, along with the eruption of the first person during the most intense scenes of betrayal, splits the female narrative subjectivity in two ways: into pained observer and imagined participant, into reliable or hallucinating narrator. Maria's *need* to see is most urgently expressed immediately before she witnesses a scene. For example, "No, she couldn't do without seeing them. She sees them still."[13] The divided narrative creates a space in which the reader can read two different, if compatible, stories. One version would hold that Maria witnesses Pierre and Claire on the balcony, that her vision confirms her suspicions about them and that her further speculations in the novel about their efforts to consummate their passion are to be read at face value. Betrayal, according to this version, confers lucidity.

The other version would suggest that Rodrigo's exemplary story of desire, betrayal, and violence, in which unambiguous witness turns to clear, irreversible action, transforms Maria's fear into vision. Unable to see clearly and, therefore, to act, she projects the features of her husband's betrayal onto the shifting shadows of the other balcony, creating the cinema of her (forsaken) desire. She becomes the spectator of her own erasure. Desire betrayed, according to this version, produces phantasy (*fantasme* in French, spelled "phantasy" in psychoanalysis and literary applications to distinguish it from the nontechnical "fantasy"). Throughout the novel, each time that Maria sees or imagines that she sees signs of Pierre's adultery she puts herself in his place, or Claire's; she fills in details she cannot quite see in order to feel their desire, to mark the transfer of Pierre's desire from her to Claire.

In the final chapter, Maria, Pierre, Claire, and Judith continue their trip, with Pierre driving recklessly away from the scene of Rodrigo's suicide. In the heat of the afternoon, they stop at a parador to have lunch and take a siesta. Maria, as usual, drinks far too much and stretches out to take a nap alongside Judith. In the following pages, Duras carefully maintains ambiguity so that the reader cannot say with certainty whether Maria witnesses or dreams, sees or imagines that Pierre and Claire go off, rent a room in the hotel at the parador, and consummate their passion. The stories of Rodrigo, of Pierre and Claire, and of Maria's own lovemaking with Pierre years before in a hotel in Verona merge in her mind.

> Maria closed her eyes again. It was going to happen. In half an hour. In an hour. And then the conjugation of their love would be reversed.
>
> She would like to see what happened between them so that she too would be drenched in the same light that illuminated them and to enter into this community that she bequeathed them, since the day, in fact, when she invented it, a certain night in Verona. (Translation mine; published translation *FN*, 192; *DH*, 169)[14]

At the end of the scene she sees, or imagines, Claire, unsure of Pierre's love, looking out at the landscape through the window of their rented room, the landscape from which Maria would witness their lovemaking. Then Claire turns back to the mirror, holding back tears, thinking about Maria: "Maria, dead in the wheat fields? On her face a grin that had been stopped, laughter [*rigolade*] in full bloom? Maria's lonely laughter in the wheat fields? This was her landscape. Everything was leading back to Maria: the sudden softness of the shade from the olive trees, the heat which suddenly made room for the oncoming evening" (*FN*, 194; *DH*, 174). Nowhere in the novel does the narrative voice move outside Maria's subjectivity. In this passage, the narration has not moved away from Maria to Claire; rather, Maria projects what she imagines Claire to be thinking. This is quite literally Maria's landscape, and everything leads back to her because everything in it projects from her.

In *10:30 on a Summer Night*, Duras stages a model fantasmatic scene. In their definition of phantasy in psychoanalytic language, Laplanche and Pontalis stress the relationship between phantasy and desire, and the dual role of the desiring subject as participant and observer in the fantasmatic scene. They summarize the structure of phantasy by saying that the primary function of phantasy is the *staging* of desire in which what is prohibited (*l'interdit*) is always present. Phantasies are scenarios, sequences, in which the subject is invariably present, even in the case of the "primal scene," as both observer and participant. Phantasy is also the locus of defensive strategies such as negation and projection.[15]

Maria is both observer and participant in this "primal scene" of sexual betrayal. Whether or not Pierre has betrayed her with Claire, the need for Maria to stage this scene, to see herself seeing, and to witness the substitution of another woman for herself is the central drama of *10:30 on a Summer Night*. The reader never knows whether Pierre has slept with Claire. Toward the end, as he professes his love for Maria, she hears it as an admission of guilt. He says "You're part of my life . . . I can no longer be content with a woman just for the novelty. I cannot do without you." Maria answers: "It's the end of our story . . . . The end of the story" (*FN*, 199; *DH*, 184). Duras ends the novel in a freeze-frame gesture of closure that leaves the narrative in a state of suspended animation. Claire, Maria, and Pierre go out to a nightclub to watch dancers—a man surrounded by women—in an image that is an emblem of desire:

> Plastered on his face, he had at times a chalky laugh, and at times the mask of a loving, languorous, nauseous drunkenness that made an impression on his audience.
>   In the room, among the others, packed together like the others, Maria, Claire and Pierre were looking at the dancer. (*FN*, 200; *DH*, 185)

Far from telling "the end of the story," the fantasmatic scene marks the beginning of a story endlessly retold through the texts of the Lol V. Stein cycle. The suspended animation of this novel will be replaced in the Lol V. Stein cycle by the dynamics of the fantasmatic scene. The woman subject is split within herself into observer and participant in the drama of betrayed desire. This, as she will say later, is Duras's "primal scene," engendering both desire and narrative. Duras's tendency to retell tales, already evident in *The Sea Wall* and fully developed in the three versions of *L'Amante anglaise*, will become a compulsion to repeat the same story—with variations in perspective, intensity, characters, and accessories—in the stories of Lol V. Stein. The repetitions always lead back to the same source and ultimately end in silence.

Toward a Narrative of Silence: The Lol V. Stein Cycle

Until the publication of *The Lover* in 1984, none of Duras's novels generated more critical attention than *Le ravissement de Lol. V. Stein*, published in France in 1964 and translated as *The Ravishing of Lol Stein*. Itself a story of staging and restaging, repetition and retelling, *The Ravishing of Lol Stein* in turn led Duras to renarrate characters and fragments of scenes in *The Vice-Consul* and *L'Amour*, creating the Lol V. Stein cycle.[16] These texts are not a cycle of novels in the usual sense of the word—a series of novels with recurring themes, overlapping plots, and reappearing characters. Although Duras calls *The Ravishing of Lol Stein* a novel, she does not designate any genre for *The Vice-Consul* or *L'Amour*. Themes recur, and slightly altered place names; characters reappear, though sometimes only their names are reused, and there is little or no continuity in their stories. Taken as a group, this cycle provides a good example of Barthes' definition of an open-ended text (rather than a closed work) cited at the beginning of this chapter: "multiple writings, drawn from many cultures and entering into mutual relations of dialogue, parody, contestations . . . ."

Most critical attention to these texts has shown a fascination with the characters of Lol V. Stein, Anne-Marie Stretter, or the Vice-Consul or with the porousness of the language of these texts. Absence, gaps, breaks in both characterization and language have been read as examples of *écriture féminine* or as the narrative inscription of loss—both psychological and cultural—in an alienated, dislocated, postmodern era. These readings are all justified and highlight different effects of these texts. I would, however, like to return to questions raised in Nancy Miller's discussion at the beginning of this chapter about the interplay of writing and gender and the question of agency for the woman writer. Miller's argument suggests a tension between (French) postmodernist "anonymous textuality," which destabilizes the authority of the Author and gives primacy to disembodied discursive practices, and (American) feminist "situated narrative," which highlights the cultural positioning of both writer and reader and refuses to foreclose the question of agency for the woman writer.

The texts I call interrogations of desire are, largely, stories about the making of narrative and, most often, represent a man and a woman inventing stories that inscribe their desire by retelling fragments of other stories. These are self-consciously gendered narratives. The Lol V. Stein cycle taken as a sequence tends, on the contrary, toward "anonymous textuality."

While Lol's madness and her obsessive fantasmatic scene in *The Ravishing of Lol Stein* and *L'Amour* have preoccupied readers as the center of interest in this cycle, I would argue that the drama of these texts is also Duras's struggle against an illusory ideal of anonymous textuality. The narrative structures of *The Ravishing of Lol Stein* and *The Vice-Consul* dramatize the dilemma of a (woman) writer writing through or against masculine constructions of feminine subjectivity. The creative impasse reached in *L'Amour* reveals that narrative anonymity conceals a controlling, masculine voice or gaze that risks silencing the woman writer.

The Cinema of Lol V. Stein. *The Ravishing of Lol Stein*, like *The Sailor from Gibraltar*, is narrated in the first person by a male character (Jack Hold). Like the interrogations of desire, it begins with his recollections of what a female character (Tatiana Karl, his lover and Lol Stein's childhood friend) has told him about Lol V. Stein's story. Rather than represent a dialogue between them at this point, Duras tells the story entirely through Jack's voice. The reader is put in the role of interlocutor because of the linguistic markers Jack uses and his conversational tone: "Lol Stein was born here in South Tahla, and she spent a good part of her youth in this town. . . . Lol has a brother nine years older than she—I have never seen him—they say he lives in Paris. Her parents are dead" (*LS*, 1; *LVS*, 9).[17]

The narrative structure of *The Ravishing of Lol Stein* reverses the use of gender and point of view in *10:30 on a Summer Night* (and, earlier, in *The Tranquil Life*). In the earlier novels, Duras used a third-person narrative situated in a female character's consciousness that erupted into the first person in moments of particular urgency, inscribing a split feminine subject moving from observed to observer. In *The Ravishing of Lol Stein*, told in a masculine first-person narrative, the third person erupts at moments of phantasy and desire, signaling a split masculine subject, moving from observer to observed.

From the very first words of the novel, the reader is reminded that this is being told by a masculine narrator, that this is his remembrance and invention, what he sees and what he imagines of Lol Stein. Also from the start, he presents and then denies other readings of her— Tatiana's, for example—preferring to present his version of her story, a version shaped by his desire. Before focusing on the narrative structure and the dynamics of gender and desire in this novel, a short summary is in order.

The primary event in the life of Lol Stein—at least as told by Jack Hold—takes place in her nineteenth year at the resort town of T. Beach. With her fiancé, Michael Richardson, she goes to a ball at the casino; at one point, an older woman—Anne-Marie Stretter—walks in, captures the gaze and desire of Michael Richardson, and leaves with him at dawn while Lol looks on, witness to her own abandonment. Transfixed by the spectacle of her own erasure, she is comforted in vain by her friend Tatiana, who also witnesses the event. Removed from the scene, Lol suffers a nervous breakdown. While walking alone at night, after her apparent recovery, she encounters Jean Bedford, who marries her and takes her away to U. Bridge (Uxbridge in the translation). For ten years she leads an exemplary, ordered married life; she gives birth to three daughters. Her parents having died, she and her family move back to her hometown of S. Tahla (the word evokes the Greek *thalassa* for the sea, even though the town is not represented as being by the sea, as is T. Beach). Again, she establishes a carefully ordered existence, though, according to Jack, she seems always to be imitating someone, fitting a role.

After a time, she takes daily walks, the better to relive the scene at the ball, according to Jack Hold, to recapture the moment when she was eclipsed by another woman. This, in Jack's metaphor for Lol's obsession, is the cinema of Lol V. Stein that she enters every day in her mind. Significantly, the only other mention of cinema in the novel occurs when Jack recreates for the reader (in the third person) a scene in which Lol discovers him. One afternoon, according to his story, Lol follows a man leaving a movie theater in the middle of the afternoon. She follows him to a bus stop where he meets his lover—Tatiana Karl—and then to a hotel where they have a room. She watches the window of their room, seeing them in fragments as they walk by the window. She then tracks down Tatiana Karl's address and calls on her one day saying that she had found an old photograph (which doesn't exist) and was reminded of their shared girlhood. As she meets her friend again, she also meets the man from the hotel: Jack Hold.

She begins to include Tatiana, her husband, and Jack in her social life; Jack learns that she had witnessed his meeting with Tatiana. Now, whenever he meets Tatiana at the hotel, he knows that Lol is watching the window from a field of rye. He and Lol meet at a tearoom in another town and together construct the story of his last assignation with Tatiana in the hotel and this, in turn, becomes folded in with the story of the ball at the casino. Jack and Lol return to T. Beach together, visit the casino, reconstruct the scene, and spend the night together in that town. In the last scene of the novel, they have returned to S. Tahla, Jack is with Tatiana in the hotel room and Lol watches their window from the field of rye.

The story, as they say, is in the telling. As many have pointed out, the title, *The Ravishing of Lol Stein*, in French as in English, can signal ecstasy or rape; further, Lol could be construed as subject or object of pleasure or of violation. All readings can be maintained in the book in the play of substitutions effected by the narrator. Although most readers regard the narrator as transparent, a sympathetic observer trying to understand Lol in her terms, attempting to find the word she would use to tell her story, his self-conscious construction of the narrative nevertheless reminds us of his mediating presence. I would argue that the narrative itself presents yet another ravishing of Lol Stein: the appropriation of her gaze and the substitution of one fantasmatic scene (Jack's) for another (Lol's).

Throughout the novel, Jack reminds the reader that he is building this story out of what he knows of Lol and what he imagines. Tatiana's version of Lol would locate the cause of her illness—a pathological indifference masked by thoughtfulness—long before the ball scene. Jack rejects this reading and begins his own story of Lol: "Here then, in full, and all mixed together, both this false impression which Tatiana Karl tells about and what I have been able to imagine about that night at the Town Beach casino. Following which I shall relate my own story of Lol Stein" (*LS*, 4; *LVS*, 12). He specifically excludes the story of her adolescence from his story, beginning with the night at the ball, because through this event he can incorporate her into his life. He says, "the presence of her adolescence in this story might somehow tend to detract, in the eyes of the reader, from the overwhelming actuality of this woman in my life. I am therefore going to look for her . . . at that moment in time when it seems to me she first began to stir, to come toward me . . ." (*LS*, 4–5; *LVS*, 13).

What we are reading, then, is Jack's story, not Lol's. Jack imagines that Lol has kept intact the absence of Michael Richardson, the lover of her choice, that she has not betrayed the "exemplary abandon" (*LS*, 21;

LVS, 33) in which he left her. Jack presents Lol's marriage as something that happened to her; her husband was not someone she chose, not a substitute for Michael Richardson. Significantly, Jack suggests that had she made the choice of another man (rather than submit passively to a social script), it would have amounted to "a kind of plagiarism, the crime of replacing the man from Town Beach" (*LS*, 21; *LVS*, 33). The story that Jack constructs might be read as a kind of plagiarism, rewriting Lol's story in his name. The abandoned woman, left empty, becomes the blank screen (or page) on which Jack projects his desire.

By the end of the narrative, Jack assumes the absences left by Richardson to become "the man from Town Beach." Early in the novel he tells the reader, "I know Lol Stein in the only way I can, through love" (*LS*, 36; *LVS*, 52). He reconstructs her phantasy scene for the reader as a "triangular construction of which dawn and the two of them [Michael and Anne-Marie] are the eternal sides" (*LS*, 37; *LVS*, 52). Voiceless, she cannot stop them, cannot stop the dawn. She could not stop them for want of a word. In the most often-cited passage from the book, Jack imagines what Lol's word would have been:

> It would have been an absence-word, a hole-word, whose center would have been hollowed out into a hole, the kind of hole in which all other words would have been buried . . . this word, which does not exist, is none the less there: it awaits you around the corner of language, it defies you—never having been used—to raise it, to make it arise from its king-dom, which is pierced on every side and through which flows the sea, the sand, the eternity of the ball in the cinema of Lol Stein. (*LS*, 39; *LVS*, 54–55)

Jack then goes on to provide language for what he imagines Lol must have seen every day in her reconstruction of the ball scene. He says that she fixes on the moment when Michael would have undressed the other woman, that "She was born to witness it" (*LS*, 39; *LVS*, 55). He elabo-rates the appearance, little by little, of the other woman's body and with it the replacement of Lol's: "Michael Richardson begins to undress a woman other than Lol, and when other breasts appear, white beneath the black sheath, he remains there transfixed, a God wearied by this divesting, his only task, and in vain Lol waits for him to take her again, with her body rendered infirm by the other she cries out, she waits in vain, she cries out in vain" (*LS*, 40–41; *LVS*, 57).

Having established his terms for Lol's phantasy, Jack begins a lengthy narrative in the third person: the story of Lol following "a man" leaving the cinema, meeting his mistress and going to the "Forest Hotel," the same hotel Lol had gone to with Michael Richardson. Later we learn that the man from the cinema is Jack. The use of the third person signals the entry into fiction, his inscription of himself in Lol's story, which has already been presented as his version of Lol's story. Duras, in other words, is constructing a many-layered *mise-en-abîme*: the (woman) writer imagining through the (male) narrator a (woman) character who is unknowable, or who is knowable to the reader only in the terms of a male narrator.

In his depiction of Lol's discovery of his affair with Tatiana, he says, "I think I can see what Lol Stein must have seen" (*LS*, 51; *LVS*, 69). He portrays her watching the hotel window, which has become a "narrow stage," "inventing" the lovers. In a long scene at Lol's house, which leads to Lol's declaration that she has "chosen" Jack, she first stages a conversation with Tatiana about their past. In complicity with the narrator, she sets it up so that he can eavesdrop and watch them through French doors. Once Tatiana has left, Jack and Lol have an extended conversation in which she tells him she followed them to the Forest Hotel. Then that scene becomes mingled with the ball scene and, through a series of substitutions, he becomes Richardson; Tatiana becomes Anne-Marie; and Lol, desired by Jack, becomes Anne-Marie, Tatiana, and herself as observer all at once:

> Just as my hands touch Lol, the memory of an unknown man, now dead, comes back to me: he will serve as the eternal Richardson, the man from Town Beach, we will be mingled with him, willy-nilly, all together, we shall no longer be able to recognize one from the other, neither before, nor after, nor during, we shall lose sight of one another, forget our names, in this way we shall die for having forgotten. (*LS*, 103; *LVS*, 131–32)

Just as Jack had reconstructed Lol's obsessive phantasy of the ball scene in an earlier chapter, he now represents Lol detailing his rendezvous with Tatiana. When she says to him that she saw Tatiana "naked beneath her dark hair," Jack is overwhelmed by the intensity of the image. In an extraordinary passage, the sentence explodes, the image of Tatiana expands into a hallucinatory presence in which desire and repulsion, language and image overcome the narrator until he assumes Lol's position as (voyeur) observer. The language of the passage again alerts the reader to the fantasmatic nature of the scene; we are entering into Jack's desire, he is spectacle and spectator in his (re)creation of Lol's vision. Furthermore, Lol as teller is removed from the scene, looking elsewhere as Jack enters into the power of the image:

It's true that Tatiana was as Lol has just described her, naked beneath her
dark hair. She was that way in the locked room, for her lover. The intensity of the sentence suddenly increases, the air around it has been rent,
the sentence explodes, it blows the meaning apart. . . .
Lol is still far from me, rooted to the floor, still turned toward the
garden unblinking.
The nudity of Tatiana, already naked, intensifies into an overex-
posed image which makes it increasingly impossible to make any sense
whatsoever out of it.
The void is statue. The pedestal is there. The void is Tatiana naked
beneath her dark hair, the fact. It is transformed, poured out, lavishly,
the fact no longer contains the fact, Tatiana emerges from herself, spills
over through the open windows out over the town, the roads, mire, liq-
uid, tide of nudity. . . . I am no longer afraid of Tatiana, I am no longer
afraid. There are two of us, now, beholding Tatiana beneath her dark
hair. (*LS*, 106; *LVS*, 134–36)

The next time Jack meets Tatiana at the hotel he is aware of Lol's
presence—a dark place in the field of rye—looking up at their window.
As he moves to possess Tatiana, the narrative switches abruptly to the
third person, "Jack Hold" replaces "I," as he sees himself being seen. In
a brief return to the first person, he imagines Lol watching as the window becomes a mirror in which Lol's exclusion is reflected: "she had seen
us appear in turn in the frame of the window, that mirror which reflected
nothing and before which she must have shivered with delight to feel as
excluded as she wished to be" (*LS*, 113; *LVS*, 143).
The effect of this scene is revealed in another return to the third person, another possession of Tatiana: "At one point, he spoke constantly to
some other woman who could not see, who could not hear, and with
whom, in intimate contact, he strangely seemed to find himself" (*LS*,
113–14; *LVS*, 144). Jack's fantasmatic scene—Lol watching the window
of the room where he and Tatiana make love—consolidates his subjectivity and desire. Lol as imagined observer and listener enables Jack to
"find himself." Because she cannot see or hear, he can find himself
through her in his own terms, and his projection of Lol's desire reflects
back (on) his own.
In a tearoom conversation that recalls the conversations between
Chauvin and Anne in the café of *Moderato Cantabile*, Jack and Lol together reconstruct the story of his meeting with Tatiana and incorporate the
ball scene. Jack does this by representing Tatiana as the narrator of the
ball scene while she is in bed with him. She is "headless," reduced to an

anonymous body, because he has covered over her head with a sheet; she can therefore take on the features of any woman. The final chapters in which Jack returns to Town Beach with Lol and they make love in a hotel show him assuming a place in her memory, the place held by Michael Richardson. They also show him assuming her perspective in the darkened ballroom where her abandonment had taken place. Having absorbed her fantasmatic scene, Jack's phantasy is replayed at the end of the novel. Lol, a dark spot in the field of rye, watches the window of the Forest Hotel where he has met Tatiana again.

At one moment toward the end of the novel, Jack is interpreting Lol's feelings for Tatiana at a dinner party at Lol's house. Tatiana says, "How do you know such things about Lol?" The narrator, in an internal monologue, adds: "She means: how do you know these things in the place of a woman? in the place of a woman who could be Lol" (my translation; *LS*, 140; *LVS*, 174). Duras is reminding us again that it is Jack speaking, putting himself in the place of a woman and giving her the name of Lol. We have a masculine version of what a woman knows, a masculine construction of "woman" serving his desire.

The *Vice-Consul* and the Beggarwoman from Battambang. In *The Vice-Consul*, Duras's narrative of desire rejoins the colonial narrative through the story of the beggarwoman from Battambang. *The Vice-Consul* is the first of Duras's texts set against the background of India, specifically an imaginary Calcutta. In *The Ravishing of Lol Stein*, Calcutta is named as the city to which Michael Richardson follows Anne-Marie Stretter. The most important European woman character in *The Vice-Consul* is named Anne-Marie Stretter and she has a lover named Michael Richard (*sic*), but when he tells the story of their love it does not correspond with the story in *The Ravishing of Lol Stein*; there is no mention of Lol Stein in this novel. In other words, Duras takes fragments of the earlier novel and attaches different meanings to them. The film *India Song* will merge the narratives of *The Ravishing of Lol Stein* and *The Vice-Consul* in what Duras calls a new narrative region, creating still other meanings and destinies, as she says, for these stories, making them cohere in a new configuration.

The Vice-Consul opens not with the story of the Vice-Consul but with the story of the beggarwoman from Battambang, a figure who will haunt many future texts and films. As in *The Ravishing of Lol Stein*, the reader has access to the first pages of *The Vice-Consul*, and to the story of the beggarwoman, through a male narrator—Peter Morgan—this time represented in the process of writing: "She walks on, writes Peter

Morgan" (*VC*, 1; *LVC*, 9). The reader is reminded less frequently than in *The Ravishing of Lol Stein* that this story is being constructed by a male narrator who has bits of information about a woman who is unknowable to him, that he is piecing together a narrative that is his invention. Nonetheless, in every chapter that tells the story of the beggarwoman there is at least one discrete reminder: "writes Peter Morgan." In the beginning of the third chapter, "Peter Morgan has stopped writing" (*VC*, 18; *LVC*, 29) and becomes a character in another narrative, the story of the ex-Vice-Consul of France, assigned to Lahore, brought to Calcutta because of "unfortunate events," to be reassigned to another post by the French ambassador, the husband of Anne-Marie Stretter.

The Vice-Consul presents a novel within a novel in which the secondary story (the beggarwoman's) precedes and is then incorporated into the primary story (the Vice-Consul's). Of the twenty-one unnumbered chapters in the novel, five are explicitly "written" by Peter Morgan. He invents the story of a Cambodian girl, rejected by her family when she is found to be pregnant, who walks for ten years from Indochina to India in search of food and a place to be. When she has her child, she sells him to a white woman. She is a figure signaling marginalization and alienation: Her pregnancy and her hunger alienate her from her body; her mother rejects her, thus alienating her from her family; her native land is colonized, dominated by a foreign power; she cannot communicate in the language of the country in which she chooses to stay. Her utterances, undecipherable to those who hear, are reduced to saying "Battambang" (the name of her birthplace), singing songs and laughing. Peter Morgan writes her story in part because the whites of Calcutta are haunted by the sounds of her uninterpretable cries in the night.

When Peter Morgan stops writing for a moment in the beginning of the novel he goes out of his room, into the embassy grounds, and sees the beggarwoman in front of the residence of the ex-Vice-Consul of France to Lahore. The Vice-Consul, whose childhood in France is recounted in the primary narrative, is a source of scandal and embarrassment to the whites of Calcutta. While in Lahore he took a gun and shot into an undifferentiated mass of lepers gathered outside his residence in the gardens of Shalimar. In a gesture that seems to shock the whites of Calcutta even more, he is rumored to have turned his gun on the mirrors in his residence in Lahore, shattering reflections of himself—and, I would add, reflections of a colonial, European presence in Lahore.

At the center of the primary narrative is a reception at the embassy to which Anne-Marie Stretter has invited the Vice-Consul. In the descriptions of the reception, disembodied fragments of gossip about the Vice-Consul, Anne-Marie Stretter, and others punctuate the narrative. These voices anticipate the use of offscreen voices during the reception scene in *India Song*. One of the disturbing stories told about the Vice-Consul by the crowd is that he has never had any liaisons with women. At the reception he is, like the other men, fascinated by Anne-Marie Stretter and wants something to happen between them. Peter Morgan ejects him from the reception and in the streets he cries out his desire for Anne-Marie Stretter, shouting "Keep me with you for just one night" (*VC*, 116; *LVC*, 146). His cries mingle with the cries of the beggarwoman, also roaming the streets outside the embassy gates. It is not clear in the novel whether the guards and gates are meant to keep the lepers and beggars out or to close the whites of Calcutta in.

The two stories are related in multiple ways.[18] The narrator of the secondary story is a character in the primary story; the mysterious, mad beggarwoman from Cambodia who inspires Peter Morgan's narrative is part of the crowd of lepers and indigent beggars who surround the embassy looking for food in the primary narrative. In the story Peter Morgan invents, he incorporates an anecdote told to him by Anne-Marie Stretter concerning the sale of a child to a European woman in Savannakhet, Laos. He makes this an episode in the life of the beggar-woman, thereby linking the stories of Anne-Marie Stretter and the beggarwoman from Battambang. The themes of colonialism, poverty, death, leprosy, and hunger, among others, run through both stories. But the narrative structures of the two stories are different. While the narrator of the beggarwoman's story is clearly localized, the narrator of the Vice-Consul's story is unmarked, undefined, shifting in perspective from one character to another. It is impossible to answer "who is speaking" in the chapters that are not Peter Morgan's.

There have been compelling readings of *The Vice-Consul* using Lacanian or French feminist models that focus on the inscription of femininity, maternity, and the exclusion of the female subject from the (masculine) symbolic order.[19] These readings, however, tend to minimize the (re)appearance of the colonial subject in this novel and its continuing presence in the Lol V. Stein cycle. The female colonial subject is structured in this text in the same way that Lol Stein is in *The Ravishing of Lol Stein*: She is the projection of a male narrator, a feminine figure who is, to the narrator, enigmatic, blank, unknowable. In one of the chapters in which Peter Morgan slips from his function as narrator to his presence as character in the primary story, the unmarked narrator says: "Peter

Morgan would now like to substitute, in the place of the destroyed memory of the beggarwoman, the bric-a-brac of his own memory" (my translation; *VC*, 55; *LVC*, 73).

In a later chapter, when again Peter Morgan has the status of character in the primary narrative, he is explaining his desire to write the story of the Cambodian woman to the other European men:

> "In Calcutta, will she be a . . . dot at the end of a long line, the last distinguishable fact of her own life? With nothing left but sleep and hunger, no feeling, no correlation between cause and effect?"
>
> "What he means, I think," says Michael Richard, "is something even more extreme. He wants to deprive her of any existence other than her existence in his mind when he is watching her. She herself is not to feel anything."
>
> "What is left of her in Calcutta?" asks George Crawn.
>
> "Her laugh, drained of all colour, the word 'Battambang' that she repeats incessantly, the song. Everything else had evaporated." (*VC*, 146; *LVC*, 182–83)

The parallel with Jack Hold's appropriation of Lol Stein is striking here and points to an identity between "woman" and the colonial subject in the imagination and desire of European masculine subjectivity and language. The violent, inarticulate act of the Vice-Consul, seen as an embarrassment by the colonial powers, strikes out both at the misery of the colonies massed outside his residence and at the reassuring narcissism enclosed within the residence: mirrors reflecting him back to himself. The beggarwoman, Anne-Marie Stretter, and the Vice-Consul are all scandals that cannot quite be contained by the colonial powers that be. They figure death within a discourse of power and containment that will be explored in later texts.

The alternative to Peter Morgan's narrative is the unmarked narrative voice of the primary story—a fragmented, shifting perspective that is mobile rather than omniscient. Further, several of the characters are portrayed as would-be narrators—Charles Rossett, who has been called in to investigate the Vice-Consul, to piece together his story; the (male) Secretary of the European Club, who is the Vice-Consul's interlocutor; and Michael Richard, who tells and interprets the story of Anne-Marie Stretter. She, on the other hand, is repeatedly portrayed as a reader. She receives packets of books from Europe, and her reading is one of the few things the other whites know of her daily activities; she is portrayed reading at several moments. The effacing of a specific narrative voice in the primary narrative signals an effort at "anonymous textuality" in this novel, though the reader infers that anonymity is masculine. Significantly, all the narrators Duras represents in the text are male; the beggarwoman cries out in a language no one understands; Anne-Marie Stretter reads. At several moments, the Vice-Consul's voice is described as false, like the voice in a dubbed movie, disturbingly out of synch. I would argue that this is also the case with the primary narrative voice in *The Vice-Consul*. It is both masculine and anonymous; a female speaking subject has yet to emerge in its own terms in Duras's narrative.

L'Amour: **The Screen of Anonymity.** The anonymity of the narrative voice in *The Vice-Consul* is taken to extremes in *L'Amour*. *L'Amour* returns to the story of Lol V. Stein in the most stark, abstract terms. No names are used except for S. Thala (*sic*), where the story is located; however, in this text, S. Thala is not like the S. Tahla of *The Ravishing of Lol Stein*, but like Town Beach, a resort town by the sea. In the narrative, normal syntax is elided, persons and objects appear to be unmediated, revealing an underlying geometry of desire:

> A man.
> He is standing, he looks: the beach, the sea . . .
> Between the man who looks and the sea, just at the edge of the sea, far, someone walks. Another man.(*LA*, 7)
> . . .
> To the left, a woman with closed eyes. Seated.
> The man who walks doesn't look, nothing, nothing but sand in front of him. His step is constant, regular, far off.
> The triangle closes with the woman with closed eyes. She is seated against a wall that marks the beach near the end, the town. (*LA*, 8)

A few prepositions suggesting stage directions ("to the left") and several uses of the pronoun "one" ("one sees him . . . one hears," *LA*, 10) suggest a place for the narrator in the text and, therefore, a place to situate the reader. But most of the text represents an effacement of both narrator and reader behind a veil of anonymity. While this text distills the story of Lol Stein to an essence of betrayed desire and love and memory lost, it is only readable, I think, when placed back in the context of the Lol V. Stein cycle.

After writing *L'Amour*, Duras temporarily abandoned written narrative as her primary means of expression and turned to film, making *Woman of the Ganges* in 1972–73. *Woman of the Ganges* is based on *L'Amour* but introduces an entirely new narrative instrument—offscreen (feminine) voices. When *L'Amour* is read in the context of the other two texts of the Lol V. Stein cycle, the anonymity of the narrative voice, the radical refusal to locate it in any personal terms, can be understood as the effort of the woman writer to write outside or beyond the terms of masculine desire and discourse portrayed through Jack Hold and Peter Morgan. The anonymity is, however, a screen for masculine discourse that continues to structure the narrative. In the three texts of the Stein cycle, the woman writer writes through a masculine construction of female desire that reflects back on himself, constitutes him as desiring subject. She arrives in *L'Amour* at abstraction without memory, without a voice, her own "hole word," or absence at the heart of a masculine language. Only when she discovers the use of voices offscreen, outside the screen of projected male desire (the window/mirror of Lol, which becomes an illuminated rectangle in *L'Amour*), can she begin to imagine a narrating voice in the feminine—tentative, whispered, fragmented, with imperfect memory *but* in the feminine.

Chapter Four
Film Fictions

Duras turned to filmmaking because she found the films made from her books so bad that she thought she could do as well "or rather, I could only do better."[1] Initially she adapted written texts to film,[2] but eventually films engendered written texts rather than issued from them. Although dissatisfaction with the film adaptations of her texts by other filmmakers may have led Duras to decide to make her own, deeper narrative needs compelled her virtually to abandon writing for cinema as her primary means of expression during the seventies.

Feminist film theorists provide particularly useful tools for understanding Duras's films because they distinguish conventional films, like the adaptations Duras scorned, from experimental films while defining the role of gender in both the creation of films and in cinematic representation. In *The Acoustic Mirror*, Kaja Silverman builds on earlier theorists who concentrated on the construction of woman as the object of the male gaze in classic cinema. She widens the analysis to examine the representation of the female voice and the issue of authorship, particularly ways of inscribing a female authorial voice in film.[3] Duras's most important cinematic innovations involve the separation of the voice from the image tracks and the emergence of a female authorial voice that will lead her back to a new kind of writing in the eighties.

Kaja Silverman observes that "Film theory has been haunted since its inception by the specter of a loss or absence at the center of cinematic production, a loss which both threatens and secures the viewing subject" (Silverman, 2). Silverman argues that the preoccupation with lack in psychoanalysis, film theory, and classic Hollywood cinema is really "a preoccupation with male subjectivity" (Silverman, 2). Duras's cinematic production is also informed by the ideologies expressed in psychoanalysis, film theory, and classic cinema, but at the same time her films expose those ideologies. Duras's films develop a female subjectivity and a female authorial voice that are complicit with masculine order and yet disruptive of it. Filmmaking for Duras, particularly in the 1970s, was more than the temporary diversion of a writer. Film production provided a new narrative apparatus with which to explore her recurring themes and obsessions: putting both writer/filmmaker and reader/spectator in new "narrative regions."[4] Gradually in her films, Duras finds ways to tell a woman's story with women's voices.

In this chapter, I review aspects of feminist film theory, particularly Kaja Silverman's formulations, that help us to read Duras's films. Then I look at Duras's major films in three groups: setting the terms in *Hiroshima mon amour* and *Nathalie Granger*; literalizing the metaphor of the "cinema of Lol V. Stein" in the Indian cycle; and becoming "Duras" on screen and off in *The Truck* and the short subjects made in 1979. My discussion focuses on voices (narrating and authorial), the split female subject, and the relation established between the filmmaker and the spectator. Throughout I look at displacements, substitutions, and splittings: persons and places shifting and substituting for each other on screen, in mirrors and on the sound track, and the splitting of the sound from the image track, which is one of Duras's most striking cinematic innovations.

Laura Mulvey, in one of the founding essays of feminist film theory, locates the pleasure of traditional cinema in the look, or gaze. She breaks down the look of traditional films in the following way:

> There are three different looks associated with the cinema: that of the camera as it records the profilmic event, that of the audience as it watches the final product, and that of the characters at each other within the screen illusion. The conventions of narrative film deny the first two and subordinate them to the third, the conscious aim being always to eliminate intrusive camera presence and prevent a distancing awareness in the audience. Without these two absences (the material existence of the recording process, the critical reading of the spectator), fictional drama cannot achieve reality, obviousness and truth.[5]

Duras, like other experimental filmmakers, will refuse to privilege the third look described here, the look among characters within the screen illusion. Rather she will heighten awareness of the camera's look and complicate the spectator's look, challenging the terms of pleasure as maintained by conventional cinema and exposing the artifice of the reality and truth it purports to represent. Duras's films establish a sometimes disturbing tension between the filmmaker and the spectator, a tension that is often explicitly gendered—the female filmmaker and the male spectator—placing the female spectator in a different relation to the film. Duras generates this tension largely through the invention of a distinctly inflected female authorial voice.

Kaja Silverman reads both psychoanalysis and film theory to account for the female voice in cinema, building on the work of other feminist film theorists, like Laura Mulvey, who have analyzed woman as spectacle. Her basic thesis, following Lacan, is that "there is a castration which precedes the recognition of anatomical difference—a castration to which all cultural subjects must submit, since it coincides with separation from the world of objects, and the entry into language" (Silverman, 1).

Silverman argues that all subjects, male and female, experience symbolic castration (separation from the mother that coincides with entry into language) before the discovery of anatomical difference. She tries "to articulate the relationship between . . . symbolic castration and the traumatic discovery anatomized by Freud" (Silverman, 1). Freud's "anatomical literalism" distances the male subject from the notion of lack and projects it onto the female. By conflating symbolic castration with anatomical difference, the male subject is able to disavow that he "is already structured by absence prior to the moment at which he registers woman's anatomical difference—to concede that he, like the female subject, has already been deprived of being, and already been marked by the language and desires of the Other" (Silverman, 15).

In classic cinema, Silverman argues, male lack is easily displaced; it may, for example, be projected onto female characters as "anatomical deficiency or discursive inadequacy" or equated with the concealed site of production.[6] In classic cinema the male voice is located "at the point of apparent textual origin," and may be a "voice-over," occupying a different (superior, narrative) order from the film fiction (or diegesis). The male voice can, thus, be identified with the cinematic apparatus, the technology (camera, recorder) and ideology that produce and control the terms of the film. The female voice, in contrast, is most often situated firmly within the fiction, synchronized with characters on screen or a "voice-off" that is contained within the fiction, not located outside it. Voices identified as "outside" the story are synonymous with the cinematic apparatus[7] and almost exclusively male; voices "inside" the story are both male and female (Silverman, 54).

The necessary split of the site of production from the scene of the story or fiction is covered over in classic cinema; surrogates are found to shield the viewer from his absence from the site of production. Silverman maintains that "the shot/reverse shot is generally deemed to be particularly well suited to this purpose, since the second shot purports to show what was missing from the first shot; together the two shots seem to constitute a perfect whole. Moreover, typically one of those shots depicts someone looking, while the other seems to provide the object of the gaze" (Silverman, 12).

Duras almost never uses the shot/reverse shot and, in fact, accentuates the split between the site of production and the scene of the fiction. Often Duras further splits the scene of the fiction, creating a precarious, threatening space for the spectator and establishing an entirely different relation between the filmmaker and the spectator from that maintained in classic Hollywood cinema.

An innovation of Duras's cinema that will significantly influence her writing in the eighties is the gradual inscription of the filmmaker in the films and the emergence of a strong authorial voice. In a lengthy discussion of authorship and subjectivity in the wake of Barthes' sounding the death knell of the author in literature, Silverman delineates the various ways in which the filmmaker is inscribed "inside" the text. The text here is taken to mean more than the story or fiction; it includes the means of production as well as the film statement itself (the *énonciation* as well as the *énoncé*). For the literary question "who is speaking," film theorists have substituted "who is looking" and have uniformly responded: the camera, meaning the cinematic apparatus (Silverman, 200). In a gesture typical of Hitchcock, for example, the camera may be turned on the filmmaker's face (or the tape recorder to his or her voice) to create an "authorial citation" within the film (Silverman, 213). Another primary means of inscribing authorial subjectivity is through the "libidinal coherence" of the film by a particular director—"the desire that circulates there, more or less perceptively" (Silverman, 212). The author "outside" the text is the biographical subject who creates the text, the director who signs the film; the author "inside" the text is a creation of the film whose signature is inscribed within it. Silverman suggests reversing the conventional relation of author "inside" or "outside" the text by suggesting that the author "outside" the text may find the mirror for which he or she is looking in the "body" of the text (Silverman, 215).

Finally, just as the filmmaker, the author "inside" the text, is identified with the cinematic apparatus, the spectator becomes a part of the apparatus in the reception of the film: "Implicit in the reception of the cinematic spectacle is the viewer's identification not only with the camera, but with the projector and the screen. . . . The viewer is held in the 'pincers' of the cinematic apparatus, and thus inserted into its technology" (Silverman, 23).

I have insisted on these aspects of a much longer argument because they help to define and interpret aspects of Duras's cinema that are resistant to a strictly literary reading and yet are essential in the development of narrative strategies that Duras will use in later written texts as well as films.

Hiroshima mon amour and *Nathalie Granger*: Setting the Terms

Hiroshima mon amour, written by Duras and directed by Alain Resnais in 1959, is the film for which Duras is best known in the United States. *Nathalie Granger*, made thirteen years later, was one of the first full-length films both written and directed by Duras and conceived of as a film, rather than an adaptation of a play or written text. The scenario of *Hiroshima mon amour* clearly reflects the narrative concerns expressed by Duras in her novels and short stories of the late fifties. *Nathalie Granger* begins to experiment with the narrative concerns that will characterize her films in the seventies. Considered together, these two films help put into focus the terms that shift as Duras makes the transition from novelist to filmmaker. Voices, female subjectivity, and the relation between the filmmaker and the spectator are treated quite differently in these two films, in part reflecting the collaborative nature of *Hiroshima mon amour* versus Duras's more central role as director in *Nathalie Granger* but also demonstrating Duras's development as a storyteller in the sixties.

Duras wrote *Hiroshima mon amour* a year after *Moderato Cantabile* and in it reworked many of the themes and obsessions expressed in the earlier work: a man urging a woman to tell (or invent) a love story leading to physical or social death, the scandal of female sexual desire and infidelity to provincial moral order, and a narrative that interweaves crime and love, violence and desire. While *Moderato Cantabile* is only vaguely situated geographically and historically—in a more or less contemporary provincial port in France—and Chauvin urges Anne to invent a story based on what they have partially witnessed, *Hiroshima mon amour* is carefully situated, and the Japanese man extracts the Frenchwoman's most private story from her while she seeks to understand the public scandal of Hiroshima, his city.

Hiroshima mon amour has been summarized in many different ways. I should like to propose a brief summary of the two interweaving stories that shape the film. The first story is placed in 1957: A French actress, played by Emmanuelle Riva and never named in the film, is in Hiroshima to play the part of a nurse in a film for peace, twelve years after the bombing. The day before she plans to return to France, she has a brief affair with a Japanese man played by Eija Okada and also never named. The first images the viewer sees are of embracing bodies (from shoulder to waist) abstracted so that we cannot tell whether they are making love or in pain. The ambiguity is heightened because the Japanese man ("he") and the actress ("she") are discussing off screen the atrocities of the bombing of Hiroshima. He says, "You saw nothing in Hiroshima. Nothing." She insists, "I saw everything. Everything."[8] As she then describes the things she has seen (the hospital, the museum), the viewer sees what she has seen—the wounded and sick in the hospital, documentary photographs and artifacts of the bombing in the museum. This first story—of their love affair and her efforts to see and therefore know Hiroshima—is contained within the twenty-four hours before her departure.

The second story concerns her very private experience of the war. As a young woman in Nevers, she fell in love with a German soldier. On the eve of the liberation of her town, her lover is shot as he waits to meet her by the river. She lies next to him for hours as he dies. The scandal of their affair leads to condemnation by the town (they shave her head) and punishment by her parents (they lock her in the cellar). For two years she is mad, imprisoned, and tortured by the memory of her dying lover. After she regains some sanity, in their eyes, her mother sends her off to Paris in the middle of the night with a bicycle and some money. When she arrives in Paris on a glorious August day, the headlines tell of the bombing of Hiroshima. She has never told her story to anyone. The Japanese lover gradually coaxes it from her—his possession of her story being more intimate than his possession of her body but both signaling betrayal to her first love in her eyes.

The film moves back and forth narratively and in the images from one story to the other so that the story of Nevers and the story of Hiroshima—private and public scandals of the war, intense desire and massive destruction, personal loss and historical disaster—are merged.

Even though Alain Resnais was the director of *Hiroshima mon amour*, some of the most striking cinematic effects anticipate Duras's films made more than a decade later. The offscreen voices of the beginning, only gradually identified for the viewer, place the viewer in an uncomfortable, ambiguous position at the start: voyeur of a one night stand? witness, with the actress, of an event removed in time and reconstructed to remind those who share historically in the guilt of the bombing? As *Hiroshima mon amour* progresses, it becomes clear that, although the production was equally shared by French and Japanese crews, the viewer is presumed to be European. The Japanese man speaks excellent French and wears Western clothes; we see Hiroshima through the Frenchwoman's eyes. Okada was chosen in part because he has a

"Western look." Duras explains in a portrait of the Japanese character published with the scenario that she did not want an actor who looked too Japanese because it might lead to a distracting exoticism and an "involuntary racism." She says: "The spectator should not say 'How attractive Japanese men are,' but 'How attractive *that man* is.' This is why it is preferable to minimize the difference between the two protagonists" (*HM*, 109; *H*, 136).

Disembodied voices accompanying images of bodies in pleasure and in intense pain give the viewer a first sense of the title of the film: This is about the horror of Hiroshima and it is about a love story. Deborah Glassman argues in a convincing analysis of *Hiroshima mon amour*[9] that the film traces the story of the feminine subject as history writer moving through three stages. First, the French actress tries to keep her German lover alive with her body. Then she and the Japanese assume the roles of her younger self and the German, acting out the story with their bodies and dialogue. Finally, she gains narrative control of her earlier experience of loss and rebellion, but while her telling records and communicates the events, it also contains and domesticates them, betraying her former self. In Glassman's analysis, "the feminine subject can write her story at the price of her own dislocation" (Glassman, 53).

Judith Mayne shows, further, how in the manipulation of the visual motifs and the interweaving of the two stories, Duras inscribes a split female subjectivity in the film. Mayne observes: "Like the Japanese hospital patient who looks at the camera with distant interest, the Frenchwoman becomes both the central focus of the narrative and an observer who witnesses flashes from her past as a film over which she has no control."[10] This split female subjectivity anticipates the fantasy scene that structures much of the Lol V. Stein cycle and informs the films of the Indian cycle. The female subject, ravaged by desire for a lover who has been taken from her (or, in the case of Lol, who betrays her), obsessively relives the scene of separation. She is both participant and observer in her fantasy—watching her former self at the moment of greatest desire and pain. As Glassman points out, the female subject gains control of the past as she assumes control of the narrative. But control is also betrayal; the end of her narrative and of the film (he is named Hiroshima by her, she becomes Nevers for him) provides formal closure without entirely taming the disruptive character of her desire or the destruction contained in the rebuilt Hiroshima of 1957.

Another feature of *Hiroshima mon amour* that will characterize Duras's later films is her refusal (with Resnais) to allow the viewer to forget the cinematic apparatus and the controlling power of the filmmaker. From the opening shots the actress insists that she can "see" and therefore "know" the reality of Hiroshima by seeing reconstructions and meeting witnesses. The Japanese man insists just as vehemently that reconstructions do not allow one to see or know anything. The viewer, meanwhile, has been presented with a series of images (the embracing bodies, shadows on rock, maps) that only gradually come into focus and assume meaning. When the lovers go out into the city, the city has itself become a stage set where the film on peace is being made. The viewer sees the lovers swept up into a staged demonstration for peace in which actors carry placards bearing the very same images shown in the opening shots of the film, representing the hospital or the museum. We are constantly reminded that these are, in fact, reconstructions, fragments of an experience too horrible to be remembered or forgotten; our experience is intensely mediated by the filmmaker.

The fragmentation of images disrupts the spectator's sense of continuity in the beginning; similarly, the couple moves from one public place to another as the first story unfolds and discontinuity marks the narrative of the second story, which is told in nonchronological fits and starts. While they move from one public, anonymous place to another (the hotel room, a bar, the train station, another bar where another Japanese attempts to pick up the Frenchwoman using the time worn clichés of heterosexual seduction), she recounts her story following an emotional logic rather than chronology. Judith Mayne notes the absence of a grounding of vision in *Hiroshima mon amour* that results in "the refusal of *Hiroshima mon amour* to bring the spectator into an assigned place, a comfortable vantage point from which she/he can witness the unfolding of cinematic spectacle" (Mayne, 52). The refusal to provide a comfortable vantage point for the spectator that marks *Hiroshima mon amour* will become overt antagonism in later films as Duras assumes more fully the role of filmmaker. The tension between the spectator and the filmmaker in later films is often compounded by sexual antagonism between the female filmmaker and the assumed male viewer.

At first viewing, *Nathalie Granger* seems to represent an entirely different sort of film from *Hiroshima mon amour*. *Hiroshima mon amour* has the vast scope of documentary and historical commentary as well as the intense intimacy of love denied, punished, and betrayed. *Nathalie Granger* recreates for the spectator a day shared by two women in a house. But there are similarities that emerge on closer examination. *Nathalie Granger*, like *Hiroshima mon amour*, borrows motifs from *Moderato Cantabile* and sets terms that will mark her other films. As in

Moderato Cantabile, a middle class mother wants her rebellious child (this time a daughter) to study the piano, and the child's piano practice is heard at intervals throughout the film. Like the novel too, *Nathalie Granger*, behind a façade of quiet domesticity, tells a story of crime and violence. While the violence of *Hiroshima mon amour* is both spectacular and intimate, central to both of the stories told in the film, violence in *Nathalie Granger* is subdued, erupting in domestic gestures or invading the house in radio news flashes.

One of the major differences between the two films is the mediation of narrative. While *Hiroshima mon amour* maintained the narrative structure used in *Moderato Cantabile* of a man urging a woman to tell her story, the narrative in *Nathalie Granger* is no longer mediated in that way. The camera or, by extension, the filmmaker assumes the role of narrator. Except for the cliché role of the newscaster on the radio, men as interpreters or mediators of experience are eliminated from the story as soon as the father leaves the house after the first few minutes of the film.

Nathalie Granger may be summarized as follows. The film tells the story of a day in the house of Isabelle Granger (played by Lucia Bose), a bourgeois woman who lives in a village in the Yvelines (the department west of Paris where Duras's house at Neauphle-le-Château is located) with her husband and two daughters, Laurence and Nathalie. She has a heavy Italian accent that is never commented on in the film but that links her to other foreigners or socially marginal characters. She spends the day with her friend, played by Jeanne Moreau (who is never named), who is visiting. Two events set this day apart. First, Isabelle must decide whether or not to send Nathalie to a special school because she has displayed violent, antisocial behavior at school. Second, beginning with the opening shots at the breakfast table, the radio news tells of two young boys who are terrorizing the region by shooting at random. They have already killed and might kill again for no apparent reason. By the end of the day, we learn that they have been caught and that Isabelle has decided against sending her daughter away. The violence of the boys has been contained; the rebelliousness of the daughter has been adopted and, in a sense, protected by the mother.

These external and internal events establish the emotional tension of the day and most of the interaction between the inside of the house and the outside world, but they are not the focus of the film narrative. The focus is the house itself, as Duras has said in her notes to the film text and in interviews about the making of the film. It is, in fact, her own house in Neauphle-le-Château, the first property she bought for herself, paid for with income from the movie adaptation of *Moderato Cantabile* (*EVC*, 12). She says in her 1984 interview with Dominique Noguez that the house is the text on which the film is based. She also says that in the making of the film she learned to read her house, its history and meanings. The film text, published a year after she made the film, is enriched by that knowledge.

In *Moderato Cantabile*, Anne Desbaresdes' identity risks being subsumed into that of generations of women who have occupied her house and her room. Duras seeks to discover in reading her own house the generations of women who have occupied it. She is careful to distinguish her possibilities as a woman from those of the other women who have lived in this space:

> there is a continuity of women who have passed through here, who died here, who said nothing, who lived here in a kind of equivalence, finally, to what we live. With the difference, of course, that as for me, I write. . . . These women are not my sisters. I'm not fraternally bound to them. . . . I'm not a woman who inhabits the house. They are the ones who inhabited it, the ones who came before me. . . . we are confronted with an important fact, the occupation of places by woman. . . this doesn't necessarily correspond to a sorrow in the lived experience of woman, it corresponds to a function that she had for thousands of years up until thirty, forty years ago, until your mother's life and mine, until my own life as a young woman. Then, suddenly, it was over. (*EVC*, 13)

While she explores the mute, ancient, and ageless presence of woman through the two central characters, she also begins in this film to define her own feminine subjectivity, her presence as filmmaker.

The most obvious way in which Duras inscribes herself as filmmaker in *Nathalie Granger* is by exploring her own house. But there are two other markers of her presence that will become increasingly important in later films. First, she makes a brief cameo appearance, in the manner of Hitchcock, on the sound track. Toward the beginning of the film Isabelle calls the special school where Nathalie might be sent to see if she can ensure that her daughter will continue her piano lessons. The voice we hear speaking for the school is Duras's, saying that the school refuses to impose such a choice on the children and that they are free to choose whether or not to learn what is offered them.

More important, though, is the use of the camera and the particular way of controlling the spectator's gaze that Duras begins to establish in this film. Two types of shots dominate. Long, stationary camera shots with little action force the viewer to stare at objects; traveling shots associated with the women, a cat, and, briefly, a traveling salesman explore the presence of the house. In the long, stationary shots particularly, the filmmaker provides little guidance on how to read what we are forced to contemplate. Catherine Portuges, in an excellent article entitled "The Pleasures of *Nathalie Granger*," describes the use of the camera and the editing of *Nathalie Granger* as a "highly controlled openness" that puts the viewer in a different sort of relation to the film than he or she is used to: "The Durassian viewer is thus not forced to decode or decipher, but can instead be borne along by the fluidity of the editing which exerts the minimum of effort to control change of camera position, rapid cutting, or technical virtuosity of an exhibitionistic kind. In such a way the *viewer* becomes the locus of openness; what ensues is the creation of a state of desire that links viewer and film in an unconscious collaboration."[11] Portuges is careful to point out that what is pleasurable for the female viewer may not be so for the male viewer, using a hostile review by Vincent Canby as a case in point.

One ten-minute scene in the middle of the film provides a sharp contrast to the rest of the film and, indeed, to Duras's other films. The only male character to come into the house (other than the voice on the radio) is a traveling salesman played by Gérard Depardieu. His entrance is presented as an invasion of the women's space because he comes into the house—and the room where they are sitting—without being shown in or invited. Before long, though, he is overcome by the presence of the women, which he experiences as an aggression, an undermining of his identity. What sets the scene apart is that it is one of the rare sequences in which Duras uses a shot/reverse shot technique and in which, for an extended period of time, characters appear to address each other. That is to say, the camera technique and the elements of the film fiction are more conventional than the rest of the film. Duras seems to place this long sequence at the middle of the film precisely to undo its terms even as the terms that structure the salesman's identity are undone by the women.

Depardieu comes into the room, says he is representing a washing machine company, and begins his sales pitch. The women do not move, but they allow him to sit down. He is visibly nervous, delivers his lines like a learned script, mimicking conviction but conveying anxiety. The conventional role for women faced with such obvious male distress would be to put him at ease, to help him play his role, to enter into the discourse he is trying to deliver. Instead they are silent. They listen and stare. Finally, first the friend and then Isabelle say, "You're not a traveling salesman,"[12] articulating the challenge to his identity that their silence had already established. He tries to prove who he is by showing his police permit and his company's brochure, but he is obviously discomfited. After what seems an interminably long scene, with Depardieu becoming increasingly devastated and the women refusing to relieve his pain, he asks to see what kind of machine they have so that he can better address their needs should they change their minds. He returns to tell them that they already own the model he was trying to sell them. He leaves the house defeated and dejected.

The discomfort and tension of the scene are heightened for the viewer because, although Duras uses the familiar shot/reverse shot technique, each shot is unrelievedly fixed and protracted so that the viewer begins to share the salesman's discomfort and feel trapped by the situation. Further, as Silverman points out, "the most paradigmatic of all shot/reverse shot formations is that which aligns the female body with the male gaze. This two-shot not only covers over the absent site of production, but places the male subject on the side of vision, and the female subject on the side of spectacle" (Silverman, 27–28). In Duras's use of the shot/reverse shot in this scene, the female subject(s) are placed on the side of vision and the male subject on the side of spectacle. The (male) viewer, insofar as he is associated with Depardieu, is removed from a familiar position of power and subjected to the female gaze.

This can be read as a highly comic scene—but only if the viewer dissociates from Depardieu, who, like the viewer, is a stranger to this house and is slowly overwhelmed by it. To accept the women's terms, the viewer, like Depardieu, might be absorbed into this space at the price of his identity, or at least an officially sanctioned fiction of identity that is reassuring.

In the final scenes of the film, Depardieu returns, defeated, to confess that the women were right, he really isn't cut out to be a traveling salesman. He then wanders through the house and garden, following the other dominant traveling shots associated earlier with the women and with a cat who also is "at home" in this space. Finally, though, he flees the house, apparently afraid of being absorbed by it. One of the last images we see from inside the house looking out through a frame is his car driving rapidly away.

The beginning of the initial scene with the salesman could have set up a violation of the women's space by the man. It ended with a violation of his assumed identity by the women's refusal to go along with it. The tension between men and women suggested by these scenes is developed by other representations of power and violence in the film. For example, the spectacular, random violence of the two teenage boys told throughout the film by radio broadcasts is both likened and contrasted to the smoldering potential for violence in Nathalie. Nathalie expresses her rebellion by refusing her assigned role: She dumps over a doll carriage, she tells her sister that she wishes she (Nathalie) were an orphan, a Portuguese orphan, in other words marginalized rather than a comfortable middle class girl. Finally the mother embraces the daughter's rebellion rather than send her away; she shares in her refusal rather than try to tame it.

Throughout the film, the representation of female presence and power is complicated by the double presence of Isabelle and her friend. They speak as one to the salesman but elsewhere are contrasted. Visually one is dark, the other blond, one speaks with a heavy accent, the other doesn't. The friend urges Isabelle to forget about Nathalie; Isabelle refuses, finally, to give Nathalie over to the authorities. Even though Moreau is the guest, she seems more at home in the house, more accustomed to the ritual daily tasks than Isabelle.

Nathalie Granger, both thematically and in Duras's cinematic choices, represents female power as subversive of social order, as a threat to conventional identities and disruptive of familiar fictions. The film sets other terms that will become central in later films. The use of offscreen voices, particularly her own voice, is barely alluded to here but will provide an important narrative strategy in the Indian cycle. Similarly, mirrors and mirrored space are almost parenthetical in *Nathalie Granger* but will assume greater importance. Most important, in this film Duras assumes as filmmaker the narrative role played by male intermediaries in earlier fictions. In her next films she returns to the unresolved obsessions of the Lol V. Stein cycle to explore this new way of seeing and telling.

The Indian Cycle: The Making of the Filmmaker's Voice

The loss or absence that Silverman observes at the center of cinematic production provides for Duras a particularly apt new "narrative region" in which to pursue the story of Lol V. Stein, centered as it is on the "hole-word" ("le mot-trou") or absent word named by the male narrator, Jack Hold. The metaphoric "cinema of Lol V. Stein" constructed in *The Ravishing of Lol Stein* and related texts is literalized in *Woman of the Ganges*, *India Song*, and *Son nom de Venise dans Calcutta désert* which culminate the Lol V. Stein cycle, turning it into the Indian cycle. Anne-Marie Stretter eclipses Lol V. Stein to become the center of fascination for the filmmaker as well as for the male characters Michael Richardson and the Vice-Consul. India is invoked in the title *Woman of the Ganges* and becomes the imaginary site for the other two films. The reader of Lol's texts becomes a spectator, much closer to the figure of Lol the voyeur, imagining or reconstituting the moment when she is replaced by Anne-Marie Stretter in her lover's gaze.

Film theory and readings of Duras converge in efforts to define fantasy. In a particularly useful reading of the Indian cycle, Deborah Glassman summarizes readings of phantasy in Freud and Lacan in relation to Duras: "The function of fantasy . . . is to stage desire. . . . Fantasy is about looking from and for a place. This place . . . is what Lacan would describe as the place of the subject."[13] "Fantasy," Glassman argues, "is a story about the displaced subject" (Glassman 1988, 36). The subject, in and of phantasy, is staged as both observer and participant in the fantasmatic scene, as we saw in *10:30 on a Summer Night*. The scene is both a projection and reflection of the subject's desire. The subject is situated at the "focal point from which everything is ordered, and which defines the vanishing point at which everything converges" (Glassman 1988, 37). The fantasizing subject is necessarily (and impossibly) split: absent and present in the fantasmatic scene. Lol's phantasy continually reconstructs the scene in which she was replaced; she would be voyeur of the moment when she is eclipsed by another woman.

The much-commented-upon "hole word" at the center of Lol's story is often read as the wound of female sexuality, the empty chasm of female desire discovered and abandoned by the male lover, then recovered and spoken by the male narrator. The "hole word" can also be understood as the focal point/vanishing point of phantasy—the split site of the fantasizing subject who creates the scene that defines and destroys her. Read as female sexuality, the absence at the center of Lol's story reveals more about male than female subjectivity. As we saw in chapter 3, in *The Ravishing of Lol Stein*, Lol as split subject, as insistent voyeur of her own destruction, is made accessible to the reader through the mediation of the male narrator. In the films of the Indian cycle, the filmmaker replaces the narrator, and the mediation of the fantasmatic scene is explicitly linked to the camera as well as to language, the visual as well as voice. Read as the focal point/vanishing point of the fantasmatic scene, the absence at the center of Lol's story begins to define a site for female subjectivity—a doubled, reflecting site created, perhaps, by male desire and abandonment, but opening up a field for female desire, a woman's gaze. Cinematic production allows Duras to combine these two meanings of the absence at the center of Lol's story. She reveals a female sexuality and subjectivity within the story created by male desire and fear. At the same time, the filmmaker exposes the ways in which this construction of female sexuality and subjectivity is potentially disruptive of male subjectivity.

Woman of the Ganges. As she has admitted in interviews, even after writing *The Ravishing of Lol Stein*, *The Vice-Consul*, and *L'Amour*, Duras had not yet rid herself of the need to explore the story told in the Lol V. Stein cycle. Significantly, one of Duras's first films in the seventies was *La Femme du Gange* (*Woman of the Ganges*), based on *L'Amour*; the film itself engendered another written text, published with the text of the film *Nathalie Granger* in 1973. Duras did not, in fact, abandon writing for film in the seventies; while exploring the narrative possibilities of cinema, she also used film as a support for writing and invented a new genre, which has been called a *film text*.[14] A *film text* is a text written after the film has been made; more than a scenario, a film text includes the script, descriptions of the film images, and additional written commentary.

Originally intended to be the screen adaptation of *L'Amour*, *Woman of the Ganges*, filmed at Trouville-sur-Mer in November 1972, has been called a "first draft" of *India Song*.[15] In *Woman of the Ganges*, Duras discovered the possibility of radically separating voices and images, a technique she perfected in *India Song* and then used to different effect in *Son nom de Venise dans Calcutta désert*, the short subjects *Césarée*, *Les Mains négatives*, and the *Aurélia Steiner* series. *Woman of the Ganges*, however, is more than a draft for future films. It is the last narrative in which Lol V. Stein is a central figure and the first example of film text. I would argue that *Woman of the Ganges* does not work well as a film, but that, when considered along with the film text it generated, the film opens up new narrative possibilities for Duras as a filmmaker.

A summary of the film text helps to focus the discussion. The primary characters include "the woman in black" and the "wife of the traveler," who are both played by Catherine Sellers. The traveler, Lol V. Stein (also known as the young girl of S. Thala), the Fool, another man on the beach, a male Casino attendant, and the traveler's children (a boy and a girl) complete the cast. Two female voices speak on the "film of the Voices" that accompanies the image film. The film opens with a cityscape, an empty square, where the traveler arrives, suitcase in hand. Eventually he arrives at the shore, and only music is heard on the sound track (the tune "India Song"). The woman in black and the Fool watch the traveler; another woman, Lol V. Stein, does not watch him, but looks to the ground. At this moment the second film, the film of the Voices, begins, as the two women interrogate each other about the people the spectator is watching. Eventually we understand that the traveler is (and is not) Michael Richardson, the man who abandoned Lol V. Stein many years before at the ball at S. Thala. He has returned from India—to which he had followed Anne-Marie Stretter—to the Casino where the event had taken place. The Voices invoke the love and desire of that story.

S. Thala is in flames, associated with Lol's desire, and the waves of the sea recall heartbeats. The landscape is obviously the space of Lol's fantasy. India, the beggarwoman, the Vice-Consul are all invoked as the story is reconstructed in fragments. There is a brief mention of Anne-Marie Stretter's death in India. The continuing life of Lol V. Stein is recounted—her marriage with a musician, children, her second breakdown in a field of rye while she watched another couple in a hotel. Returning to the Casino, the traveler sees Lol V. Stein. When he asks the attendant who she is, he identifies her and then adds that it cannot be Lol; Mademoiselle Stein had died ten years before. The traveler repeats the name of Michael Richardson and says that they are all dead now. The last actor on screen is the Fool; the music fades out at the end as the image of the sea also disappears.

In the preface to the film text of *Woman of the Ganges*, Duras describes her discovery of creating two simultaneous, related but separate, films: the image film and the film of the Voices (her capitalization). While the image film was planned for, she says, the film of the Voices just happened, after the fact. She states in the preface that the films should be considered as totally autonomous even though they are linked materially by the celluloid they are both inscribed on and they are meant to be viewed at the same time. One could say, as Ropars-Wuilleumier does of the sound-film in *India Song*, that the Voices belong to the narrative and the actors' dialogues belong to the fiction (or diegesis); the Voices are telling the story, the actors embodying it (Ropars-Wuilleumier 1980, 248–49). The film of the Voices is not meant to be a commentary on the image film, the voices "don't facilitate the unfolding of the film, on the contrary they impede it, trouble it" (*NG*, 102). Duras goes on to associate the Voices with Lol and the *hole-word* of the Lol V. Stein narrative by saying that the film of the Voices could have been associated with an entirely different film than this one, provided that "it were vacant, poor, made of holes" (*NG*, 103).

Although the two films are separate and to some degree autonomous, they are more related than Duras's statement would suggest. The Voices do not provide a commentary in the conventional sense of a voice-over, but they attempt to reconstruct the narrative of the ball at S. Thala that is the always-absent but ever-determining tale of origin in the Indian cycle. The creation of the separate film of the Voices runs exactly counter to two of the characteristics of classic Hollywood cinema described by Silverman. The Voices being outside of the story, the film fiction, are associated with the authority of the cinematic apparatus. At the same time, they are double, female and hesitant, recreating a story by fragments, drawing attention to the gaps as much as to the story. Later in the film, their dialogue becomes entangled with the story through the desire that circulates from one film to the other. They are, therefore, both inside and outside the story, authoritative and tentative, expressing a knowledge riddled with desire.

If classic cinema seeks to disguise or cover over the absent site of production, the invention of the second film of the Voices serves to accentuate that absence, to vocalize a space beyond the screen. The spectator is put into a contradictory, precarious position, having to keep the films separate and to integrate them at one and the same time. The two films are inscribed on the celluloid; the spectator is the site of their convergence in the reception of the film.

The uncomfortable space in between where the spectator is placed is further accentuated by the camera shots used. All the camera shots (152 during the ninety-minute film) are stationary, the spectator is locked into the rectangle of the camera's viewfinder, which is doubled by the rectangle of the screen. No traveling shots or camera movement provide the illusion of escape from the fixed (fixated) view of the camera. One stationary shot replaces another, substituting one view for another, closing the spectator in each time.

In the film text of *Woman of the Ganges*, Duras adds another voice— the filmmaker's voice—that inscribes a model spectator. The additional filmmaker's voice in the film text adds an interpretive function to its narrative role: Links are made between places, characters, and key images. In establishing one shot, for example, the filmmaker's voice says "A white building, a hotel, closed shutters, squared off form: bunker (blockhaus) of memory, impenetrable" (*NG*, 147). The layering of values and associations instructs the spectator in how to see and understand the images in the film. The hotel—scene of intimacy and betrayal—is also a bunker, a World War II ruin scattered on this beach in Normandy; the tomb of the memory of military invasion is interchangeable with the public house that holds the memory of emotional and erotic desertion. As in *Hiroshima mon amour*, intimate desolation and public devastation are linked. This interpretation is available only in the film text, adding another triangle (filmmaker/ spectator/ image) to the geometry of desire and meaning.

The filmmaker's voice in the film text is analogous to the function of the camera itself in the film. Elisabeth Lyon has summarized the look of the camera in *Woman of the Ganges* as "the articulating presence, the link between the disparate spaces that the characters occupy. The presence of the look of the camera and of Duras as controller of the look, conventionally the suppressed term in filmic discourse, is stressed . . . through this function of liaison operated by the position of the camera. The term literally absent from our view (the camera) is thus put forth as presence, as subject of the filmic discourse."[16] In *L'Homme atlantique*, also filmed at Trouville, Duras will explore further the connection between the presence of the look of the camera and the controlling voice of the filmmaker.

The innovations of the *Woman of the Ganges* film text—the film of the Voices and the filmmaker's voice—provide new means to inscribe a split female subject. After the male narrators represented in *The Ravishing of Lol Stein* and *The Vice-Consul*, the narrator is effaced in *L'Amour*. The multiple female voices of *Woman of the Ganges* take on the narrating function; for the first time since *The Tranquil Life*, female voices articulate a woman's story. The disembodied women's voices are characterized by Duras as circulating in the body of the film, afflicted with an incoherent, mad knowledge. The voices enter the film at the moment that all eyes are turned to the traveler who has arrived in the visual space of an early shot.

The structure of the film of the Voices is interrogatory, recalling *L'Amante anglaise*: One asks questions of the other, and the spectator tries to reconstruct a narrative through these fragments of speech. At the beginning of the film the first voice asks questions and the second has some memory, though it is incomplete and she sometimes asks questions of herself. About a third of the way through the text, the voices change roles: The one that remembered now forgets, the one that had asked questions informs (*NG*, 127). Identity, like memory, is fluid in the film of the Voices. Neither is ever named; they could be the same woman at different moments, a dispersion of Lol's identity, perhaps. The first voice belongs to the actress Nicole Hiss, who plays the role of Lol V. Stein in the image film. Because she is voiceless as Lol, however, that link can be made only by the reader of the film text. Or the voices could be read as an effort to create a female narrating voice outside any character but obliquely related to the story being told. The narrative of origin passes through these voices, incomplete but persistent, directing their gaze and ours. Some phrases, fading into silence, are repeated like a litany charged with an emotion so strong that repetition recreates the burning memory for both the voices and the spectator: "*Voice 1*: When one thinks of what was . . . So much love . . . So much desire . . . " "*Voice 1*: Do you still want to die? . . . *Voice 2*: Yes. And then, I forget . . . I watch . . . *Voice 1*: He still loved her . . . *Voice 2*: . . . through the other woman, the other love" (*NG*, 130). The desire unleashed in the moment of betrayal circulates through the voices and remains forever trapped: created and held by loss.

Desire for the beloved becomes a desire for death until the voices speak to each other rather than obliquely in reference to the image film. By addressing each other in this way the voices create a second film fiction—an adjacent story—not included on the image track but, in a sense, absorbing it. At this climactic moment in the film of the Voices, the filmmaker's voice is interleaved, providing both description and interpretation for the reader of the film text:

Voice 2
You are so young and I love you so . . .
                                                    No answer.
Voice 2, imploring.
I love you more than anything in the world.
                                                    Break.
[Filmmaker] Voice #2 asked that one be allowed to live.
No answer. Silence.
Voice #1 speaks very slowly, very low, she is exhausted.

Voice 1
If I asked you, would you agree to kill me?

[Filmmaker] The answer to the request for death is slow in coming. It comes. It is affirmative. It bears witness to the *complete, mortal desire* that, similarly, joined the heroes of the ball at S. Thala.

Voice 2
Yes.

[Filmmaker] . . . The voices are silenced for ever. It is probable that the ultimate request has been granted. (*NG*, 182)

The filmmaker then provides a detailed interpretation of the film of the Voices, filling in as they no longer speak. She says:

> The desire expressed by the burned-out Voice (#1) is the only moment when the image film joins the film of the Voices. The image film *touches* the film of the Voices here. It lasts the length of a phrase. But this contact *provokes death*. The film of the Voices is also killed.
>
> The desire of the Voices—that expressed by the burned-out Voice, that accepted by Voice 2—is quenched by the desire of S. Thala. This desire of S. Thala, *mortal* by nature, *entire*, had been shared out (distributed?), entire, mortal, to each of those who was prey to it: therefore it was impossible to break it down, therefore it was unlivable. (*NG*, 183)

When the gap between the outside and inside of the film story is bridged, there is death.

Duras then, in the filmmaker's voice, interpolates a lengthy analysis of the relation between the Anne-Marie Stretter/Michael Richardson couple and Lola Valérie Stein, explaining the madness of L.V.S. She explains that if Michael and Anne-Marie had heard Lol crying out to them it would have shown that they were still capable of hearing anything outside of their desire. Lol, recognizing the strength of their desire, that it was impenetrable, called out to them *because* they were no longer capable of hearing anything. The filmmaker's voice says: "It's within that perimeter, in that *absurdity*, in that disequilibrium—balanced—between three terms that could never, in any case, be rejoined, that L.V.S. remained. Wrenched apart between the wrenching terms of desire. Her madness was to have thought it possible, if only for the moment of a cry, that this torture could break open to welcome her" (*NG*, 183–84). She goes on to say that it was in this precarious gap that the Voices were located as well. They, like Lol, are "voyeuses." The site where L.V.S. had been rejected is where the burned-out Voice dies, and L.V.S. at last dies with that Voice. The filmmaker specifies that the death of the Voice coincides with the image on screen of L.V.S. who follows the traveler; the death of the Voice coincides with the beginning of the end of the film, the return of the traveler to the Casino of S. Thala, where he had abandoned Lol for Anne-Marie.

The gap between the Voices and the image track is substituted for the distance between Lol and the lovers, the absence that structures her fantasy scene. To close over that gap is to foreclose desire, to shut out the fantasmatic scene. Lol, focal point and vanishing point of the scene of her desire, disappears with the silencing of the Voices.

Transferences and substitutions of women and places in *Woman of the Ganges* reveal a nesting of meanings, one within another, that might otherwise seem unrelated. The projection of one woman onto another, of one place onto another, begins with the title, *Woman of the Ganges*. Although seeming to refer to a specific woman and place, the terms of the title are polyvalent in the context of the film.

In *L'Amour*, identities were stripped away so that Lol became "the woman," Michael Richardson "the traveler," and a third male figure simply "the Fool." Lol reclaims her name in *Woman of the Ganges* but loses her voice; the character called "the woman" in *Woman of the Ganges* is a shadow Anne-Marie Stretter, but who is the woman of the Ganges? No Indian women inhabit the Indian cycle. European women's voices and the remembered cries of the Asian beggarwoman suggest that the woman of the Ganges is at once Lol, the beggarwoman, and Anne-Marie. But "woman" as told in *Woman of the Ganges* is more than any single character; she is multiple voices and a figure through which pass desire and death. The woman of the Ganges is a phantasm, a projection of desire. In this film, "woman" figures the "geometry of desire"—the triangle of the woman abandoned, the man and the woman pursued—burning in the memory of the woman abandoned. In the filmmaker's voice, Duras says that Lol's discovery of the geometry of desire compels her "to see, to follow the lovers" (*NG*, 136).

The Ganges, named in the title, is absent from the film except as part of a fiction that neither Lol nor the spectator sees. Michael Richardson, having left Lol for Anne-Marie Stretter at the ball at S. Thala, followed her to Calcutta. To keep her desire intact and to control her place in relation to Michael Richardson and Anne-Marie Stretter, Lol needs to see and to follow the couple that took her place. The coincidence of the Voices interrogating each other about the ball, the scene of betrayal, and Michael's return from India in the image film, as "the traveler," sets this narrative in motion and brings the absent couple of the Ganges back to S. Thala.

In the syntax of Lol's desire, the traveler provides the link between the "conjugated nights of the Ganges and S. Thala" (*NG*, 161). In all three of Duras's "Indian" films, Calcutta, the Ganges, and India are imagined against a distinctly French landscape: a landscape in ruins—whether revealed in the traces of World War II on the beach in Normandy in *Woman of the Ganges* or in the crumbling Rothschild Palace in *India Song* and *Son nom de Venise*. India is an imaginary site. The Asian beggarwoman links the imaginary India to Indochina in the other two Indian films. By filming an imaginary India against a French landscape (and architecture in the other two films), Duras displaces the Indochina of her childhood and generalizes the colonial experience, revealing it to be a projection of Western European fantasy now situated in desolation and ruins. The colonial dream, the European fantasy of the exotic, which fascinates but threatens and must be dominated, is played off a European landscape that signals its own destruction. In *Woman of the Ganges*, as in the text of *L'Amour*, the landscape is enveloped in flames. The exotic folds into the erotic as the colonial outpost and the site of erotic betrayal merge in the logic of the film's images and the filmmaker's voice.

Having pushed narrative to its most abstract in *L'Amour*, Duras needed to return to the story again in *Woman of the Ganges*, layering narrative voice on narrative voice in an effort to control and understand the meaning of Lol's madness. The "narrated narrator"[17] of *The Ravishing of Lol Stein*, Jack Hold, is replaced by three female voices—the Voices and the filmmaker—and, in addition, the spectator sees the image film, which presents another access to this retelling of the story of Lol V. Stein. With film, Duras can put the reader in the role of spectator, like Lol and the Voices, a voyeur of unattainable desire.

For all the layers of narrative and interpretation, the reader/spectator of the *Woman of the Ganges* film text is left with the effort to understand rather than understanding, the fascination of fragments of memory and desire that yield a more intense need to know. Lol could not leave S. Thala and is absorbed back into the site of her betrayal. The innovations of *Woman of the Ganges* are as literary as they are cinematic; the film text adds significantly to the film and helps us to read the film. *India Song* takes the spectator to the imaginary site of India as the Vice-Consul replaces Lol as voyeur of Anne-Marie Stretter. Unlike *Woman of the Ganges*, *India Song* stands alone as a film and, in many ways, surpasses the texts associated with it.

India Song. In *India Song*, Duras takes the cinematic innovations of *Woman of the Ganges* one step further. In *Woman of the Ganges* the image film has a sound track of its own in which the actors address one another; their voices are synchronized with their on-screen images, though dialogue is very sparse. In *India Song*, Duras separates the sound track entirely from the images. Even when the actors address each other their voices are disembodied, "off" in the same way that the film of the Voices is "off" in both films. The filmmaker's voice, which exists only in the film text of *Woman of the Ganges*, becomes part of the film *India Song* as Duras's voice speaks in the epilogue.

The radical separation of the visual from the sound track situates the viewer in an even more profound gap than that created in *Woman of the Ganges*. The "story" is split, both on and off screen, while the site of the narrative apparatus is also signaled off screen. Again Duras refuses any illusion of continuity to the spectator. There are no comforting shot/reverse shot sequences, no synchronization of voice and visual to support the illusion of a "real" presence. The film fragments all illusions of continuity against a background of a French monument in near ruin.

India Song occupies a privileged position in the work of Marguerite Duras. Together with *Son nom de Venise dans Calcutta désert* (which uses the same sound track), it completes the Indian cycle and the narrative of Lol V. Stein. *India Song* is generally acknowledged to be Duras's most important film and has generated considerable commentary. All the elements of the Lol V. Stein story come together in *India Song*. The "place" of the film is the French embassy in Calcutta—which, as Duras is quick to point out, does not exist. Michael Richardson, who left Lol V. Stein at the ball in S. Thala, has followed Anne-Marie Stretter, the ambassador's wife, to Calcutta. The French Vice-Consul, shunned because he shot at lepers from his balcony in Lahore, has come to Calcutta to pursue Anne-Marie Stretter. The Asian beggarwoman, whose story was first told in *The Vice-Consul*, seems to have followed Anne-Marie Stretter to Calcutta and, like the Vice-Consul, circulates around the embassy, piercing the air with her cries, laughter, and song. The beggarwoman's look and cries signal an indictment of the colonial order and Anne-Marie Stretter's place within it even as the Vice-Consul's look and cries signal fascination and death.

The story of Michael Richardson's abandonment of Lol V. Stein for Anne-Marie Stretter is alluded to in the prologue of the film. Although *India Song* exists as a written text, I want to focus discussion on the film. The written text was intended to be the basis of a theater production and is not a film text like *Woman of the Ganges*. In the film, Duras fully realizes new narrative possibilities that are not adequately represented in the written text.

The film resists summary because the meanings are articulated through voices, music, sounds, and images rather than through a conventional story; it is nonetheless useful to give an overview. The film is divided into three parts: a prologue, the reception scene, and an epilogue.[18] The prologue consists of twenty-seven shots and lasts for thirty minutes. First the viewer sees an extended, stationary shot of a landscape at sunset and hears the cries of the Asian woman. Two Frenchwomen's voices interrogate each other about Anne-Marie Stretter and the Asian woman. One of the voices belongs to Nicole Hiss, who had been one of the voices in *Woman of the Ganges* and had played the voiceless Lol in the same film. Through a play of tenses the viewer understands that Anne-Marie Stretter is no longer alive. In the first interior shot, a male Indian servant is the first actor on screen; he comes to light incense at an altar placed on a piano that seems to be a remembrance of Anne-Marie Stretter, surrounded by articles of her clothing, a hairpiece, and other traces of her person. Actors whom the viewer comes to recognize as Anne-Marie Stretter (Delphine Seyrig), Michael Richardson (Claude Mann), the Vice-Consul (Michael Lonsdale), and other male guests (Matthieu Carrière, Didier Flamand, and Claude Juan) eventually come on screen, overwhelmed by heat and, possibly, by desire.

In one of the most famous scenes of the film, Anne-Marie Stretter, Michael Richardson, and another man, unable to sleep because of the oppressive heat, stretch out on the floor of a salon and are watched by the Vice-Consul. The camera fixes on Anne-Marie Stretter's uncovered right breast in two extended shots—one medium-range, the other close-up. The story of Lol is told while the spectator watches Anne-Marie Stretter's breast.

The reception scene at the embassy consists of thirty shots and lasts nearly an hour. Offscreen voices—sometimes the voices of characters we see, sometimes disembodied voices of guests—tell the story of the Vice-Consul while various characters move in and out of the visual field. The primary visual field of the reception scene is a "double rectangle": a salon where the piano and "altar" are located, perfectly reflected in a mirror so that the viewer is not always certain which is "real" space and which is reflected space. Because of the camera angle, actors disappear and reappear as they move from one rectangle to the other, creating a visual gap at the center of the film. During the reception the Vice-Consul confesses his love for Anne-Marie Stretter. She tells him she cannot love him because of Michael Richardson. The Vice-Consul says that he loves her in her love for Richardson. He wants to spend just one night with her. She refuses and he then adds to the scandal of his presence at the party by crying out her name and his desire for her outside the embassy so that all can hear him. He shouts her Venetian name "Anna-Maria Guardi," which recalls her name before marriage, her foreign origins, and her status as "spectacle," "Guardi" meaning "Look."

In the epilogue (sixteen shots lasting twenty-three minutes), two voices (this time a man asking questions of an authoritative woman, the woman's voice easily recognized as Duras herself) recount the events that followed the reception. A party consisting of Anne-Marie Stretter, Michael Richardson, and several other men go off to an island resort. Eventually the Vice-Consul disappears; there is no continuing record of his whereabouts, though he is not, probably, dead. The spectator is told that Anne-Marie Stretter walked into the sea to her suicide, leaving her clothing on the shore. During the epilogue, Duras's voice places the film in historical time, situating the events in 1937, referring to political events in China, Russia, and Germany. Until then, although the music is reminiscent of the 1930s, nothing would situate the film in historical time. The costumes—particularly the men's clothing—are distinctively of the 1970s, and nothing else provides a clear marker. Even as the female voice of the epilogue situates the fiction in historical time, the image track locates the film in a mapped geography. The final images in the film are a close-up of a map retracing the trek of the Asian woman back to Savannakhet from India while we hear her voice again. The camera closes in on the map so that the image becomes fragmented. The voice fades into a piano playing the tune "India Song."

As in *Woman of the Ganges*, many of the camera shots are stationary. Traveling shots are used for the exteriors, façades, and gardens, but, with one or two exceptions, the shots of the actors are done with a stationary camera. This is especially marked in the reception scene in which the two shots of the "double rectangle" fix a carefully delineated visual field. Aside from the sunset at the beginning and the resort hotel toward the end, most of the images are of the interior and exterior of the Rothschild Palace near Reims, which is taken to be the embassy at Calcutta. The palace is in a state of near ruin and the camera focuses on crumbling façades. Exterior shots (nearly all nocturnal) usually follow the Vice-Consul and include abandoned tennis courts where he sees Anne-Marie Stretter's red bicycle, gardens, and empty paths.

Images of fragmentation—the crumbling palace—and the fragmentation of cinematic reception for the spectator created by multiple voices and the separation of sound from image tracks are further accentuated visually and temporally. The "double rectangle" of the reception scene frames a gap into which the actors disappear momentarily as they move from real to reflected space, undermining the solidity of both. In one of the most striking uses of the double rectangle, Anne-Marie Stretter faces her image, alone, in the mirror. The Vice-Consul comes up behind her. Because of the angle of the camera and mirror, only the reflected image of the Vice-Consul is seen by the viewer. Anne-Marie Stretter turns to

look at him and in so doing her "real" image must turn her back on her
reflected image. Recalling Francine's moment of self-discovery (or invention of self) in the mirror scene of *La Vie tranquille*, Anne-Marie Stretter
turns her back to the reflection of herself to meet the male gaze. She is
split into two images in direct visual contrast to the unitary male image.
Yet the viewer is limited to the image of the reflected male gaze; the
"real" image of Anne-Marie Stretter stares out beyond the frame to the
"real" Vice-Consul whose image we do not see.

Meanwhile, the viewer has been told that Anne-Marie Stretter is
buried in the English cemetery; the altar to death in the very space that
frames the reception scene is a reminder that the "time" of the reception
is a phantasy time, both before and after the death of Anne-Marie
Stretter. Whose phantasy is this? Who is looking, talking in this film?
The first response would have to be "the filmmaker," especially because
the voice of Duras is inscribed authoritatively at the end and relocates
the story in historical time. A second answer, compatible with the first,
might be "female subjectivity" as imagined by Duras.

In *Woman of the Ganges* female subjectivity was inscribed primarily
through the two female voices on the film of the Voices, the voiceless Lol
and the voice of the filmmaker in the film text. The voices have replaced
Jack Hold's mediating access to Lol, although the figure of Michael
Richardson is a mediating presence within the story. Defined by desire,
absence, and the male gaze in *The Ravishing of Lol Stein*, female subjectivity in *Woman of the Ganges* is further defined by the gaze of the filmmaker, with the complicity of the viewer. In *India Song*, women's voices
(the Asian beggarwoman and the two French voices of the prologue)
provide access to the story while retaining an oblique relation to it.
Anne-Marie Stretter, the only woman represented on the screen, fascinates all of the male characters. She is a projection of their desire, created
by their desire. This explains, in part, the Vice-Consul's affirmation that
he loves her in her love of Michael Richardson. But Anne-Marie Stretter
is also, in a sense, an object of desire and fascination for the filmmaker.
The viewer is again caught between the (often fixed) rectangle of the
camera's viewfinder and the rectangle of the screen, both of which mark
out the filmmaker's gaze.

The material conditions of the production of both *India Song* and *Son
nom de Venise dans Calcutta désert* confirm in a curious way the controlling
role of the filmmaker and the transformation of cinematic conventions.
Bruno Nuytten was the cinematographer for both films. In interviews
about the films, he stresses that Duras made him do things with the

camera that were entirely unprecedented in his years of training and previous cinematic practice. He especially mentions the breast scene in *India Song* as a "regard sur la femme" that was different from anything he had ever done or been taught. He thought that the scene was intensely erotic (*EVC*, 30). Although it would be unwise to generalize too quickly, it is interesting to note that some women spectators of the film have found that scene to be violent, unbearable rather than erotic.[19] In *Son nom de Venise dans Calcutta désert*, too, Nuytten says that Duras controlled the camera, making him do things he had thought were impossible.

In both these films, female subjectivity and desire are produced by male subjectivity, but the gradual substitution of the filmmaker's gaze (and voice) for the male narrator exposes the terms of this construction of female subjectivity and begins to map out another model for female subjectivity. This new model does not represent a radical departure from the figure of woman as absence but rather a variant in which "woman" would speak her subjectivity rather than be an "echo chamber" or an expression of male lack alone.

In chapter 1, I talked about the story that Duras tells of Elisabeth Striedter, the model for Anne-Marie Stretter, whom she saw when she was about eight. Duras never saw the woman up close, only framed in windows, gates, car windows. The gossip about Elisabeth Striedter was that a young man in another colonial outpost had killed himself because of his desire for her. In an interview with Xavière Gauthier, Duras tries to explain the force of this woman on her imagination by saying "it was like the primal scene that Freud speaks of. The day I learned about the young man's death was perhaps my primal scene. . . . She was the mother of little girls who were my age, and she had a body with the power to bestow death" (*DD*, 79). She goes on to situate the explosive power of this woman in the context of colonial society: "With the very established, very visible colonial ostentation that surrounded me, this power of woman was not apparent; it was unexpected, it exploded just like that, like a bomb, but silently, you see. This accident wasn't ascribable to anything, nor could it be classified; it was natural, it had the fantastic violence of nature. . . . all of a sudden there was this accident within this order which had nothing to do with the kind of arrangement of white social life in the posts" (*DD*, 80).

Duras has also said, repeatedly, that the Vice-Consul and Anne-Marie Stretter are the same, that he embodies a "feminine principle" as the bearer of death in *India Song*. In the film, she shifts crucial characteristics of each figure, significantly changing the story she tells about the people

whose lives she took as models. Anne-Marie Stretter, rather than the
Vice-Consul, commits suicide. The Vice-Consul's scandalous desire for
her is linked to his shooting at lepers, a detail entirely of Duras's invention. The shooting is as much a disruption of order as his crying out for
Anne-Marie Stretter at the reception. Anne-Marie Stretter is described as
a "leper of the heart" on several occasions during the film. While the
Vice-Consul, in Duras's terms, might be a "feminine principle" in that he
is disruptive, an exile, and a scandal to colonial order, it is the death of
Anne-Marie Stretter that forecloses his desire and she who pays the price
of disruption.

Inscribing an Authorial Voice. The way Duras inscribes her own
authorial voice in *India Song* and *Son nom de Venise* will shape future films
and written texts. As Silverman points out, there are many ways in
which the author may constitute himself or herself as a speaking subject
in the text of the film (Silverman, 202). Cameo appearances in the manner of Hitchcock, for example, establish a position for the viewer or create a complicit relationship between the filmmaker and the viewer who
is now "in the know."

As mentioned earlier, Silverman argues that as the concept of cinematic apparatus as the enunciating agency of film has replaced the
"auteur" in film theory, there has been "a much greater emphasis upon
both the productive role of the technological and ideological apparatus,
and the strategies for concealing this apparatus from general view"
(Silverman, 11). The filmmaker's voice offscreen might signal his or her
presence at the site of production "outside" the fiction and yet close the
gap between the apparatus and the story. The association with the cinematic apparatus makes the authorial voice more authoritative than the
voices within the story. Duras, as we have seen, in the invention of the
film of the Voices draws attention to this apparatus rather than conceal
it. In *India Song* she identifies the zone of cinematic production with her
own voice in the epilogue, giving herself the most authoritative voice in
the film of the Voices and situating, in her voice, the film fiction in historical time and geographical space. Hers is not the only voice heard offscreen at the end. All the voices—whether inside the story or outside
it—are "off" in *India Song*. Although the tone of her voice is more
authoritative, it has the same status as the questioning male voice, and
the voices associated with the story—including the Asian beggarwoman's—that close the film. In that way she refuses to reassure the
viewer of special access via the author's voice.

Silverman also speaks of another more dynamic and less localized kind of authorial inscription: "the libidinal coherence that the films by a particular director can sometimes be said to have" (Silverman, 212). Duras often uses the language of desire to speak of her need to make the Indian cycle films, to retell the Stein/Stretter obsession. She describes her own "urgent" need to unburden herself of these stories, to work through this "primal scene" in her films. At the level of the story, the libidinal coherence of the Indian cycle films, and the Lol V. Stein texts before them, was maintained through male subjectivity constructing female desire. Several simultaneous narrative events shift the principle of libidinal coherence in the two last films of the Indian cycle and reshape all Duras's texts to come. First, the female filmmaker gradually replaces the male narrator. At the level of the story, Anne-Marie Stretter, who had eclipsed Lol as the object of male desire, kills herself, and the Vice-Consul, who in some ways was the filmic equivalent of Jack Hold, disappears.

Although female sexuality will continue to be defined in Duras's work by male desire, the story of female sexuality—and male desire—will be told through an explicitly female subjectivity. The eclipsing of the male narrator and the ascendancy of the female filmmaker are further marked in *Son nom de Venise*, which closes the Indian cycle. In what may be an entirely unprecedented gesture in film history, Duras used the sound track of *India Song* and a new image track to create *Son nom de Venise*. Duras has said that *Son nom de Venise* is "the most important thing I've done in cinema" (*EVC*, 33). She had the impression that she had not yet finished off *India Song*, and that in *Son nom de Venise* Anne-Marie Stretter's death is finally accomplished.

The image track of *Son nom de Venise* returns to the scene of *India Song*, the Rothschild Palace, now in an even greater state of disrepair than when *India Song* was made two years earlier. Duras also uses interiors of the palace—rooms crumbling with time, in fragments. The palace had been used by Goering during the Occupation, and the Rothschilds, after his presence had defiled the place, wanted nothing to do with it again. Again, the site of this Indian cycle film contains traces of World War II occupation and violence even as it is used to represent a colonial outpost that stages the disruption of desire.

The image track consists entirely of these depopulated exteriors and interiors, sometimes shot in such close-up that the images on the screen are abstract designs of cracks, fissures, and gaps in the walks and walls. Clearly this site is beyond human habitation. Actors are nearly entirely eliminated. The only appearance of human forms is in the last eight minutes of the two-hour film. In five shots lasting a little more than four minutes, we see two women (Delphine Seyrig and Nicole Hiss) framed by a window looking out from the interior of the palace. In some shots they are together, in others separate; in some their features are distinguishable, in others they are just silhouettes. Having removed all images of the male actors, Duras closes off these two actresses who played Lol and Anne-Marie Stretter in the earlier Indian cycle films.

The reuse of the *India Song* sound track confirms the primacy of the voices and underscores the arbitrary nature of the link between image and sound in film. It also reconfirms Duras's voice as filmmaker, as shaper of meanings and controller of the cinematic apparatus. In her next film, *Le Camion* (*The Truck*), she appears on screen with Gérard Depardieu in an effort that further stresses the arbitrary nature of film representation by staging a reading of the filmscript, intercut with scenes that represent the film's fiction.

The Truck, Caesarea, Negative Hands, and the Aurélia Steiner Series

Le Camion (*The Truck*)[20] is the kind of French film that American movie reviewers love to hate. During the week it was screened at the New York Film Festival in September 1977, Janet Maslin in the *New York Times* and Pauline Kael in the *New Yorker* both observed that *The Truck* did not fulfill moviegoers' expectations.[21] For Maslin, *The Truck* was a talky film that did not say much, though she praised its "stern and unrelenting . . . visual style." Kael, on the other hand, while acknowledging intense viewer anger against *The Truck* at the Cannes film festival, and anticipating the same in New York, turns Duras's denial of viewer expectations into a virtue. The refusal to ease the tension between the film's fiction and the cinematic apparatus, the precarious gap in which she situates the viewer, is at the heart of the frustration that Duras creates for the viewer of *The Truck*.

A brief summary is in order for the film that Kael calls "an end-of-the-world road movie" (Kael, 124). In *The Truck*, Duras again presents two films, linked this time by an insistent use of the past conditional ("This would have been a film."). The first film the viewer experiences is the film that would have been, dominated by images of an enormous blue diesel truck, seen first negotiating the square of a town and then rumbling through the barren waste of the French industrial landscape west of Paris. The Beethoven "Diabelli" variations orchestrate this film with varying intensity. The other film, which alternates with the first and dominates it, takes place entirely in what Duras calls "the black room," or the "reading room" (*C*, 11), a camera obscura located in her own house at Neauphle, the house that provided the setting for *Nathalie Granger*. Duras and Gérard Depardieu are seated at a round table with manuscript pages in hand, and they read and discuss "the film that would have been."

Contrary to what some critics have suggested, they do not read the film script, playing the roles of the truck driver and of the mad, old woman hitchhiker he picks up. Rather, they imagine what the film might have been and move imperceptively in and out of the characters of the driver and the hitchhiker, and the roles of actor and filmmaker. Duras's voice, as at the end of the Indian cycle, is the authoritative one; Depardieu asks questions and seems very tentative. The contrast between them is all the more striking because of her diminutive size and aged face and his physical bulk and youthful strength. She has said that it was a cold reading for him, that he had never read the script before.

The "story" of the film that would have been tells of an old woman who resembles Claire in *L'Amante anglaise*, the mother in *The Sea Wall* and *L'Eden cinéma* and with whom Duras explicitly identifies in several interviews. The woman hitches a ride, ostensibly to visit her daughter who has just given birth to a son in a remote village. The woman does almost all the talking; her topics range from a repudiation of communism to fear that giving her grandson a Jewish name—Abraham—will cause serious problems for him in life. The truck driver is alternately uninterested in the woman and suspicious that she may have escaped from a psychiatric hospital. The woman, like Claire, has many ideas jumbled up; she finds it hard to give logical sequence to her ideas, though she insists that apparent confusion does not mean she lacks a logic of her own. Her strongest, repeated statement is "May the world get lost" (*Que le monde aille à sa perte*). In an interview with Dominique Noguez, Duras claims that she did not mean this as a nihilistic statement, and that loss should not be equated with death. She meant to say that justice should return, that by the "loss" of the world she meant that the world should expand, equality should spread through the world, "common" destiny should truly become common (*EVC*, 48).

The viewer is repeatedly frustrated by *The Truck* because, as Kael points out, every time the truck and landscape are on the screen the viewer gets pulled into the story, wants to believe that "now the real movie will begin." And yet we never see the driver or the woman, we are constantly brought back to the camera obscura with Duras and Depardieu at the table. The story is told by them (primarily by Duras) in the past conditional—a taunting mode in that it provides an image even while denying its reality. The film ends as they imagine her getting out of the truck in a depopulated landscape. He takes off again and the story is over because "They could only exist in relation to each other" (*C*, 67). They exist, in other words, only as inventions for the purposes of this film.

Viewer response was so intensely angry in part because Duras does not let the viewer maintain the illusion of the film and in part because she repeatedly asserts the primacy of the filmmaker's voice and vision. In her interview with Noguez, Duras says that the film "renews the place of the author" (*EVC*, 43), and that the use of the past conditional in particular "steals away from the spectator a certain kind of representation" (*EVC*, 49). The published scenario is presented with an epigraph from Grévisse's *Le Bon usage*, the bible of French grammar, on the past conditional. The citation recalls, among other things, that the past conditional is used to indicate "a simple imagination transporting events, as it were, into the field of fiction (in particular, a preludic conditional used by children in their game propositions)" (*C*, 7). Duras insists that *The Truck* renews the "grammatical role of the camera" (*EVC*, 44). The filmmaker plays with the viewer in a game in which she retains all control, reminding the viewer constantly of his (or her) precarious status; like the characters in *The Truck*, the viewer exists only in relation to the film.

Duras denies that the truck is symbolic, insisting instead that it is "a pure truck" (*EVC*, 43). Given the play between the two films contained in *The Truck* and the relations she establishes in earlier films between the "inside" and the "outside" of the story, however, it is hard not to read the truck as the engine of cinema, embodying the technological apparatus of cinema. The viewer learns (but does not see) that a second driver sleeps, hidden from view. The driver who is awake, associated with Depardieu, moves from the space of the fiction to the author's room while the woman, a hitchhiker, appropriates a place for herself within the enclosed cabin of the truck. She is transported by it but is not in the driver's seat.

Reading the truck as a metaphor for cinema is upheld by a number of references in the scenario that suggest a slippage between the cab of the truck and the author's room or between the place of the passenger and the spectator. At one point the viewer is watching an image of the truck stopped at a crosswalk while Duras's voice off screen discusses the woman's ideas. The woman maintains that "everything is in everything, everywhere, at the same time" (*C*, 26). Duras's voice then adds that the woman says:

> It's there in front of us on the screen.
> That's what I think.
> He asks:
> What screen?
> She says:
> There, in front of us:
> The road.

The films that Duras made after *The Truck* have not received much popular attention, although some would argue that they are her most beautiful cinematic achievements. The films have not been distributed very widely and it is difficult to get them in the United States even though they exist on videotape. Most of her films since *The Truck* have been short subjects.[22] Four of the best-known short subjects, all made in 1979, are structurally similar though focused on different narrative concerns: *Césarée* (*Caesarea*), *Les Mains négatives* (*Negative Hands*), and two films called *Aurélia Steiner* (one is subtitled "Melbourne" and the other "Vancouver"). *Caesarea* is a meditation on classical history with Racinian overtones; *Negative Hands* speculates on the meaning of a prehistoric, man-made image and links it to the present moment through desire; the Steiner series turns to a remembrance of World War II, particularly the concentration camp experience as imagined by the daughter, or granddaughter, of Jews who died in the camps.

In each of the short subjects the image track and the sound track are seemingly independent of each other. The image tracks include, primarily, Parisian monuments, nearly empty cityscapes, other depopulated landscapes, and ocean images; there are no actors, no represented characters in the image tracks. The sound tracks consist of monologues by Duras that were all published as written texts after the films. Just as the exteriors and images of architecture and gardens in the Indian cycle films were presented in moving camera shots—panoramas and traveling shots—most of the image tracks in these short subjects consist of shots in motion.

Caesarea, Duras's first short subject, is an eleven-minute film, in color, made from takes left over from the filming of *Le Navire Night* (*The Ship Night*), a full-length film released in 1979. All the shots were made in Paris on a single day in July. Duras has said that the film is structured around the word *Césaréa* (*EVC*, 53). *Caesarea* recalls many organizing motifs from *Hiroshima mon amour*: the importance of place and of name, the substitution of one place for another (or the grafting of one city's memory onto the image of another), the blend of personal passion and political event, the haunting fear of historical amnesia, and the juxtaposition of different historical moments. The narrative of *Caesarea* is a brief prose poem meditation on Caesarea and on Bérénice, abandoned by Titus. Bérénice, never named, is evoked by traces of her story—the queen of the Jews, taken into exile by a Roman ship, repudiated "by reason of the State." Duras's enduring interest in this story, particularly the Racinian version, led her to make an hour-long film based on Bérénice, called *Dialogo di Roma*, for Italian television in 1982.

The images are primarily of the Maillol statues and other sculptures (marbles and bronzes) in the Tuileries gardens in Paris, of the Louvre, of the Place de la Concorde (especially the obelisk in the center), and of quais along the Seine as seen from a boat; often it is the reflection we see, not the buildings per se. Duras explained in an interview with Dominique Noguez (*EVC*, 53) that the film was inspired by a trip she had taken to Israel, specifically to Caesarea, where she was struck by the intense blue of the water and images of columns. While those images appear in the text of *Caesarea*, the film also corresponds to narrative needs evident in other texts and films by Duras: retelling a familiar story, focusing on a woman abandoned by her lover, radically separating sound from image tracks to signal the presence of the filmmaker and draw attention to the constructed nature of the film. She further interrupts the illusion of continuity in the image track by having the screen turn to black between shots. Toward the end of the film, this device becomes naturalized as the black sequences coincide with the passage of the boat bearing the camera under the bridges of the Seine as the camera captures the quais or, more precisely, the reflection of the Conciergerie in the Seine.

Perhaps the most important innovation in *Caesarea* is Duras's monologue. Beginning with the film of the Voices in *India Song*, where her voice is an authoritative presence toward the end, and continuing with her image and voice in *The Truck*, Duras assumes an increasingly important presence in her films. In *The Truck*, her voice is both authorial and narrating, confusing distinctions between the film fiction and the site of production. In the short subjects, hers is the only voice, by now recognizable to the spectator as the filmmaker's voice but staying within the role of narrator: narrating the poetic monologue that accompanies the images, while remaining separate from them. The monologue creates verbal images—the sea, the desert, the columns, the repudiated woman—that are echoed indirectly by the statues and cityscape but are more often in a point-counterpoint relation to the visual images. At the very end of the film she brings the sound and image tracks together by invoking Paris instead of Caesarea: "The weather's bad this summer in Paris. Cold. Foggy."[23] Yet the cold, foggy image she creates verbally is in direct contrast to the splendid sun-filled images of the film.

All the shots of the Tuileries in *Caesarea* were taken in the morning and the shot of the Concorde in the afternoon of the same July day (*EVC*, 54). The images of *Negative Hands*, an eighteen-minute short subject, were made the night and dawn preceding that day but show a very different Paris: the boulevards moving from the République toward the center of the city at dawn. Whereas *Caesarea* contains some stationary shots (broken by the black transitions mentioned earlier), most of the shots in *Negative Hands* are traveling, moving shots. The film opens with a black screen and Duras's voice explaining the title. Then we see images of late night and dawn when the only people visible are workers—street cleaners, Portuguese cleaning women, Arab and African workers. Duras has explained that the sight of this "colonial presence of humanity," which silently dominates the streets at dawn led her to create her monologue about "the negative hands" (*EVC*, 55).

The image of the title refers to "paintings of hands found in the caves of . . . Europe along the south Atlantic coast. The hands—posed wide open on the stone—were dipped in color. Most often blue or black. Sometimes red. No explanation has been found for this practice" (*NN*, 93). Later, Duras corrected herself: The hands were held up to the stone, and color was painted around them, outlining them. (*EVC*, 55). The essence of the image remains intact in either case: the inscription on stone of a prehistoric human presence—which Duras takes to be male—enduring to the present but unreadable; the hands signify identity without our being able to name it.

What exactly is the link between immigrant, Third World workers in contemporary Paris and traces of prehistoric man? One link that Duras's monologue suggests is the unchanging nature of desire and the anguish of having one's identity stripped away, by time or by colonial power. Her voice speaks the anguish of the man she imagines leaving this indelible sign on the stone. He cries out his love to a woman who has a name, who is endowed with identity: the filmmaker perhaps. In the monologue he identifies himself as "he who calls out . . . who called and cried out thirty thousand years ago" (NN, 97). His cries are surrounded by images of immensity—the sea, forests, the wind—and remain unanswered except by the presence of this film and the monologue invented and articulated by the filmmaker who would imagine his cries piercing through all those thousands of years.

The circulation of desire through the film of the Voices in *Woman of the Ganges* and among the various voices in the other films of the Indian cycle is now specifically linked to the filmmaker. The monologue she imagines and speaks for the prehistoric man calls out to a woman who is known and who, therefore, can confer identity. The filmmaker as creator of both the image and sound tracks sets in motion a circulation of desire that is, ultimately, self-referential. The dispersal or diffusion of desire among the several voices of the Indian cycle films is now focused in the filmmaker's voice as she assumes the power of articulating the desire of the nameless man.

Another link between the "colonial presence of humanity" and the prehistoric man is suggested by the juxtaposition of the verbal and visual images and by comments Duras made about the film. She said that the film is at once about a prehistoric cave and about Paris, signaling a profound timelessness: of desire, sexuality, and crime. In her sympathy for the blacks she sees cleaning the streets at dawn, she acknowledges the erasure of identity that their situation imposes. At the same time, however, by simultaneously speaking the prehistoric man's desire in her own voice and maintaining in the long traveling shots the distanced point of view of the privileged—who might travel the boulevards at dawn but are not a part of them—she tends to reify the status of the blacks as nameless, without distinct identity. In her interview with Dominique Noguez about this film she says:

> I think that everything is there, as it has always been there, for all time.
> . . . Sexuality, the sexuality of monsters as well as of normal people, has
> not changed, it is still intact. It is there, like before, as it has always been
> for thousands of years. Crime is also part of society in the same way. And
> I believe that those people, those Blacks, call out to be loved, to be rec-
> ognized like other living beings, as much now as in the beginning of the
> world. (*EVC*, 55)

The line between a sympathetic despair at the timelessness of injustice, on the one hand, and, on the other, a fatalistic essentialism that maintains a privileged viewpoint and assumes the situation of the powerless to be immutable is a delicate one. The ambivalence of Duras's treatment of blacks and other Third World laborers is all the more intense because she links desire, which is always a privileged term in her work, with crime and the robbing of identity, which are recurrent sources of anguish in her work. The blacks of *Negative Hands* recall the Asian beggarwoman of the Indian cycle: a nameless person from a colonized culture whose words are unreadable by the Western observer, whose story is imagined or invented by the whites in the colony but who also serves as a constant reminder of the scandal of colonization.

The problematic nature of Duras's representation of the "other" continues in the *Aurélia Steiner* series, in which she tries to understand Jewish identity. As in *Negative Hands*, the increasingly dominant voice of the filmmaker assumes the identity of those who might otherwise be voiceless when confronted with oppressive power. The two films called *Aurélia Steiner* are a thirty-five-minute short subject in color, filmed in Paris, called *Aurélia Steiner (Melbourne)* and a forty-eight minute black and white film shot at Honfleur and Trouville, called *Aurélia Steiner (Vancouver)*. A text referred to as *Aurélia Steiner (Paris)* completes the series and is published with the texts of the two films, although Duras never filmed it. In the *Aurélia Steiner* series, Duras focuses with increased intensity on the question of Jewish identity while she stages the (Jewish) woman writing. Earlier texts and names (Lol V. Stein, Stein in *Destroy, she said, Abahn, Sabana, David*, for example) suggest Duras's interest in Jewish identity, but the *Aurélia Steiner* series makes it a central concern. Later, in *La Douleur (The War: A Memoir)*, Duras writes extensively and painfully of her husband's return from a concentration camp, barely alive, and the Holocaust is, through her account of his experience, personalized in a way that is analogous to the bombing of Hiroshima in *Hiroshima mon amour*. But it is through the multiple figures named Aurélia Steiner that Duras, in her characteristic retelling of one story and simultaneous telling of several juxtaposed stories, first focuses her narrative attention on what it means to be Jewish.

In her discussion of the *Aurélia Steiner* films with Dominique Noguez, Duras says that she does not want to associate them with the other short subjects, because the *Aurélia Steiner* series, unlike the other films, is about Jews. She "identifies" the character(s) called Aurélia Steiner as the grandchild of Jews killed in the camps whose children escaped the Holocaust. The children, the second generation, were sent far away to cities like Melbourne and Vancouver to be protected from the Nazis. "And these two people (in one), these two Aurélias, this same Aurélia, would have been born there" (*EVC*, 55). She insists again and again that the story of Aurélia is the story of all Jews throughout history, every-where and nowhere, wandering, dispersed throughout the world, a sur-vivor and yet part of the death chain of the camps.

If one had only the film or text of *Aurélia Steiner (Melbourne)*, without reference to the other film or to Duras's comments about the series, the centrality of the Jewish theme would be difficult to discern. Filmed in Paris from the Seine, the image track is in motion and filmed almost entirely into the light so that the human figures one sees on bridges and on the quais are back lit and, therefore, seen as silhouettes, without clear features. Just as the workers at dawn in *Les main négatives* were at once seen and invisible, perceived but without identity, the distinctive features of people caught by the camera in this film are erased. The river, Duras has said, is central to this film in every way, recalling the many French Jews who were deported, swept away during the war. The river creates "a void in the middle of the image" (*EVC*, 57). The black screens that punctuated the images of *Caesarea* are replaced in this film by passages under the bridges that subdue the light without turning to total darkness.

The sound track is stark, without music and with many moments of silence. A monologue, spoken in Duras's voice in the first person and representing Aurélia Steiner, situates her immediately as a writer addressing an absent "you." "I write to you all the time, always that, you see" (*NN*, 105). The "you," absent and unidentified at the beginning, could be the spectator just as the "I" writing could be identified with the filmmaker, especially because it is spoken in her voice. Desire for the absent "you" is expressed by the speaker, as well as the impossibility of reaching the absent one.

The image and sound tracks are linked through the image of the river. The speaker situates herself in a room looking out at a garden filled with roses about to fade. Several times she invokes a river, associat-ed with death. The monologue is an effort to reach out to the absent loved one; she asks questions, tries to imagine his fate. The recurring themes are separation, fragmentation, dispersal. In a reverse gesture from *Negative Hands*, the woman (who is ultimately given a name) speaks to the absent man, who is never identified except as he who is desired, whose love was, probably, never realized. References to the Holocaust are dispersed in the text, death camps are mentioned along with other places—islands off the coast of France, London, Siberia, Cracow—the whole creating a verbal Diaspora. At the very end of the monologue, the female speaker identifies herself:

My name is Aurélia Steiner.
I live in Melbourne where my parents are teachers.
I'm eighteen years old.
I write. (*NN*, 120–21)

In *Aurélia Steiner (Vancouver)*, both Jewish identity and the staging of the woman writer are more explicitly developed; two interwoven narratives, spoken again by Duras, constitute the sound track. The frame narrative, in the first person, is about the woman who writes, by the sea, awaiting a sailor who will be her lover. The second narrative, which she recalls or invents, tells the story of her grandparents when they were her age (eighteen) in a concentration camp. In the white rectangle of the central courtyard the mother gave birth to "Aurélia Steiner" as the father was hanged in punishment for stealing soup for the child. He was so frail that he would not die until an officer shot him on the third day. Desire motivates both narratives and links them: The woman who waits for her lover also longs for her grandfather, who died when he was her age. She has the same name as her grandmother and, as is often the case in Duras's texts, the identities of the women are merged through desire and the telling of these stories: the story of the camp by Aurélia Steiner, the story of the film by Duras.

The image track, filmed completely in black and white, opens with images of the sea that correspond to what Aurélia Steiner describes in her monologue. Interior shots then replace the seascape as Aurélia Steiner situates herself in a room looking out. The opening monologue merges the seascape and the process of writing:

I am in this room where every day I write to you. . . . In front of me is the sea. . . . Between the sky and the water there is a wide black line, like coal, thick. It covers the entire horizon, it has the regularity of a large, sure handed erasure, and the importance of an insuperable difference. It could be frightening. (*NN*, 125)

Seeing erasure (forgetting) and difference (separation by geography and historical moment) in the seascape, the writer projects on the world she observes the terms that will structure desire and writing and that will articulate her identity in her connections with her mother, her grandmother, her lover, and her grandfather. In the second paragraph of the monologue, a mirror image doubles the image of the woman who writes in a gesture that recalls the proliferation of self-images experienced by Francine in *The Tranquil Life* and the doubling of Anne Marie

Stretter in the mirror of the double rectangle in *India Song*: "In the mirror of my room, upright, veiled by the dark light there is my image. I am looking toward the outdoors" (*NN*, 125). The perception of both images of the writer would be possible only in the eyes of another person—the camera or the spectator.

A few moments later, she turns to look at herself but can see herself only dimly. The effort to discern her image turns immediately to an expression of her desire for the one who is not there: "I love you with all my strength. I do not know you" (*NN*, 126).

The monologue establishes the subjectivity of the woman who writes as split and as motivated by desire for the absent or unknown lover. As she sits down to write, she goes away from the mirror but looks at herself—her blue eyes and black hair—through the imagined eyes of the absent "you." She imagines that "you" are seeing her in her beauty. She then identifies herself: "My name is Aurélia Steiner. I am your child" (*NN*, 127).

Having situated herself as a writer, Aurélia Steiner begins the second narrative, specifying that lovers the age of her grandfather at his death substitute for him and enable her to meet him beyond death, to recognize her resemblance to him through the chance experience of desire. As the story of the camp is told, the image track shows an abandoned train station, logs piled alongside train tracks, a port, a bunker on the beach. The name "Aurélia" written in Duras's hand, in a long, stationary shot, fades out to "Aurélia Steiner—2000095," reinforcing the substitution of one Aurélia Steiner for another across time, space, and the insuperable distance of death.

Toward the end of the film her anonymous sailor lover comes to her room and, as she comes to the conclusion of the concentration camp narrative, she says: "Trembling with desire for him, I love you" (*NN*, 140). The grandfather, before dying, had cried out the name Aurélia Steiner again and again so that she would be remembered. After his death the words are no longer cried out in the camp but are dispersed in the world.

When the sailor finds Aurélia Steiner in her room, she tells him her name and writes it out for him. He speaks it as he undresses her, discovering her body as he repeats her name. As they make love, he says, "Juden [Jew], Juden Aurélia, Juden Aurélia Steiner" (*NN*, 146). The possession of her name and her story are synonymous with the possession of her body. Like the Japanese at the end of *Hiroshima*, the sailor wants to stay with her, but she asserts that she belongs to no one in particular.

Like the other *Aurélia Steiner* film, this one ends with her assertion of her own identity:

> My name is Aurélia Steiner.
> I live in Vancouver where my parents are teachers.
> I am eighteen years old.
> I write. (*NN*, 147)

Both narratives are inventions, imagined by the woman who writes and the woman who films, the narrating subject of this film being split between the woman writer within the fiction, Aurélia Steiner, and the filmmaker whose voice tells the story and whose camera creates the images.

The filmmaker, however, is not Jewish, but is trying to imagine Jewish identity through the figure of the woman writer/lover that will become increasingly dominant in her work. Even though Duras's identification with Aurélia Steiner is more closely articulated than her identification with the prehistoric male artist or the contemporary immigrant workers of *Negative Hands*, she still encloses Jewish identity within terms set by the oppressor. Victim, wanderer, isolated in a foreign land, the Jew in Duras's work resists only by crying out or, perhaps, by writing. Again, the line between sympathy with an oppressed group and appropriation of their story, between empathetic representation and fatalism, remains problematic.

The *Aurélia Steiner* films give a new dimension to a figure that recurs in many of Duras's films: the rectangle. At once viewfinder, screen, mirror, and blank page, the (white) rectangle becomes in the *Aurélia Steiner* films the place of death as well as the place of writing. The writer writes so that death will not be forgotten, so that the scandal of the death camps (or of Hiroshima) will be recalled. But the white rectangle is also the bed of desire, the bed where the sailor possesses Aurélia Steiner or the Japanese possesses the Frenchwoman in *Hiroshima*. As the Indian cycle made clear, the woman's body is both bearer of life and bearer of death.

The films of the seventies enabled Duras to develop a narrative voice in the feminine signed "Duras." Her break with writing in the early seventies and her subsequent withdrawal from filmmaking and return to writing in the early eighties are not precisely defined moments but, rather, part of a process that moves gradually from one type of narrative

and representation to another. Her films—particularly the short subjects—are increasingly "written," as she has said; the films are texts to be
spoken, to be voiced, but are increasingly texts nonetheless. "I've had a
stronger desire to write, for several years," she said in 1984, "And my
films are more and more 'written,' they are books . . . though they are
texts to be said. By a voice. Therefore, they are not completely 'written'"
(*EVC*, 59).

One of the most distinct characteristics of the narrating female voice
signed "Duras" that emerges from the films is the apparent will to control: to control the spectator's experience, to control readings of the film
by asserting authorial presence. Control is asserted in spite of divisions
within the writer's subjectivity (signaled by the separation of image and
sound tracks) or, perhaps, because of those divisions. Duras did not cease
making films altogether after the seventies, for *L'Homme atlantique*
(*Atlantic Man*) and *Agatha* are two important films made in the eighties.
The tension between the female "I" and the male "you" of the *Aurélia
Steiner* series and the controlling look and voice of the female filmmaker
that gradually dominate in her films in fact reach new intensity in
L'Homme atlantique. Because the film is dominated by a black screen with
only occasional glimpses of images and because the text enacts a particularly interesting dynamic between the (female) writer and the (male)
reader, I discuss it in the context of the written texts of the eighties. That
text, like the other narratives written after 1979, would have been
inconceivable without the cinematic experiments and the narrative
regions they opened up for Duras in the seventies. Before making her
own films, Duras could only imagine male appropriation of a woman's
story. The films develop a distinctly inflected female authorial voice
telling a woman's story and in some of the short subjects speaking male
desire. The texts of the eighties further emphasize the tensions between
female and male, narrator and reader, as Duras explores the possibilities
of erotic texts and autobiography and as she reflects more explicitly on
the act of writing itself.

Chapter Five

Return to Writing: Duras Becomes "Duras"

Suddenly I see myself as another, as another would be seen, outside myself, available to all, available to all eyes, in circulation for cities, journeys, desire.

Marguerite Duras, *The Lover*

Duras's experiments with a split, female, narrative voice in her films, her increasing gestures of narrative control, and her persistent fascination with desire, particularly desire for the absent one, have informed her return to writing since 1980. With the publication of *L'Amant* (*The Lover*)[1] in 1984, Duras became a national phenomenon. The immense popularity of *The Lover* has led readers back to earlier texts even as Duras continues to reinvent them in new ways.

At least part of the reason for the explosive popularity—and scandal—of her work in the last decade is that it feeds two related reader appetites: for erotica and for autobiography. Although desire has always been one of Duras's organizing themes, her texts in the 1980s, such as *L'Homme assis dans le couloir* (*The Seated Man in the Passage*), *L'Homme atlantique* (*The Atlantic Man*), and *La Maladie de la mort* (*The Malady of Death*), go beyond the representation of desire to an explicit representation of sexuality. Similarly, her life has always informed her work, but as she develops the narrative "I" in *L'Amant* (*The Lover*), *La Douleur* (*The War: A Memoir*), and *L'Amant de la Chine du nord* (*The North China Lover*), for example, readers tend to read her texts as confession and then to reread earlier fictions in that light. In interviews and journalistic pieces, Duras has seemed to make herself increasingly available as a public spectacle; her companion Yann Andréa's book, *M.D.*, describing her painful treatment for alcoholism in 1982 further encouraged readers to feel that they had access to the person as well as the texts.

The erotic texts stage aggressive assaults on the reader, male and female, though in different ways. The autobiographical texts, which are themselves highly erotic, border on exhibitionism, creating the illusion of unmediated access to the writer. The shifting erotic and narrative power unleashed by these aggressions toward the reader and exhibitions of the writer have intensified debate about Duras. Discussions of Duras in the popular press, however, present these texts as personal revelations rather than as artistic representations—a confusion Duras has colluded with. Consequently, Duras is often attacked (or adored) as a woman (writer) rather than read as a (woman) writer.

As in the films, the gaze often structures these works; the image (in *The Lover*, the photograph) is an organizing metaphor. The illusion of an unmediated gaze, like the immediacy of a photograph, further seduces the reader into a sense of uncomplicated referentiality. But these texts are far from transparent or uncomplicated. The split (female) subjectivity of Duras's early narratives and the separate voice and image tracks of her films assume a different configuration in her more recent texts. The narrating female voice in the erotic texts is both filmmaker and spectator, a voyeur of images, sometimes incorporated into the text, sometimes withheld from the reader, that raise questions about the representation of sexuality. In the autobiographical texts, female subjectivity is doubled again into the first and third person as Duras represents the self. In recent fictional texts, such as *Emily L.*, *La Pluie d'été* (*Summer Rain*), and *Yann Andréa Steiner*, Duras reflects on problems of reading and writing, in fictional representations of writing itself.

As Duras becomes an increasingly public figure, participating in televised interviews, for example, we begin to see her fascinated by the product she has become, a spectator of her own spectacle. Since 1980 her writings have been marked by shifts from split female subjectivity to objectification of the female body to commodification of "Duras." These shifts maintain "woman" as "Other" while repositioning the female speaking subject. The problematic tension between empathetic representation and essentialism masquerading as fatalism that we noted in the discussion of the *Aurélia Steiner* films persists in these representations of "woman."

To consider the representational character of the erotic and autobiographical texts is to recontextualize them, to understand the ways in which they inscribe and express cultural constructions of sexuality, power, and gender. This, in turn, helps us to read recent fictions that focus explicitly on problems of reading and writing. In this chapter, I look at the difficult dynamic between writer and reader in Duras's texts since 1980. I pay special attention to the ways that the gender of both writer and reader complicate interpretation of these texts. When we read these texts that represent sexuality, the self, and writing in a North

American context, problems of the cultural construction of gender and desire become even more acute. Recent debates about sexuality and pornography among North American feminists and theorizing about gender and autobiography among French and American literary critics have changed the ways we read sexuality, gender, and autobiography. These are all, to be sure, contested sites; Duras's texts—and the intense responses they provoke—enable us to understand better the stakes involved in both writing and reading desire, sexuality, gender, and the (female) subject.

Representing Sexuality: *The Seated Man in the Passage, The Atlantic Man,* and *The Malady of Death*

Three intensely erotic texts written in the early eighties combine cinematic and narrative technique to arouse or provoke the reader. Underlying each text is a violent, disturbing representation of sexuality that, in retrospect, is consistent with Duras's earliest novels. *The Seated Man in the Passage,*[2] a short narrative published in 1980, is emblematic of many of Duras's texts written after her work as a filmmaker. Duras's story about the origins of the text reveals the impact of her cinematic discoveries. In a short article she wrote for a special issue of *Les Cahiers du cinéma* in 1980,[3] Duras discusses writing *The Seated Man in the Passage.* She claims—as she will five years later for *The War: A Memoir*—that this is a found text, a rediscovered draft of a story that she must have written in 1959 around the time she wrote the scenario for *Hiroshima mon amour.* In the original draft of *The Seated Man in the Passage,* she says, she wrote the phrase "You destroy me, you're so good for me" ("Tu me tues, tu me fais du bien") that became a refrain for the affair between the Japanese man and the Frenchwoman in the film. In other words, when she took up this draft again in 1980, she was reinventing a text that was centered on violent desire in which the woman equates her own destruction with her pleasure.

Duras says in her essay that it was the experience of making the *Aurélia Steiner* series that helped her to understand what to do with the draft of *The Seated Man in the Passage.* She decided to incorporate an immense and yet undefined landscape and to add love. Significantly, she observes that having made the films, "I discovered that the lovers were not isolated but seen, probably by me, and that this seeing was, had to be mentioned, integrated into the facts. And then that the orgasm had taken place, whereas it hadn't taken place in the initial form" (*GE*, 42; *YV*, 60–61). She concludes that she rewrote the text entirely, except for about ten words that may remain from the first draft.

The discovery of her own gaze as a part of the story and, in her telling of it, linked to orgasm, to "jouissance," marks not only *The Seated Man in the Passage* but many other texts she has written since 1980. The incorporation of the writer's gaze is effected here through a triangular narrative: An offstage female voice, specified as "I," is both voyeur and director of the scene; the lovers are the other terms of the triangle. The narrator imagines partial access to the thoughts of the characters. Toward the beginning, she says, "She knows he is looking at her, that he sees everything. She knows it with her eyes shut just as I do who am looking" (*M*, 268; *HA*, 9). The narrator is aligned with the male gaze, but at the same time, the man is the object of her gaze and imagination.

The intense, harsh landscape by the sea is as much an extension of the lovers as it is a setting. The terms used to describe the landscape are nearly interchangeable with the terms describing the bodies of the lovers; its harshness also reflects their brutality.

In the narrative, the woman colludes in her own rape, inviting both violation of her body and violence to her person; the man complies. But she is not merely a passive object of male desire and brutality; she invites his desire by displaying herself; she intensifies his desire by performing oral sex. Toward the end, after orgasm, as their desire rekindles, as the ultimate erotic request, she begs him to beat her, which he does until she is either unconscious or dead. The narrator does not know.

In the article that accompanies her translation, Mary Lydon speaks about the difficulty of translating this text, not only because of linguistic features that have no parallel in English but because it challenges in the most blunt terms feminist efforts to imagine a "nonviolent sexual union" (*M*, 261). If we read this text looking for feminist erotic alternatives to pornography, Lydon is certainly right. This text stages a blatant affront to women; it colludes with a vision of violent, phallic heterosexuality in which punishment and pain are inextricably linked to a woman's pleasure and violence to a man's.

If, however, we do a feminist reading of the representation of sexuality within the text, rather than expect the writer to provide a feminist alternative to violent desire, the full implication of Duras's discovery of the writer's presence as voyeur becomes clearer. Paradoxically, this text confirms radical feminist critiques of pornography and the culture that produces it. Catharine MacKinnon, for example, in an analysis of sexuality and gender, links objectivity with the male standpoint and argues that objectivity leads to objectification and control: The act of control is itself eroticized. She writes, "In the society we currently live in, the content I want to claim for sexuality is the gaze that constructs women as objects for male pleasure. I draw on pornography for its form and content, for the gaze that eroticizes the despised, the demeaned, the thereto-be-used, the servile, the child-like, the passive, and the animal. . . . I'm saying femininity as we know it is how we come to want male dominance, which most emphatically is not in our interest."[4] Femininity, as our culture constitutes it, depends on the objectifying gaze; eroticism in this context requires women's submission, pain, and punishment at the hands of men.

In this perspective we can understand that *The Seated Man in the Passage is* a pornographic text. The woman participates in her own objectification; she is beaten to unconsciousness, if not to death. Her exercise of erotic power is in the service of her own annihilation. But it is a pornographic text with a difference. Even as she stages pornography, Duras twice destabilizes its terms. First, the objectifying gaze is appropriated by the female narrator, who punctuates the text with "I see . . . I see" as she presents the spectacle to the reader. Her appropriation makes the blunt brutality of the gaze even more blatant. Further, toward the end of the text, Duras suggests, through a curious solidarity of imagined women, that this is a shared experience of "femininity as we know it." In a merging of landscape and violent desire that recalls both *Moderato Cantabile* (the man, weeping, is stretched out on the woman's inert body) and the Lol V. Stein cycle, the narrator says:

> I see that the violet color is advancing, that the sky is overcast, its slow progress toward the vast expanse brought to a halt. I see that other people are watching, other women; that other women now dead have likewise watched the summer monsoons rise and play themselves out beside rivers bordered by dark rice-fields, facing wide, deep deltas. I see that a summer storm is blowing up out of the violet color. (*M*, 275; *HA*, 35–36)

The seeming inevitability of this experience of "femininity as we know it," as ineluctable as the dusk and the gathering storm, is undercut by a second destabilizing strategy common in Duras's texts: the use of the past conditional. As we saw in *The Truck*, the past conditional has a privileged place in Duras: It signals a "simple imagination transporting events, as it were, into the field of fiction" (*C*, 7). The use of the past conditional in the very first line of the text posed a special difficulty to the translator. The French "L'homme aurait été assis dans l'ombre du couloir" is literally "The man would have been seated in the shadow of the corridor." Lydon, however, sensitive to Duras's frequent use of the past conditional, wanted to maintain the ambiguity of the mode. She chose "Say the man were seated in the obscurity of the passage." She explains her choice by saying that "it preserves the ambiguity of the French, hinting at the fictional, disputable character of the conditional mode, the 'Say' a gesture in the direction of the *conditionnel préludique* that French children use in setting up their games" (*M*, 265–66).

In other words, *The Seated Man in the Passage* is presented as a self-conscious fantasy, a play of words. This representation of sexuality is a product of imagination and language—a game for adults that is deadly, but a game nonetheless, a product of culture rather than nature, an invention, not an inevitability. Duras accomplishes in narrative what MacKinnon proposes in theory: a stark representation of heterosexual desire as it is structured in the unconscious by contemporary Western culture in which "woman" is desired and despised. And yet, for all the destabilizing features of this narrative, Duras's representation differs from MacKinnon's in at least two respects. Duras's refusal to name the man or woman or to particularize this episode (to name a specific country or moment, to indicate any attachment to a culture) underscores that Duras's subject is the unconscious, as Lydon maintains (*M*, 261). But Duras remains ambiguous about the status of the unconscious: Is it a cultural product or an ahistorical, essential feature of the human psyche, indifferent to historical or cultural context?

MacKinnon's analysis is the basis for an activist agenda: to change desire and power and the relation between them, to dismantle the hierarchy of power that determines gender in our culture. Duras's text is a representation rather than an analysis. As such, it contains ambiguities that Duras refuses to resolve: Is she challenging this construction of the erotic and the definition of "woman" it depends on, or is she complicit with it? Is she destabilizing the male gaze or adopting it, exposing pornography or exploiting it? Does *The Seated Man in the Passage* challenge pleasure or give it, and who does Duras imagine the reader to be?

L'Homme atlantique (*The Atlantic Man*),[5] a 1982 text based on a forty-five-minute film Duras produced in 1981, proposes some resolutions to these ambiguities. In *The Atlantic Man*, the ambiguity of the past conditional is replaced by the urgency of the imperative mode and a willful, controlling future tense. The filmmaker/voyeur and the woman lover of *The Seated Man in the Passage* are collapsed into the subjectivity of the filmmaker/narrator, who constructs this text in rage against the lover who has abandoned her. The man, absent, is addressed as "vous" (you). The violence at the heart of *The Seated Man in the Passage* is transmuted in this text into the rage of the abandoned woman as she addresses the absent lover. The insistent use of the imperative links the reader to the absent man, but has the effect of positioning male and female readers differently.

Beginning with "You will not look at the camera. Except when one requires it of you," (*HAt*, 7), the filmmaker asserts control of the camera and of the man's gaze. In a reversal of the convention that represents woman as erotic object of the (male) filmmaker's gaze, the woman filmmaker offers the camera as a lure and a threat: The male lover is invited to look at the camera as a desired object and as an instrument of death.

Initially, the reader, whether a man or a woman, is the object of the filmmaker's aggressive imperative. "You," however, is explicitly masculine. The woman reader needs to make a conscious effort to realign with the filmmaker and not accept identification with the "you" who is being addressed. Once extricated from "you," the woman reader can become a spectator of this film of absence allied with the speaking female voice. The male reader can detach less easily from "you." In MacKinnon's terms, the male reader has become a pornographic subject: He is forced to witness his own absence or to assume a sympathy with the narrative voice that is contrary to his interest as a man.

As in *The Seated Man in the Passage*, Duras does not try to cover over or disguise the imaginary status of this narrative; the text is offered to the reader as a product of the unconscious or of the imagination. The imaginary material of *The Atlantic Man*—the image of the absent lover—is explicitly presented as a projection of the filmmaker's desire rather than as a representation of the other. The lover's absence provides a blank screen on which the narrator can project her desire and her rage. At the heart of the woman's voice in *The Atlantic Man* is not passivity or a fetishistic reification of the absent love object (as in *The Sailor from Gibraltar* or the Lol V. Stein cycle) but an aggressive articulation of the radical discontinuity between the speaking subject and the other. The antagonism and resistance that characterized the relationship between the woman subject and the male interlocutor in earlier texts such as *L'Amante anglaise* is transferred here to the relationship between the narrator and the reader, with varying effects for male and female readers. The narrative shifts effected in *The Atlantic Man* intensify the reader's collusion in the making of the narrative even while stressing the (erotic) antagonism implied by that relationship.

Considering Male Homosexuality. A cluster of related texts—*La Maladie de la mort* (*The Malady of Death*), *Les Yeux bleus cheveux noirs* (*Blue Eyes, Black Hair*) and *La Pute de la côte normande* (*The Whore from the Coast of Normandy*)—have male homosexuality as a theme for the first time in Duras's work. This coincides with the arrival of Yann Andréa in her life and has inevitably led readers to consider them, especially *Blue Eyes, Black Hair*, which is dedicated to Andréa and was published after the success of *The Lover*, as an insight into their life together. The theme of male homosexuality is a screen, however; like the other erotic texts, these texts interrogate a particular construction of (hetero)sexuality as imagined through a feminine subjectivity. Duras uses the figure of the male homosexual to confirm that sexual union is a cruel deception, that sexuality reiterates an essential isolation of the individual, a disconnection between lovers. Absence, violence, and solitude have always marked what Duras has called the tragedy of passion. Desire in the Lol V. Stein cycle depends on absence and the mediation of a third; *The Seated Man in the Passage*, representing sexuality, confronts the reader with the violence and misogyny that were only suggested in earlier representations of desire. *The Malady of Death* takes the radical solitude of the desiring subject that was developed in *The Atlantic Man* one step further.

It is hardly surprising that many careful readers of *The Malady of Death* failed to identify the male character as homosexual until *Blue Eyes, Black Hair* reworked whole sections of the narrative into a longer, more detailed, and explicit novel four years later. The text opens in the familiar conditional mode of the woman narrator's imagination. As in *The Atlantic Man*, she addresses a male "you." The first paragraph is an unambiguous image of male desire: an erection in search of a woman. "You wouldn't have known her, you'd have seen her everywhere at once, in a hotel, in a street, in a train, in a bar, in a book, in a film, in yourself, your inmost self, when your sex grew erect in the night, seeking somewhere to put itself, somewhere to shed its load of tears."[6]

But whose desire is this, the female narrator's or the male character's? The narrator is creating the scene, telling "you" what you would have or should have desired. The progression from the anonymity of public places to the lure of language and image (a book, a film) to the deepest

layers of the unconscious traces the narrator's imagination as she leads
the reader to her projection of male desire, which signifies, at the end of
the paragraph, solitude and sorrow. Duras then repeats the voyeurism of
The Seated Man in the Passage and reintroduces the prostitute, the saving
figure of female sexuality in "The Boa." The narrator imagines the man
paying a woman to spend several nights—or months—with him in a
hotel by the sea to teach him "to love."

The text is the story of those nights. Or, rather, as Duras said in an
interview: "There is no story in *The Malady of Death*. I take people, I put
them there, I make them approach each other, but there is no knowledge, no sentiment. It's a desert, *The Malady of Death*."[7] The narrator
centers on the man's *lack* of pleasure with a woman; she is fascinated by
the discontinuity between his desire and woman, the lack of connection
between this man and this paid woman that persists even though there
is sex, even though there is "jouissance." The woman leaves him at the
end of their contract, her absence more palpable than at the beginning
of the story, confirming his solitude. All that remains are the words she
used to describe his sickness: "the malady of death." There is no "story"
without heterosexuality, without "woman," even though the only story
possible may revolve around the scandal of destruction the woman har-
bors within her desire, her capacity to bear death as well as life.

But the man in this text is a reflection, or projection, of the narrator.
The anguish, the isolation and anonymity, even the "jouissance" that
mark *The Malady of Death* are feminine. As in *The Seated Man in the
Passage*, the woman's body calls out to be raped: "The body's completely
defenseless, smooth from face to feet. It invites strangulation, rape, ill
usage, insult, shouts of hatred, the unleashing of deadly and unmitigated
passions" (*MD*, 16; *MM*, 21). But more significantly, even for this
"homosexual" male character, it is within the woman's body that the
"malady of death" originates: "You realize it's here, in her, that the malady of death is fomenting, that it's this shape stretched out before you
that decrees the malady of death" (*MD*, 34; *MM*, 38).

How can this character be read as homosexual, and what does "homosexual" come to mean in this text? There are oblique references to male
lovers. When the paid woman takes pleasure in him and talks about it,
he silences her: "one doesn't say such things." The woman then asks "if
they talk about it" (*MD*, 10; *MM*, 16). In the French, "*they*" is in the
masculine. Later, she wants to know if he has ever loved anyone to the
point of wanting to destroy him:

> She says: The wish to be about to kill a lover, to keep him for your-
> self, yourself alone, to take him, steal him in defiance of every law, every
> moral authority—you don't know what that is, you've never experienced
> it?
>   You say: Never.
>   She looks at you, repeats: A dead man's a strange thing. (*MD*, 42;
> *MM*, 45)

In chapter 4, I suggested that representations of blacks, Third World
workers, and Jews border on essentialism in Duras's films. Even while
expressing sympathy for the oppression suffered by these groups, she
seems to suggest that this is their destiny, that this is what defines them,
this is who they are, "other" to the defining voice of the filmmaker.
Similarly in this text, male homosexuality is defined by lack, as a sort of
living death.

In the Durassian libidinal economy, homosexuality is literally incom-
prehensible, unrepresentable. All the narrator/author can "see" in male
homosexuality is the absence of woman: The text begins with the lack of
a woman and ends with the absence of the prostitute. The word *homosexual* is never used, the desire of a man for men is only glancingly referred
to. But, again, this text is not about homosexuality: It stages heterosexuality using the figure of a male homosexual. Duras never uses the word
heterosexual in her work. It would be redundant. There is only one construction of sexuality, endlessly explored, considered from different perspectives but at the heart of every "story."[8]

Blue Eyes, Black Hair, published four years later, is dedicated to Yann
Andréa and rewrites *The Malady of Death* in an amplified narrative that
incorporates other familiar Durassian concerns. This narrative begins
with a gesture that places it in the imaginary: "A summer evening, says
the actor, would be at the heart of the story."[9] At various moments the
text is punctuated by stage directions to emphasize its status as a scenario, to be performed. In this version of *The Malady of Death*, the man
does not pay the woman to stay with him; she says she is a kind of prostitute but that she doesn't charge anything. At one point, she says "I'm a
writer" (*BE*, 26; *YB*, 39). Her story is more fully developed here, particularly the story of her sexual initiation by an anonymous man on a beach
where girls knew they could go to be touched.

Three new or newly emphasized aspects of this text set it apart from
The Malady of Death. First, Duras explicitly reintroduces the obsessional
triangulation of desire explored in the Lol V. Stein series. The man is first
drawn to the woman because her blue eyes and black hair remind him of

a lover he has not completely left. His desire is aroused as she discusses sexual encounters she has with other men, specifically one man she goes to regularly before coming back to the hotel room: "she has told him about him. He too gets extreme pleasure [jouit très violemment] from her desire for another man" (*BE*, 58–59; *YB*, 78). She also tells him that sex with the other man is followed by insults, blows. Even more than in *The Seated Man in the Passage* or *The Malady of Death*, the woman's sex is presented as morbid and dangerous. The woman displays herself, saying: "it's velvet, vertiginous, but also, make no mistake, a wilderness [désert], something bad [malfaisante] that also leads to murder and madness. She asks him to come and see, says it's something horrible, criminal, like murky water, dirty, bloody. She says that one day he'll have to, even if only once, have to rummage in that common place" (*BE*, 35–36; *YB*, 51). Finally, in a gesture that recalls the sheet that Jack Hold pulled up over Tatiana's face in *The Ravishing of Lol Stein*, the woman here emphasizes the interchangeable anonymity of women and her link to death by veiling her face with a black silk scarf in sleep or in sex. Early on, the man asks her what the silk is for: "'The black silk is like the black bag—it's to put the condemned man's head in'" (*BE*, 25; *YB*, 37).

Shortly after the publication of *Blue Eyes, Black Hair*, Les Editions de Minuit published a curious little booklet signed Duras, barely twenty pages long, called *La Pute de la côte normande* (*The Whore from the Coast of Normandy*). Beginning with an ellipsis, it is presented as an interrupted conversation with an unspecified interlocutor in which Duras explains the difficulties she was having with a theatrical adaptation of *The Malady of Death* to be done in Berlin. The point of the booklet, however, is to give a vivid description of the turbulent life she and Yann Andréa were living in the summer of 1986 as she wrote *Blue Eyes, Black Hair*. Anticipating *Emily L.*, she presents the anecdote recounted in the text as "this episode at Quillebeuf," a moment when she was trying to write about warm nights of summer. She describes his fits of shouting and her persistent efforts to work. His sorties to hotels on the Norman coast to pick up men were followed by screaming fits at her, or he would type what she had managed to write in his absence. At one point he yells at her: "You've been abandoned by everyone. You're crazy, you're the whore of the coast of Normandy"; he would then insult her more and they would laugh.[10] It is a barely coherent text, more like a spontaneous, unedited letter. She claims that it was not her idea to publish it. One can only assume that the publisher was responding to the nearly insatiable appetite for details about the writer's life in the mid-1980s. Between *The Malady of Death* and *Blue Eyes, Black Hair*, after all, there had been *The Lover* and *War: A Memoir*. Duras had joined the ranks of autobiographers and had become an internationally best-selling writer.

Representing Self: *The Lover, The North China Lover*, and *The War: A Memoir*

The year 1984 was a watershed year for Duras. A videocassette critical edition of her films was published along with lengthy interviews with Dominique Noguez on tape and in print, making her most important films available to a larger public for the first time. The publication of *The Lover* met with instant success in early September; in late September, Duras did a lengthy interview with Bernard Pivot on the popular French literary television program "Apostrophes"; in November, *The Lover* won the prestigious Goncourt Prize, which had been denied to *The Sea Wall* more than thirty years earlier; within a short time the book became a best-seller in English as well as French.

What accounts for this success? *The Lover* was promoted as confessional literature: revelations about the scandalous interracial adolescent affair of a famous woman writer. The "Apostrophes" interview cultivates this reading of the book. Pivot asks questions as if it were a document of the writer's childhood and a source book for her fiction; photographs from the 1930s of Duras and her family fade in over the image of Duras as she gives the interview, layering past on present.

At first, *The Lover* seems to follow Philippe Lejeune's definition of autobiography: "Retrospective prose narrative written by a real person concerning his own existence, where the focus is his individual life, in particular the story of his personality."[11] *The Lover* is the first text since "The Boa," thirty years before, in which the "I" of the narrator coincides in biographical detail with Duras's personal history; it is also the first text in thirty years situated in the Indochina of her childhood. The appearance in 1991 of *The North China Lover*, which rewrites *The Lover* in a more extended narrative, both confirms and unsettles the autobiographical status of *The Lover*. Although in the later work Duras gives more detail to some episodes, seeming to reconfirm their historical status, she contradicts and reinterprets other episodes.

The primary narrative line in both books—the story of the fifteen-year-old white girl's affair with an older, Chinese man in Indochina—suggests a model of intense sexual passion that informs most of Duras's work. The love is obsessive, forbidden, and abruptly terminated; because of the impossibility of the affair, each lover remains an erotic presence, permanently determining the terms of the other's desire, a third person who will mediate all future passions. Interwoven with this story of sexual initiation are other stories we can recognize. The most obvious is the story of her family, retold from *The Sea Wall* but now in the first-person. Like the mother in *The Sea Wall*, the narrator's mother is mad, a victim of her poverty and of injustice inflicted by corrupt colonial powers. The character of Joseph is replaced by two brothers: Pierre, a corrupt, cruel older brother, and Paulo, called "the little brother," who inspires incestuous longings in the narrator. Returning to *The Sea Wall* after reading *The Lover*, we can see that "Monsieur Jo's" race was barely disguised. His big, black, chauffeur-driven Morris Léon-Bollée is the Chinese lover's car, "as big as a bedroom" (*L*, 17; *A*, 25), that the girl in *The Lover* first sees on the Mekong ferry.

While *The Lover* poses as an "original" for Duras's fictions, it is, rather, a reworking of these now familiar themes and characters in a new narrative mode. Instead of answering the question "What is the source in your life for your fictions," it poses another "what if" question: What if desire were explored from within the self? The narrator plays with references to Duras's other texts, creating the expectation that this book will "tell all" not only about the writer but about her work. She says after the first description of the lover's car, "The black Lancia at the French embassy in Calcutta [Anne-Marie Stretter's car] hasn't made its entrance on the literary scene" (*L*, 17; *A*, 25). We do discover in *The Lover*, however, the "original" Anne-Marie Stretter and Vice-Consul, presented, respectively, as the Lady of Savanna Khet and the young man who shot himself because of their impossible love. As in her other texts, the story of the colonial administration is interwoven with the story of the beggarwoman, whose laugh is a constant reminder to the whites of the scandal of the colonies. In *The Lover*, the beggarwoman's story is further tied in with those of the mother and the Lady of Savanna Khet; they embody three figures of motherhood: the outcast, the madwoman, and the woman who bears desire and death.

To read *The Lover* as a confession that reveals the writer's sexual secrets and the sources of her stories, however, tends to obscure the narrative complexity of the book: the self-conscious play between fiction and confession, fantasy and memory within the text itself. Ambiguities and tensions in the narrative structure subvert any single reading of *The Lover*. The narrative voice is split into first and third person. Although

autobiographies often play with splits in the narrative voice that correspond to the present self and the past self, the narrating and narrated
self, in *The Lover* the correlation is not temporal but visual: the self as
spectator and spectacle. Further, the book refuses to conform to the cri-
teria of a single genre. The flood of commentaries, from book reviews in
the popular press to scholarly articles, have read the book variously as
autobiography, *bildungsroman*, and novel; all of these categories fit, but
none fits completely.[12]

The "autobiographical pact" that Lejeune defines as a necessary condition for autobiography requires that the author, narrator, and protagonist be identical (Lejeune, 14). Neither the narrator nor the protagonist
is named in *The Lover* or *The North China Lover*. In *The Lover* the narrative
moves back and forth between first and third person; *The North China
Lover* is all in the third person, with the narrator standing outside the
text and never identified as "I"; the protagonist is called only "the child."
Duras concludes the preface to *The North China Lover* by saying, "I
became a novelist all over again," distancing the text from the "autobiographical pact."

In her study of women's autobiography, Sidonie Smith understands
the "autobiographical pact" differently, claiming that "the generic contract engages the autobiographer in a doubled subjectivity—the autobiographer as protagonist of her story and the autobiographer as
narrator."[13] As the epigraph to this chapter shows, Duras uses autobiography to explore the split feminine subjectivity that characterizes her
other fictions: "Suddenly I see myself as another, as another would be
seen, outside myself, available to all, available to all eyes, in circulation
for cities, journeys, desire" (*L*, 13; *A*, 20). The self Duras discovers in *The
Lover* is seer and seen, narrating and narrated, an image and a fiction
constituted by the gaze and by stories. Duras's project seems to take as a
starting point Sidonie Smith's assertion that "the self" is not "an *a priori*
essence, a . . . 'true' presence but rather a cultural and linguistic 'fiction'
constituted through historical ideologies of selfhood and the processes of
our storytelling" (Smith, 45). In *The Lover*, Duras's discovery of her self
as split, "I" and "another," coincides with her assertion that she will be a
writer.

A double *bildungsroman*, *The Lover* tells of Duras's coming of age as
woman and writer, object and subject, generating desire and discourse
while transgressing the conventions of the colony and her culture. This
bildungsroman explores the making of the woman and the writer primarily through images. Dedicated to Bruno Nuytten, the cinematographer

for most of Duras's films, *The Lover* had as its first title *The Absolute Photograph*. In interviews she has said that this was originally a commissioned work; she was asked to comment on a family photo album, and, inspired by the images of her past, she wrote this text.[14] The words *image* and *photograph* punctuate the text with great frequency. The narrator focuses as much on the construction of images as on what they represent. A close look at key images helps to clarify the "truth-value" of this autobiography as well as the meaning of "woman" and "writer": the self-portrait that opens the book, the "absolute photograph" of the girl on the ferry crossing the Mekong, the image of the lovers in the apartment, the narrator's fantasy-image of her friend Hélène Lagonelle with the Chinese lover, and the lover's image of the girl's body.

The self-portrait that opens *The Lover* is mediated by an unnamed man: "One day, I was already old, in the entrance of a public place a man came up to me. He introduced himself and said, 'I've known you for years. Everyone says you were beautiful when you were young, but I want to tell you I think you're more beautiful now than then. Rather than your face as a young woman, I prefer your face as it is now. Ravaged'" (*L*, 3; *A*, 9). The reader's introduction to the narrator is as the object of the male gaze. The narrator's identity as woman and as writer is incorporated in the portrait. Her aging face, admired by the man, reminds us of her body while his recognition of her in a public place hints at her status as a public figure.

The next paragraph switches from this publicly available, male-mediated image to a private image, known only to the narrator: an image from her youth in contrast to the old woman we have just seen. Several pages later, after establishing the period of her youth that will constitute the heart of this narrative, the narrator returns to her private image. This is the "absolute photograph," the photograph that was never taken, that exists for her alone—generator and product of her writing. It is precisely because the photo never existed that it is powerful; its absence is the space in which representation, writing, can happen. Absent, it is without contingency, it is absolute: "And it's to this, this failure to have been created, that the image owes its virtue: the virtue of representing, of being the creator of, an absolute."[15]

The absent photograph—property and product of the imagination—subverts another convention of classical autobiography. Elizabeth Bruss, in her founding work on the genre, observed that an autobiographical text has a "certain implicit situation, a particular relationship to other texts and the scene of its own enactment."[16] One parameter defining this situation is its "truth-value": "An autobiography purports to be consistent with other evidence; we are conventionally invited to compare it with other documents that describe the same events" (Bruss, 299). Duras repeatedly invokes the "evidence" of photographs in this text; reviews of the book often include photographs that resemble portraits she describes in the book. But the most important image, the one that defines the text and nearly named it, does not exist. It exists only in the past conditional, Duras's preferred mode: It could have been taken ("elle aurait pu être prise," 16), but it was not.

The absent photograph is invoked repeatedly in the first half of the book, accumulating detail and subjected to varying interpretations. The photo that does not exist would portray the narrator at fifteen, on a ferry crossing the Mekong river—leaving her mother to go back to school, leaving her family to take a lover, leaving her childhood to become a woman. The image the narrator sees of her younger self reveals that she is made up of bits and pieces borrowed from her family or chosen as bargains to express her individual sense of style:

> I'm wearing a dress of real silk, but it's threadbare, almost transparent. It used to belong to my mother. . . . I'm wearing a leather belt with it, perhaps a belt belonging to one of my brothers. . . . This particular day I must be wearing the famous pair of gold lamé high heels. I can't see any others I could have been wearing, so I'm wearing them. . . . I'm wearing these gold lamé shoes to school. . . .
> It's not the shoes, though, that make the girl look so strangely, so weirdly dressed. No, it's the fact that she's wearing a man's flat-brimmed hat, a brownish-pink fedora with a broad black ribbon.
> The crucial ambiguity of the image lies in the hat. (*L*, 11–12; *A*, 18–19; emphasis mine)

As she describes the hat, signaling that "the crucial ambiguity of the image lies in the hat," the narrator switches, briefly, from first to third person. The man's hat on a young girl paradoxically draws attention to her femininity and helps to define it. The narrator suggests that the man's hat changes her perception of her body from that of awkward child to desirable woman as it gives the shapelessness of childhood meaning and form. The hat transforms "the thin awkward shape, the inadequacy of childhood" from an "imposition of nature" to a "choice of the mind." The man's fedora enables her to say "I see myself as another," to discover her split subjectivity.

Elsewhere the narrator says that this costume makes her resemble a prostitute, condemned and admired by her mother, who colluded in assembling it. This is the image that attracts the future lover's gaze; it is by assuming the image of a prostitute, "available to all," that the girl in *The Lover*, like the girl in "The Boa," claims her sexuality and redeems her body. Her costume and role as prostitute allow the girl to perform her gender and to be both player and spectator in the performance.

As the reader approaches the representation of sexuality in this book, the images become even more self-consciously constructed, fantasmatic scenes situating the narrator/girl as both observer and participant in desire. When the Chinese and the girl go to his apartment for the first time to make love, she asks that he treat her as he treats other women; consistent with her costume as prostitute, she wants to be anonymous, to become an object of his desire interchangeable with other women. The scene is described in the third person, returning to the first person after they make love. The description of sexual initiation in the third-person present tense has the effect of putting the reader in the position of pornographic spectator, with the girl as spectacle. The return to the first person gradually reestablishes the distance of memory and places the narrator in the position of spectator on her own past.

The apartment, scene of desire, is presented cinematically with the lovers as audience in the darkened room:

> The noise of the city is very loud, in recollection it's like the *sound of a film turned up high*, deafening. I remember clearly, the room is dark, we don't speak, it's surrounded by the continuous din of the city. . . . There are no panes in the windows, just shutters and blinds. On the blinds you can see the shadows of people going by in the sunlight on the sidewalks. . . . The shadows are *divided into strips by the slats of the shutters.* (L, 40; A, 52; emphasis mine)

Memory recreates this scene with the discontinuity of cinematic production. The world outside is seen as shadows on a screen above the heads of the lovers and, like images on celluloid, light and shadow alternate as the images go by.

The narrator goes on to say: "The bed is separated from the city by those slatted shutters, that cotton blind. There's nothing solid separating us from other people. They don't know of our existence. We glimpse something of theirs . . ." (L, 41; A, 53). In this configuration, the world is spectacle and the lovers are hidden. But the status of the blind is ambiguous. The white cotton blind acts as a screen in both senses, protecting the lovers from the gaze of the outside world as well as capturing the shadows of the crowd for them to observe.

The construction of this image also suggests, however, that the hidden scene, the scene of their desire is an imagined projection, disconnected from the reality of the city. Later, the narrator says, "I can still see the face, and I do remember the name. I see the whitewashed walls still, the canvas blind between us and the oven outside" (*L*, 44; *A*, 56). The image becomes more internalized, the narrator's property; the "canvas blind" resembles the "white rectangle" of the movie screen we have already encountered in Duras's fictions. The discontinuity and alternating of shadow and light in this cinematic image is reflected in the overall construction of the narrative of *The Lover* in which sequences are separated by blank spaces. Temporary illusions of continuity are disrupted as the narrator intercuts other sequences. Narrative juxtapositions suggest relations between sequences that must be completed by the reader.

Erotic and narrative power are exercised in a fantasy image in which the narrator appropriates the power of the male gaze. The only other white girl in the boarding house where the young narrator stays is Hélène Lagonelle. The girl is dazzled by the beauty of Hélène's body, even though Hélène herself seems blind to it. Some readers have taken this to be a rare expression of lesbian desire in Duras's work: "I'm worn out by the beauty of Hélène Lagonelle's body lying against mine. Her body is sublime, naked under the dress, within arm's reach" (*L*, 71; *A*, 89). The desire for Hélène is, rather, a desire for control of the heterosexual erotic. Through Hélène the narrator desires not a woman's body, but male desire; she seeks to control the terms of her own pleasure. She imagines Hélène as a stand-in, the "other woman" through whom she could experience pleasure by assuming the role of voyeur and of director of the scene. She says:

> I want to take Hélène Lagonelle with me to where every evening, my eyes shut, I have imparted to me the pleasure that makes you cry out. I'd like to give Hélène Lagonelle to the man who does that to me, so he may do it in turn for her. I want it to happen in my presence, I want her to do it as I wish [selon mon désir], I want her to give herself where I give myself. It's via Hélène Lagonelle's body, through it, that the ultimate pleasure [la jouissance . . . définitive] would pass from him to me. (*L*, 74; *A*, 91–92)

As the French more clearly states, Hélène's body is a "detour." This passage shows that, like *10:30 on a Summer Night*, *The Lover* stages a fantasmatic scene, this time using the autobiographical subject. As we saw in the earlier novel, "phantasies" are scenarios in which the subject is always present as participant and observer. In *10:30 on a Summer Night*, Maria needed to see herself seeing in a "primal scene" of sexual betrayal. *The Lover* is an originary love story (that is, a love story that is the origin of other such stories) in which the narrator stages herself as the "other woman" before the fact, a shadow in the Chinese lover's future marriage. The Hélène Lagonelle fantasy scene shows her preparing this mise-en-scène, deriving pleasure through the substitution of another woman's body for her own.

The male gaze redeems the body of the girl in another projection of desire that recalls "The Boa." The narrator writes: "Ever since he'd been infatuated with her body the girl had stopped being incommoded by it, by its thinness" (*L*, 98; *A*, 120). But there is more in this text than a simple transfer of value from the male gaze to the female body. In an image that follows the summary of the girl's changing perception of her body, the reader can see that the girl's body and the lover's desire create each other in a symbiosis invented, finally, by the narrator:

> He looks at her. Goes on looking at her, *his eyes shut*. He inhales her face, breathes it in. . . . Less and less clearly can he make out the limits of this body, it's not like other bodies, it's not finished, in the room it keeps growing, it's still without set form, continually coming into being, not only where it's visible but elsewhere too, stretching beyond sight, toward risk, toward death, it's nimble, it launches itself wholly into pleasure as if it were grown up, adult, it's without guile, and it's frighteningly intelligent. (*L*, 99; *A*, 121; emphasis mine)

In this passage the lover looks at the object of his desire with "his eyes shut." Like the canvas blind in the apartment, his eyelids screen out reality, allowing him to project his desire.

This passage demonstrates that the lover's fantasy is the narrator's creation; she is imagining what he would have seen behind his closed eyes. The girl's body becomes powerful through his fantasy, but his fantasy is the invention of the narrator. The girl becomes a woman in a passage that ultimately reveals that the erotic is an invention of narrative. The passage shows that the girl has become a writer as well as a woman, the image being a product of the mature narrator's "frighteningly intelligent" invention.

The Lover is less a source book to guide the reading of earlier texts than a reinscription of familiar themes and obsessions within the first-person feminine. "Woman" in this text, as in earlier texts, is given form and power through the male gaze. But through narrative the writer can appropriate the power of the male gaze, controlling the terms of desire.

The structure of *The Lover* and the construction of the images suggest that the originary passion it depicts is a phantasy, a projection of desire, even though the story maintains the illusion of a lived reality remembered. The narrative maintains this ambiguity. Twice in the French text, Duras uses the English word *experiment* to refer to the affair with the Chinese (*A*, 9, 28). In her "Apostrophes" interview as well, she insists on this word. Whether it signals a sexual or a narrative experiment, the word choice tends to reinforce the writer's control while maintaining the ambiguous status (documentary or fiction) of the narrative. The last scene is entirely in the third person and ends as a fairy-tale fantasy of romantic love. Years later, the Chinese comes to Paris and telephones "her": "And then he told her. Told her that it was as before, that he still loved her, he could never stop loving her, that he'd love her unto death" (*L*, 117; *A*, 142).

The North China Lover plays on the ambiguous status of autobiography and fiction, memory and invention in an entirely different way: The text literalizes the fantasmatic episodes of *The Lover* even as a removed narrator (who uses the first-person, signed "Marguerite Duras," only in the preface) self-consciously stages or "directs" the story. The narrator assumes greater control as she removes herself from the first-person; the text, though repeatedly "documented" with footnotes, becomes more explicitly a fiction.

The circumstances surrounding the composition of *The North China Lover* further complicate our reading of the text as memoir and fiction. In the preface, Duras says that she abandoned everything else she was working on in order to write *The North China Lover* between May 1990, when she learned that the Chinese lover had been dead for several years, and May 1991, when she thought she had finally written "the story of the North China lover and of the child," a story not yet there in *The Lover*. She says she spent a year circulating in the story with these people. She ends the preface with the remark: "I became a novelist all over again."[17]

What the preface does not mention is that Claude Berri had bought the movie rights to *The Lover* from Duras and was producing a film based on the book, directed by Jean-Jacques Annaud. At first, Duras participated in the production. She made several attempts at screenplays, but they did not satisfy Annaud. As disagreements intensified, she broke off all involvement with the film. One of her chief complaints was that Annaud was making a "filmed biography," that he took *The Lover* to be a memory book rather than a literary text. Meanwhile, Annaud was the one who told her that the Chinese had died several years earlier, and she resented having to learn it from him.[18]

As control over the film slipped away from her, Duras started to adapt the screenplays she had prepared and they became *The North China Lover*. The notes and comments within the text as to how it should be staged or filmed reveal its origins, but they also show how important it was to Duras to reassert narrative control over her story, to "become a novelist again" rather than a scriptwriter or a figure in someone else's film. The narrative in *The North China Lover* reads alternately like a film scenario and a novel and recalls the directing presence of the filmmaker in *The Atlantic Man*. Duras includes a postface about images to use if the book is ever made into a film and how to relate them to the narrative.

Although *The North China Lover* tells the story of the girl's sexual initiation and anticipates that she will become a writer, it does not read as a *bildungsroman* in the way *The Lover* does. The screenplay origins of this text redirect the focus. In *The Lover*, the cinema as metaphor shaped key scenes as phantasy projections; in *The North China Lover*, the cinema as medium requires that scenes be presented in a distanced, objectified way. Duras adds new characters and scenes and rewrites episodes from *The Lover*, at times incorporating the same language in a changed context. The effect is to literalize desire, to replace the fantasmatic scene with explicit representations that are, finally, far less evocative.

As if to warn the reader away from a simple documentary reading of the text, Duras opens not with a self-portrait but with an episode embedded in the text of *The Lover* in which the mother and children wash down their house, making a neighborhood party out of the event, with the mother playing the piano in the background. In *The Lover* the scene is incorporated in the first-person narrative: "It takes my mother all of a sudden toward the end of the afternoon . . . she'll have the house scrubbed from top to bottom" (*L*, 60; *A*, 76). In *The North China Lover* the scene is presented as a scenario: "A house in the middle of a schoolyard. Everything is wide open. Like a party. There are Strauss and Franz Lehar waltzes, but also 'Ramona' and 'China Nights' coming out the windows and doors. Water is running everywhere, inside and out" (*NL*, 3; *AC*, 13). In the opening sequence she identifies a very young girl who is dancing with her brother as "the one who has no name in the first book, or the one before it, or in this one" (*NL*, 4; *AC*, 13), further eroding the "autobiographical pact" that was barely maintained in *The Lover*. The next sequence in the book is at once sparer and more ambiguous:

> This is a book.
> This is a film.
> This is night.
>
> The voice speaking is the written voice of the book.
> A blind voice. Faceless.
> Very young.
> Silent. (*NL*, 6; *AC*, 17)

The female protagonist will be referred to only as "the child" in this text, and the narrative rarely extends beyond the period of the affair except to assert that some events will remain unforgettable.

The self-portrait of the aged narrator reflected by a male gaze that opened *The Lover* is merged with the image of the "absolute photograph" in this version and is presented well into the narrative as a mirror image rather than a man's perception. The effect of creating a split self—spectator and spectacle, the seer and the seen—is maintained:

> They walk past a standing mirror at the entrance to the restaurant.
> She looks at herself. She sees herself. She sees the man's hat made of rosewood-colored felt with a wide black band, the down-at-the-heel black shoes with rhinestones, the overdone red lipstick from the ferry where they met.
> She looks at herself—she has come up close to her reflection. She comes even closer. Doesn't quite recognize herself. She doesn't understand what has happened. Years later, she will understand: her face is already the ruin it will be for the rest of her life. (*NL*, 75–76; *AC*, 84–85)

Two new characters are added in *The North China Lover*: Thanh and Alice. In the preface, Duras says that she rediscovered the face of Thanh while writing this text, and she dedicates the book to him. A Siamese servant whom the mother saved near the plain of the ill-fated bungalow that figures in *The Sea Wall*, he is an ally of the child in this text and resembles the little brother. As such, he contributes to a portrait of the mother as hero and also—in his appearance and thematically—provides an erotic, narcissistic link between the little brother and the Chinese in the child's libidinal economy. When the Chinese sees the child, Thanh, and Paulo together, he remarks that they all resemble each other. The child confesses to having desired Thanh before knowing the Chinese and to desiring Paulo through both of the other men. Alice is the only student other than Hélène Lagonelle who is named at the Pension Lyautey, where the child is a boarder. A mixed-race child, she already works as a prostitute behind the boarding school, from which the girls sometimes watch her and speculate about pleasure. Another descendant of the girl from "The Boa," Alice seeks anonymity and finds pleasure in being called by many names. Alice provides a model in this text for the ideal sexual woman whose greatest pleasure is to be a substitute, a proxy, becoming whatever woman her client requires, a willing projection of his desire.

Alice and Thanh are linked in the erotic commerce of this text through the figure of the child. Her own prostitution is more explicit in this book than in *The Lover*; the Chinese gives her a sum of money that will enhance the family's situation and allow them to return to France. The older brother and the mother collude in the negotiations. The Chinese gives the money to the child, who sets up a meeting to pass it on to Thanh for his safekeeping. The child asks Thanh to meet her by the ditch where Alice plies her trade. They then drive to the zoological garden, again reminiscent of "The Boa," and the child asks Thanh to make love to her. Like Suzanne and Joseph in *The Sea Wall*, she is attracted to him because he resembles her little brother; he refuses her because she is like a sister.

As the addition of these characters suggests, this text is more explicit than *The Lover*; repressed longings from the first book are realized in this one. For example, the child and Hélène Lagonelle exchange passionate words and gestures that were felt by the girl but unexpressed in *The Lover*. The incestuous desire of the child for the "little brother," Paulo, is consummated and she asserts that it was the greatest pleasure the brother had ever known. As they make love, at the child's insistence, the narrator says, "It was that afternoon, in that sudden confusion of happiness, in her brother's sweet and mocking smile, that the child realized she had lived out one love between the Chinese from Sadec and her little brother in eternity" (*NL*, 194; *AC*, 201).

Rather than fantasize a triangle in which the child offers her friend Hélène Lagonelle to the Chinese in order to watch her take her own place as the object of his desire, the child tells the Chinese that she wants to give her friend to him. She is met by incomprehension and goes on to explain: "It would be a little like she was your wife, like she was Chinese and she belonged to me and I was giving her to you. . . . I'm there with the two of you. I watch. I give you permission to be unfaithful to me" (*NL*, 177; *AC*, 184). Faced with mute incomprehension, she cries out: "I want her for you, a lot, and I'm giving her to you. Don't you hear me?" (*NL*, 177; *AC*, 184). The encounter ends in silence and defeat rather than the exercise of narrative power realized in *The Lover*. The terms of the experiment—that she is preparing her own role as "other woman," that offering Hélène is a way of owning the lover's desire, that she is insinuating herself in the lover's marriage—are all spelled out with the paradoxical result that the intensity of the fantasy is dissipated.

In some cases, Duras uses this narrative to play out through the child alternative scripts that more clearly satisfy the narrator's needs. In *The North China Lover*, the mother's story repeats certain themes from *The Sea Wall* and *The Lover*, for example: She is a victim of the colonial authorities, mad but heroic in her resistance, pathologically attached to the older, sadistic and irresponsible brother. But in this version the mother supports the idea that the child will be a writer, and she explicitly colludes in her prostitution, acknowledging her child's erotic power. They are allies far more than they are in *The Lover*, in which the girl longs for the mother's attention and wants her help in protecting Paulo.

The child's vocation as writer and the link between this and other fictions by Duras are developed differently in this text as well. The child tells stories to the Chinese and claims that she will make books of them one day—especially the story of the mother. Finally it is the Chinese who confirms her vocation and its relation to their affair. Shortly before they leave each other, they imagine what will become of their lives, that they will have other loves and tell these lovers their story. Then the Chinese says:

> "And one day we'll die."
> "Yes. Our love will be in the casket with our bodies."
> "Yes. The books, they'll be outside the casket."
> "Maybe. We can't know that yet.
> The Chinese says:
> "Yes, we know it. That there will be books, that we know."
> It can't be any other way. (*NL*, 181; *AC*, 187)

The child's vocation is confirmed by the Chinese, but the narrator adds the last word: that writing is redemptive, stronger than desire. Desire is preserved (or invented) in its representation.

One scene in *The North China Lover* configures the relation between desire, language, and love in a way more reminiscent of *Blue Eyes, Black*

Hair than *The Lover.* Close to the moment of the child's departure in
this version, as in *The Lover*, the Chinese becomes impotent with the
grief of anticipated separation. Because he cannot have sex with her, he
asks her to do it for herself and to allow him to watch. She does it,
exhibits her body and her pleasure, and in her "jouissance" she calls out
his name in Chinese to create the illusion that he is the agent of her
pleasure. Through this simulated coupling in which he is spectator and
she is actor in every sense, she can say for the first time the most banal
and fictional words: "the words in the books, the movies, life, for every
lover. 'I love you'" (*NL*, 187; *AC*, 193).

In *The North China Lover*, as in the earlier autobiographical fiction, the
narrator reproduces scenes from the Lol V. Stein cycle and *The Sea Wall*.
In contrast to *The Lover*, the Lancia that belongs to Anne-Marie Stretter
does make its entrance on the ferry boat in this book. Scenes from *The
Sea Wall* that were only obliquely suggested in *The Lover* are fully recalled
here; for example, the family and the Chinese go dancing and the nightclub recalls a dance club from *The Sea Wall* in which Joseph dances with
Lina, the married woman who will save him from the poverty and madness of the bungalow. The description of the Chinese in this book is more
robust than in *The Lover* and more closely resembles Monsieur Jo.

Duras also adds a narrative device to this version that was missing
from *The Lover*. There are fifteen footnotes scattered throughout the text
in which the narrator appears to speak directly to the reader. Most of the
notes contain directions on how to stage the story, but five of them create an intertext with her other fictions or create a space for her to comment on the relations between them. For example, when Hélène
Lagonelle is introduced in the text, there is a footnote explaining that
Duras learned after the publication of *The Lover* that Hélène married,
had two daughters, and died of tuberculosis in France at the age of twenty-seven (coincidentally, the age of the Chinese during their affair and
the age at which the narrator says the little brother died in *The Lover*).
When the child tells the Chinese that one day she will write the story of
the mother, there is a footnote saying: "She kept her promise: *The Sea
Wall*" (*NL*, 88; *AC*, 97). Much later the child and the Chinese are capti-
vated by the sight of people dancing on the deck of a big ocean liner and
the child cannot comprehend her own fascination but, the narrator pre-
dicts, the child one day rediscovers the image intact in a book she hadn't
even yet imagined. A footnote says, "It became *Emily L.*" (*NL*, 141; *AC*,
149). Like *The Lover*, this text is less a source book than a new element
in a larger, fictional world that constantly reflects back on itself. The

footnotes reestablish the authority of the writer and confirm her control of the text, its relation to other texts, and its eventual representation in another medium.

One passage from *The Lover* that provoked intense controversy is left out of *The North China Lover* entirely: a recollection of life in Paris during the Occupation, organized around portraits of two women: Marie-Claude Carpenter and Betty Fernandez. The portraits seem to bear no relation to the rest of the narrative. They depict a period far removed in time and geography from the 1930s affair in Indochina. The narrator makes no particular effort to tie it in with the rest of the book except to suggest that, as her memory of Hélène Lagonelle shows, she is a fascinated observer of women, particularly women who seem absent, disconnected, or marginal.

The passage created an uproar because of the conclusion the narrator draws. After describing social events at the homes of both these women and, particularly, literary discussions at the home of Ramon and Betty Fernandez, she writes: "Collaborators, the Fernandezes were. And I, two years after the war, I was a member of the French Communist Party. The parallel is complete and absolute. The two things are the same, the same pity, the same call for help, the same lack of judgment, the same superstition if you like, that consists in believing in a political solution to the personal problem" (*L*, 68; *A*, 85). To equate Nazi collaboration with membership in the Communist Party and to seem to forgive or understand it was unacceptable to politically sensitive readers. Some condemned the entire book on the basis of this short passage, claiming that it revealed a deep-seated moral and political cynicism. Worst of all, according to some, the passage suggests that all political action is delusional compensation for personal needs, that only desire and the psyche are real. Duras refused to retract the statement and steadfastly defended it in the "Apostrophes" interview, saying "it's my opinion."

In this context, it seems a particularly fortunate "coincidence" that, a short time after *The Lover* appeared, Duras found hidden away in an armoire a couple of notebooks that chronicle her involvement in the Resistance, her husband Robert Antelme's deportation to a German concentration camp, and his return to Paris in the spring of 1945. She published the journals along with several other short texts in 1985 as *The War: A Memoir* (the French title, *La Douleur* ("Suffering"), emphasizes the personal theme while leaving out the suggestion of memoirs).[19] In the style of eighteenth-century epistolary novels, the epigraph, which claims this is a found text, grants it both authenticity and historical distance. Some critics have read the epigraph as a novelistic convention, a ploy to disguise her decision to bring out *The War: A Memoir* to answer political criticism of *The Lover*. Her own statements about the genesis of the text are vague and contradictory. In 1976 she had published a four-page text in the feminist journal *Sorcières* called "Pas mort en déportation" ("Not dead while deported") that is identical to some of the pages of *The War: A Memoir*. There too she claims to have found the text in a notebook in which she kept a journal at the end of the war. This confirms that parts of *The War: A Memoir* were "found," but it also makes the timing of its publication, after *The Lover*, seem more deliberate.[20]

In an interview for *Cahiers du cinéma* in the summer of 1985, the interviewer asked if she had really found the books or had "cheated" about the origins, as some academics had alleged. In answer, she plays on the French title, saying "I didn't cheat about the suffering." She insists that she found the notebooks but has no idea when she wrote them. She speculates that it must have been after she knew Antelme would survive, perhaps after 1946. She claims that early drafts of *The Sea Wall* and *The Sailor from Gibraltar* are in the same notebooks.[21] In an interview two years later with Jérôme Beaujour, however, Duras suggests that she wrote *The War: A Memoir* after she had published *The Lover* and had made the film *Les Enfants* in late 1984 or early 1985.[22]

The intense immediacy of certain details of daily life and of Antelme's painful recovery suggest that she did find notes written shortly after the war and that she also kept newspaper clippings about the day-by-day events leading to the liberation of Paris in August 1944 and to the fall of Berlin in the spring of 1945. Stylistically, however, the title piece resembles Duras's stark, discontinuous narratives of the 1980s more than her semirealistic fictions of the 1940s. The title piece, "The War," merges two of Duras's most important identities as a writer in the 1980s: those of the journalist and the autobiographer. Duras contributes regularly to the newspaper *Libération* and has published several collections of interviews, columns, and political commentary originally written for the popular press: *L'Eté 80* (*Summer 80*) in 1980, *Outside* in 1981, and *Les Yeux verts* (*Green Eyes*) in 1980, expanded and rereleased in 1987. *The War: A Memoir* is presented as Volume Two of *Outside*. In her pieces for the press, Duras does not pretend to journalistic objectivity, but, rather, uses the forum to personalize public events.

The War: A Memoir contains six distinct texts. "The War," the longest and most important, recounts the return of Robert Antelme, here desig-

Yann Andréa. More significantly, *Emily L.* is a novel that interrogates writing, particularly women writing and men reading. As if to prove the volatility of the project of representing gender and writing, many reviewers lashed out at the novel. It even provoked the writing of a vicious and vulgar parody, *Virginie Q.* Nonetheless, Duras has repeatedly expressed her love for *Emily L.*, enhanced, perhaps, by the efforts of some critics to "assassinate" it (Armel, 24).

Emily L.: The Purloined Poem, Lost in Translation. *Emily L.* is a complex novel weaving two stories together in a deceptively simple narrative style that plays on a chain of women writers and male readers. A brief summary is in order. Recalling the mise-en-scène of *Moderato Cantabile, Emily L.* tells the story of a French man and woman (raised in Indochina) in a waterfront café who observe a British couple and construct their story out of fragments they hear. The story is told by the French woman writer in the first person, addressing her male companion/reader as "you": "I, the woman in this story, the woman in Quillebeuf this afternoon with you, the man looking at me."[24] Her companion is a homosexual who shares her life and reads her texts. After they first observe the British couple, the narrator tells her companion that she has decided to write the story of their own affair, an affair that is "taking forever to die" (*EL*, 12; *E*, 21). He objects that there is nothing to write about. She responds to his fear and resistance by saying:

> I don't think it's our story I'm writing. . . . No. What I'm writing now is something else that will somehow include it—something much broader. . . .
>
> When it's in a book I don't think it'll hurt any more. . . . It'll be wiped out [effacé, "erased"]. That's what I find, with this story I've had with you. That writing . . . one of the things writing does is wipe things out. Replace them. (*EL*, 13–14; *E*, 22–23)

The couple whose life they reconstruct are a wealthy older woman who had been a poet and her younger husband, named "The Captain." None of the other major characters is named in the book. "Emily L." is a name assigned to the British woman by a man who loves her. Duras has explained that the name is meant to recall Emily Dickinson.[25] What is presented in the novel as Emily's favorite, unfinished poem, "Winter Afternoons," stolen from her by the Captain, is an Emily Dickinson poem, "There's a certain Slant of light." The "L.," replacing her last name, her patronymic, is a homonym in French for "elle" (she or her);

"Emily L." comes to stand for women writing, historically through the reference to Dickinson, within language through the reference to the feminine pronoun. The problem of translation and communication is established from the start because the British couple speak English, except for the Captain's very simple French, and the French couple know little English. As in *The Sailor from Gibraltar*, the British couple travel the world in a yacht, occasionally returning to the Isle of Wight, where she had grown up and he had worked for her father. Forbidden by the father to marry during her parents' lifetime, the couple had nonetheless lived together until first her mother, then her father, had died.

Within the narrative, the woman writer, the writing feminine subject, is split into two characters—the French narrator who observes, and "Emily," the English poet who is observed (or invented). Outside the narrative the woman writer is also split between the novelist Duras and the poet Dickinson. Playing on both the sameness and the difference between the two characters, the male companion says toward the end of the novel: "You're like one another, you and she. . . . It's always very moving, a resemblance between two women who are not really alike" (*EL*, 95; *E*, 131). Although the pretext for the story of each couple is a love story, the women's stories are more directly about writing and about being read by the men around them. Intersubjectivity, the ability to write one's story and to be read by an other, is explored as the men reveal themselves through their interactions with the women's texts.

The question of self and other, and the fear provoked by difference (gender, race, culture, language), is posed at the beginning of the novel in a startling image, referred to at moments throughout the novel, that seems at first entirely extrinsic to the stories being told. As the French couple arrives at the café, the woman sees a group of men who frighten her, whom she at first takes to be an hallucination: "They seem to have only one face: all their faces are the same, that's why they're so frightening. They've all got crewcuts, slanting eyes, the same cheerful expression; they're all of the same build, the same height. . . . I say, 'Why are there Koreans in Quillebeuf'" (*EL*, 5; *E*, 12)? Her companion, who had not noticed them and is not frightened, agrees that they are Asians, but asks how she can be sure they are Korean. When she says that it is because she has never seen one, he accuses her of being racist.

Because these people are unknown, and yet recall fears experienced in her childhood, because they are different by every cultural marker from the narrator, they all look the same to her and provoke terror—a terror that comes from within herself rather than from any overt threat from the "Koreans." The "Koreans" will erupt in the text from time to time, frightening the narrator. They also remind her of her distance from her companion and the other French around her who did not grow up in "Siam," an experience whose story she has not communicated adequately. More important, perhaps, the "Koreans" embody Edward Said's definition of "Orientalism": The Western observer reduces the "different" to the "other," denying individuality to the "Oriental." All "Koreans" look alike in this Western stereotype that reflects back on the observer.

The story of origins that the narrator has not told clearly enough and the story of her affair that she is trying to invent provide the frame narrative for the story of the other woman writer, "Emily," whose poems were published without her knowledge and whose most important poem was suppressed. Emily's story, and *Emily L.*, could be called "The Purloined Poem." Jacques Lacan in his homage to Duras and Lol V. Stein in 1965 said, "it turns out that Marguerite Duras knows, without me, what I teach."[26] *Emily L.* contains uncanny parallels to Lacan's essay "The Purloined Letter," the lead essay of *Ecrits* in which Lacan reads Baudelaire's translation of Poe's short story by that title and uses the reading to develop a theory of repetition compulsion. Repetition compulsion is the unconscious drive to repeat (or rehearse) a painful event from an early relationship in subsequent relationships. In psychoanalysis, according to Freud, patients may repeat or reenact painful patterns or moments with the analyst.[27]

Lacan also uses the story—a Parisian detective story about a letter stolen from a French queen that circulates among several men who have varying stakes in it and abilities to interpret it—to develop his contention that the signifier (in language) dominates the subject (the unconscious). In the Poe story, the subjects are all changed by the path of the letter to which the reader never has access. As Bice Benvenuto and Roger Kennedy say in their analysis of the essay, Lacan uses the Poe story—and Baudelaire's translation—to illustrate his contention that "the signifier, which is within the Symbolic Order, dominates over the subject. The Symbolic Order can no longer be conceived as constituted by man, but as constituting him . . . speech invests people with a new reality" (Benvenuto, 99–100). The letter is taken to be a "pure signifier."

Many elements of Lacan's reading of Baudelaire reading Poe are echoed in Duras's reading of Dickinson in a text about a French woman writer reading a British woman poet. A series of narrative coincidences between Duras and Lacan help to focus a reading of *Emily L.* and, by contrast, to highlight gender, power, and language in Duras's text. The narrator of *Emily L.* constructs the following story about Emily. Living with the Captain against the wishes of her parents, Emily composes poems for herself. The Captain does not understand the poems and feels betrayed by her writing, which omits any explicit reference to her passion for him. He is jealous of them, as if she had been sexually unfaithful: "The body that was the one thing in the world for which, before the poems, he'd probably have killed her if she'd given it to another man" (*EL*, 55; *E*, 78). He discusses his feelings with Emily's father, who asks him to copy the poems and bring them to him. Unlike the Captain, the father is pleased as he reads his daughter's poems and expresses his pleasure by transforming them into (literary) property. He turns Emily's private body of writing into a public commodity by having one of the poems published in a literary magazine. Emily is surprised to find it published, but—as if she believed that writing had a life independent of writers—accepts it without much question.

She stops writing when she loses a little girl at birth and goes through a period of silent madness. Then, one day in January, she starts her poem about winter light. While she is out, the Captain discovers the unfinished manuscript in a gesture that replicates the discovery of the letter in the Poe story. The Captain reads it as an assault because he does not find even a trace of himself or of the lost baby in the poem. To end his own suffering he throws the poem into the stove. The reader has access to the poem only through the Captain, who is as fixed on the physical characteristics of the paper and writing as he is on the verse. Through the Captain's awkward summary and the distractions caused by cross-outs and rewritings, we can plainly see that Duras has borrowed Dickinson's poem. Reading and rereading, the Captain feels wounded, the poem seems alien to him, he feels he never existed in her universe:

> At first it was about the terrible light of certain winter afternoons . . . she said that on certain winter afternoons the slanting rays of the sun were as oppressive as the sound of cathedral organs . . . she said the wounds inflicted on us by these swords of the sun were dealt by heaven. They left no visible trace, no scar either on our flesh or in our thoughts. . . . What they did was produce a new perception, an inner difference at the heart of meaning. . . . It said, or almost said, that the inner difference was reached through, and was in a way the mark of, supreme despair. After that the poem trailed off in a flight through the last valleys before the heights, the cold summer night, and a vision of death. (*EL*, 60–61; *E*, 84–85)

The Emily Dickinson poem, in its entirety, is:

> There's a certain Slant of light,
> Winter Afternoons—
> That oppresses, like the Heft
> Of Cathedral Tunes—
>
> Heavenly Hurt it gives us—
> We can find no scar,
> But internal difference,
> Where the Meanings, are—
>
> None may teach it—Any—
> 'Tis the Seal Despair—
> An imperial affliction
> Sent us of the Air—
>
> When it comes, the Landscape listens—
> Shadows—hold their breath—
> When it goes, 'tis like the Distance
> On the look of Death—[28]

Much later in the narrative—after the father has his daughter's nine-teen poems published, without letting her know, and she develops a fol-lowing of which she is ignorant, the parents both die, the Captain and Emily marry and travel around the world, a caretaker moves into their apartment, receives a copy of her book by mistake and finds the poems beautiful even though he does not understand them—Emily is led to think again about the lost poem. When the caretaker shows Emily the poems her father had published, she asks about the poem the reader knows has been destroyed. She tries to remember it, recalls fragments that echo the Captain's reading, and then remembers, intact, the most important verse: "But internal difference where the meanings are" (*EL*, 82; *E*, 114). "Winter Afternoons" would have been the poem, she says, as well as the title for the collection had she ever finished it. She becomes convinced that she dreamed it, that she never wrote the poem at all— which is, ironically, true in fact if not in fiction. They end their conversa-tion with a long, quiet kiss that recalls the deathly, adulterous kiss at the end of *Moderato Cantabile*. Emily's writing has led to betrayal of the Captain, just as he had feared.

Like the "absolute photograph" in *The Lover* and the missing word in *The Ravishing of Lol Stein*, it is the lost, suppressed (or substitute) poem that contains the most important—and most generative—meaning. Absent from the book of poems and yet central to it, the poem purloined, within the text by the husband from Emily L. and intertextually by Duras from Dickinson, both reveals and obscures the meaning of the whole. In the narrative, the book of poems that fails to contain the suppressed poem—the woman's language stolen by a jealous, narcissistic man—also defines its readers. The Captain is threatened because he fails to see himself reflected there. The father is pleased and uses his daughter's language to propagate his own name (having barred his daughter from marriage).[29] The caretaker is close to an ideal reader: He loves the poems, and through the body of writing he loves the writer without comprehension, admiring the beauty of the poetry rather than seeking mastery over its meaning. The Captain suppresses her voice and the father takes ownership, but the caretaker discovers desire for her in (her) language.

Outside the narrative, the borrowed Dickinson poem—a woman's language recovered and reinscribed by another woman writer—has also defined its readers. French reviewers failed to recognize the poem and so Dickinson's authorship was suppressed until Duras reminded her audience of the meaning of the title.[30]

The caretaker becomes the intended reader of Emily in another episode that further complicates the poet's story. After Emily and the caretaker separate, he gives her the name "Emily L." Eventually the caretaker leaves the island, travels around the world looking for Emily and catches a glimpse of her dancing on the deck of a ship: "It was on an Australian freighter moored at a port of call on its way to Korea that the young caretaker saw Emily L., among about twenty couples dancing on a dais on the upper deck. She was dancing with one of the ship's officers and wearing her old white and blue dress" (*EL*, 109; *E*, 149).[31]

In this scene, the caretaker has taken a spectator's position that recalls both Jack Hold and Lol V. Stein. A brief summary of the rest of his story shows its resemblance to Lol's: He loses track of "Emily," he goes into a deathlike coma, and his papers are stolen. Having lost both his identity and his memory, he is repatriated to Latin America, marries, and lives an apparently quiet normal life until one night he awakens and recalls the story and feels compelled to return to the Isle of Wight. He is given a letter Emily had left with her lawyer years before and that he had tried, unsuccessfully, to send to the caretaker.

The letter reverses the genders and the terms of the "purloined letter" in Poe. Written by a woman to a man, it circulates throughout the world unopened in search of the addressee. Only when the addressee and the letter return to the scene of the writing (significantly a room where wills are read) is the text made available. The narrator and her companion are also readers of this letter. The text of the letter, unlike the text of "Winter Afternoons," is included in the narrative. The letter traces a closed signifying loop: a letter in search of its intended reader but expressing in its trajectory and in its language a central absence. Emily characterizes herself as unfaithful; her unfaithfulness consists in keeping a private place within herself for solitude and love—a love "without a person attached to it" (*EL*, 99; *E*, 135). She confesses that he ("you" in the text of the letter) is what she had waited for, the "unknown part of her." She therefore expresses her desire for permanent separation from the caretaker. Separation would seal and protect their prior meeting, the always available space for love. Emily's work is constructed around the silence of a suppressed poem, her desire around absence.

From the male "you" addressed by "Emily" in the letter, the narrative switches to the male "you" signifying the narrator's companion. "You say, 'What's in that letter can't be understood by the reader. It must have been read just once by a writer who thought he understood it and put it into a book. And then forgot it'" (*EL*, 99; *E*, 136). The narrator agrees, adding that there are sometimes "things like that," beyond the writer's knowledge: "Indistinguishable from the other things in the book, and yet alien to it" (*EL*, 100; *E*, 137).

At the end of the novel, Emily and the Captain leave the café to continue their aimless voyage. The narrator and her companion return to their apartment. The final, significant return, however, is to reading and writing. The narrator wakes her companion in the middle of the night to try to explain about writing. Beautiful writing is not enough, she explains, satisfying personal or communal needs is not enough. The aim of writing should be to "get through to the body that's reading the story and wants to know the story right from the start, and that with every reading is ignorant of more than it was ignorant of already" (*EL*, 112; *E*, 153). She adds that one should not make corrections but "just leave everything as it is when it appears" (*EL*, 112; *E*, 154). She represents writing itself as a sort of "other" to be struggled with, "ejected" from oneself, "treated roughly" but also respected in its difference. In a typical Durassian paradox, the knowledge conferred by writing (to the writer and reader) is characterized as a deepening ignorance, an awareness of knowing—and understanding—less and less.

As we saw in chapter 3, in *The Sailor from Gibraltar*, Duras parodied Authorship and cut narrative practice loose from its realist moorings. The ending, and subsequent texts, however, suggest that she was searching for new means for inscribing a female writing subject. Unlike Barthes, she had not shifted narrative power entirely from the writer to language. In *Emily L.*, through textual appropriations and substitutions and through contradictory, interested readings, she undermines the Reader. The ending, though, suggests that she has not eliminated the Reader from the text, but would, rather, incorporate the reader: "get through to the body that's reading the story." In the freely circulating poems of "Emily L.," texts are cut loose from the Subject or her intentions. But Duras in *Emily L.*, unlike Lacan in "The Purloined Letter," suggests that the stakes involved in severing the Subject from the signifier vary according to gender. The Captain's misreading and suppression of "Winter Afternoons" silences her and arrests her in a state of madness. Subjects—whether reading or writing—are "interested," invested in language and exercise power through it. The path of the unopened letter also suggests that the sender and addressee matter, as does the scene of writing and reading.

One of the ironies of the novel is that so many French reviewers failed to recognize Dickinson in "Winter Afternoons" and erased her signature as though women writers were unrecognizable and therefore, like the "Koreans," "others" who were all alike and interchangeable. Both within and outside this novel, when texts are cut free from the writing subject, it is at the expense of women writers—and to the benefit of male readers.

Summer Rain: The Burned Book. When Duras decided in 1990 to retell in writing a story she had told in her 1984 film *Les Enfants* (*The Children*), which was based on her 1971 children's story *Ah! Ernesto*, she added books to the story. *Summer Rain*[32] opens with "found" books that Emilio (sometimes Enrico), the father (an unemployed Italian immigrant in the Parisian suburbs), picks up in trains or that he and the mother (Natacha, also called Hanka or Eugenia, Emilia or Ginetta, a Polish immigrant) steal from stands in front of bookstores. A biography of Georges Pompidou becomes their favorite because, even though he is famous, his life follows a pattern they can recognize, and it reassures them. The most important book Duras adds to the story had been alluded to in the film, but becomes a concrete image in the text: a found black leather book with a perfect hole burned through its pages. This book, unlike the source of "Winter Afternoons," is recognizable to French readers: the Bible, and, more precisely, the book of Ecclesiastes. The burned book, like the purloined poem, is a place where meaning is both suppressed and discovered.

In the film, Ernesto (sometimes Vladimir), the central character of the story, is seven years old and played by an actor who is probably about twenty. In the book, Ernesto is the oldest of seven children, somewhere "between twelve and twenty." His slightly younger sister Jeanne (sometimes Giovanna) is a pyromaniac, the source, perhaps, of the hole in the book. Their incestuous desire was hinted at in the film and becomes explicit in the book. Ernesto teaches himself to read (and write) by assigning meanings to the words that remain in the burned book:

> he took the shape of a word and quite arbitrarily gave it a provisional meaning. Then he gave the next word another meaning, but in terms of the assumed provisional meaning of the first word. And he went on like that until the whole sentence yielded some sense. In this way he came to see that reading was a kind of continuous unfolding within his body of a story invented by himself. . . . Only part of his story, because of the way the book had been damaged. (*S*, 10; *PE*, 16)

As the reading lesson, changing names, and arbitrary ages of the characters indicate, *Summer Rain* examines the relation between language and meaning. In a repeated, capricious linguistic gesture in the book and the film, Ernesto always refers to his siblings by means of the English words "brothers and sisters." Language is arbitrary, as much an invention of the reader (Ernesto being a kind of idiot savant) as of the writer (God?). But as the parents' reading of Pompidou's story suggests, clichés and conventions provide a reassuring order to otherwise chaotic lives and maintain the illusion for the underclass that they share a common fate with the powerful.

Another story that Duras adds to the book is the mother's. In *Emily L.*, the woman's text was separated from her body; in *Summer Rain*, the mother's body comes to be regarded as if it were a text. Her story tells of a one-night love affair on a train in Russia. The father tries to enter her story by making the children believe that he was the lover, but they learn that the story happened before she knew him, before she came to France. Again, desire, narrative and betrayal, writing and the body come together; her story and its place in her life are characterized as a work:

> It seemed to the *brothers and sisters* large and small, clearly or otherwise, that the mother fomented some inexpressibly important work inside herself every day. . . . What the mother was doing seemed without limit to others because it hadn't been named, it was too personal. There weren't any words for it, it was too soon. Nothing could contain its whole contradictory meaning. . . . But in Ernesto's eyes the mother's life might have been a work already accomplished. (*S*, 42–43; *PE*, 49–50)

This episode repeats in many details "The train from Bordeaux," described in chapter 1, which portrays the young Duras in a sexual encounter on a night train to Paris.[33]

Like Ecclesiastes, *Summer Rain* is a book about wisdom in an age of changing values and arbitrary codes. Ernesto, like the wise man of the biblical book, rejects institutions because he has achieved all the knowledge they can offer and finds it insufficient. He refuses to go to school and teaches himself chemistry and mathematics and German philosophy. Ernesto has discovered for himself the secret of the universe: Created all in one day, with everything in its place, it is like the burned book, with one thing missing. Whereas the wise man of Ecclesiastes preaches the emptiness of the world (that all is vanity on earth, that worldly goods are worthless) and the injunction to believe in God, Ernesto preaches the emptiness of the universe, "there's no point" (*S*, 32; *PE*, 38), and the nonexistence of God. Like the fragments of Dickinson around which Duras constructed *Emily L.*, recognizable pieces of Ecclesiastes are quoted by Ernesto as he reads the black book and as he elaborates his theory of the origins of the universe. In particular, the phrase "the chasing of the wind," which follows "I have seen everything that is done under the sun, and what vanity it all is" (Eccles. 1:14), recurs in both the biblical text and Duras. In Ecclesiastes, the world's vanity is denounced; in *Summer Rain*, Ernesto exposes the vanity of faith.

In spite of the bleakness of the suburban landscape and the pessimism of Ernesto's discovery, *Summer Rain* is comic. The text—again reminiscent of Ecclesiastes—turns around tautologies, syllogisms, and paradoxes, presenting the reader with riddles. For example, Ernesto refuses to return to school because they only teach things he already knows, or because they only teach things he does not know. The mother cannot remember which, and either serves as an explanation. Taken together, *Emily L.* and *Summer Rain* present the reader with a paradox about writing that underlies much of Duras's work. If we look to the figure of the writer in these works, Duras seems to romanticize and mystify writing. The writer is possessed, both in control of and controlled by the process. If we look to the figuration of landscape, writing is antinostalgic. In *Emily L.*, the landscape the narrator and her companion travel through after leaving the café is marked by ruins of a German munitions factory left over from World War II; in *Summer Rain*, the suburban ruins occupied by the immigrant working class and the unemployed will give way to the blank high rises of public housing. Duras refuses to resolve a central paradox: If we look to the writer, there is a surplus of meaning; if we look to the landscape, meaning has been erased, only traces of destruction (past or future) giving it contour. *Summer Rain* ends with a familiar narrative gesture: The writer reasserts her power by opening up the possibility of an ending different from the death and dispersal to which the text seems to lead. Using the past conditional, she says, "According to some, Ernesto would not have died. He would have become a . . . scholar" (*S*, 151; translation mine).

Yann Andréa Steiner: The Unwritten Book. In her most recent book, *Yann Andréa Steiner*, published in June 1992, Duras recombines fragments of autobiographical and fictional texts previously published in a new narrative context (reminiscent of *Emily L.*) to tell at one and the same time the beginning of her story with Yann Andréa and the story of a book that could not be written, the story of Theodora Kats.[34] As the title itself suggests, this book is a kaleidoscopic realignment of texts we have already read. In a pattern that recalls the movement from *The Malady of Death* to *Blue Eyes, Black Hair* and from *The Lover* to *The North China Lover*, *Yann Andréa Steiner* expands on earlier texts and makes explicit scenes that had been elliptical in those earlier tellings.

The book opens with a retelling of two episodes from *Practicalities* that recount her first encounter with Yann Andréa and the beginning of their relationship some time later.[35] In *Yann Andréa Steiner*, she uses a first-person narrator speaking to "vous," Yann Andréa, recalling the narrating couple of *Emily L.* In *The Sea Wall*, when Joseph begins to tell Suzanne of his fantastic love, he begins by saying "I went to the movies" (*SW*, 203). *Yann Andréa Steiner* begins as the narrator recalls a projection of *India Song* in Caen, where she met Yann Andréa; with this gesture, Duras inscribes this story into her fictions even as she places it under the sign of her cinema, specifically the story of Anne-Marie Stretter and the Lol V. Stein cycle. By recombining fragments of earlier texts (entire passages are reproduced from *L'Eté 80*, *Outside*, and *Summer Rain* as well as from *Practicalities*) in a new narrative context, Duras inscribes her story with Andréa into her work and imbues the newly recombined texts with a slightly changed significance. The recombination allows her not only to merge different texts but to make different historical moments coexist so as to reveal their commonality: the suffering of the Jews in World War II and the suffering of the Poles in Gdansk in 1980, for example.

There are, essentially, two stories in addition to the meeting with Yann Andréa that are recombined in *Yann Andréa Steiner*: the story of Theodora Kats and the story of the gray-eyed child, David, and his governess on the beach from *L'Eté 80*. In *Yann Andréa Steiner*, Yann Andréa begs the narrator to tell the story of Theodora Kats, hinted at in the final text of *Outside* and alluded to in *The War: A Memoir*. In *The War: A Memoir*, Theodora Kats was a child who was deported and never returned. In *Outside*, the text called "Théodora" is introduced by a note from Duras saying that it comes from a novel she thought she had burned but then rediscovered in an armoire "unfinished and unfinishable."[36] In "Théodora," a very short text, she imagines a hotel in the Alps after the war in which survivors, including Theodora Kats, would rediscover life and desire. She begins to imagine a story of Theodora in *Yann Andréa Steiner*, telling the story of a beautiful woman, an English Jew, who was meant to be deported but was protected by a stationmaster. She stood by the tracks every day in a white dress, waiting for the train that would take her to Auschwitz, ultimately escaping death by the power of her beauty. The narrator imagines also the scene at the Alpine hotel but then cannot tell any more of the story of Theodora Kats.

Instead, she incorporates the story of David, a six-year-old Jewish boy on the beach at Trouville whom she observes with his governess, a young woman named Jeanne Goldberg. Yann and she sit in the "dark room," the camera obscura, of her apartment, observing the boy and the young woman, imagining their story, rewriting and elaborating a story from *L'Eté 80*. Throughout this retelling, the "I" and "you" of the narrative become a "we" and then "one," a temporarily unified, neutral narrative voice. At the end, however, the narrator dissolves back into "I" and "you," with the recognition that it is impossible to tell the story of Theodora Kats: "Writing had closed itself off with her name. Her name alone was all the writing of Theodora Kats. All had been said with. This name" (Y, 138).

In *Yann Andréa Steiner*, the postmodern gesture of dissolving and recombining texts, creating a discontinuous but repetitive narrative, both undermines and reaffirms the power of the author/narrator, who is both the creator and the product of language. Even though this is the story of the unfinished, the impossible book, the narrator reasserts the power of the name and the power to name.

The many paradoxes of Duras's work, embedded in endless repetition and continual change, have created emphatically contradictory readings of Duras as writer and as woman. Like "Emily" in *Emily L.*, "Duras" is in circulation, a literary commodity consumed by readers looking for their own stories. "Duras" is a signifier, a product of language, while Duras continues to claim the authority of a subject, a creator of texts. Like the often contradictory readings of her texts, opposing readings of "Duras" tell as much about the readers as the writer.

Chapter Six

Conclusion: "Durasophiles" and "Durasophobes"

Author Duras has succeeded Simone de Beauvoir as Paris' first lady of letters.

Time, 1967

'Tis a pity she's a bore.

The Sunday Times, 1966

Response to Marguerite Duras, as suggested by the two epigraphs to this chapter,[1] has always been marked by contradiction and excess. In the popular press and in academic journals, in English and in French, readers of Duras divide into "Durasophiles" and "Durasophobes," terms coined in the French press during the fury of discussion that followed *The Lover*, the *Libération* article about Christine Villemin, and *The War: A Memoir* in the mid-eighties. Duras's position as one of the most important French writers in the second half of the twentieth century is well established. *The Lover* sold more than two million copies, was translated into over forty languages, and was on the *New York Times* best-seller list longer than any other French book in more than twenty years. Excerpts from Duras's work have been included in French national examinations and she has been anthologized in the major school textbooks. At the University of Paris at Nanterre in the fall of 1991, thirty-eight dissertations on Duras were listed as in progress, more than on any other living writer.[2]

Whereas *The Lover* was both a popular and a critical success, *Emily L.*, in 1987, was praised by some but ridiculed by others as a self-parody. When *Summer Rain* came out three years later in 1990, there was an almost palpable sigh of relief from some book reviewers that Duras had found her voice again. By and large, *The North China Lover* (1991) met with positive reviews, though some accused her of capitalizing on the publicity surrounding Annaud's film to sell a book that they took to be *The Lover* supplemented by incomplete filmscripts that the director had rejected.

146

Sharon Willis, in her excellent study *Marguerite Duras: Writing on the Body*, suggests that Duras produces emphatic and contradictory readings because she transgresses conventions, undermines expectations, and places uncomfortable demands on her reader: "In their invariable display that something is missing, her fictions are about expectations unfulfilled. Perhaps it is this potential for deception and withholding that makes her fiction alluring. This is not a passive disappointment, for Duras' force lies in her active subversion of expectation and demand."[3]

The conflicting responses to Duras are also intensified by deeply held attitudes about women, the sex of this writer who writes about sex. Having looked at split female subjectivity and how it relates to meaning throughout Duras's work, I would now like to consider exemplary readings of gender in Duras. In chapter 2, I discussed American feminist critics who have shown that the voices of women writers are articulated through a negotiation between their experience of the dominant myths and stories of their culture and their subversive experience of forbidden, suppressed, or repressed texts. Now I want to consider the negotiations effected by readers between the myths in which they are invested and the stories they find in women's texts. I borrow the definition of "negotiation" proposed by Christine Gledhill in her study of textual and social subjects in film interpretation. Acknowledging the postmodern rejection of "fixed" identity or self, Gledhill nonetheless maintains a concept of subjectivity, however unstable and changing it may be. Drawing on a range of theoretical sources, she defines negotiation as follows:

> Meaning is neither imposed nor passively imbibed, but arises out of a struggle or negotiation between competing frames of reference, motivation and experience. . . . In place of "dominant ideology" . . . the concept of "hegemony," as developed by Antonio Gramsci, underpins the model of negotiation. . . . "Hegemony" describes the ever shifting, ever negotiating play of ideological, social and political forces through which power is maintained and contested.[4]

Reading readers of Duras is a study in cultural and textual negotiations. Here, I look at three instances of negotiation that typify not only problems in reading Duras but problems in reading the figure of woman, a particularly charged "cultural sign and site of struggle," as Gledhill points out (Gledhill, 72). In each instance, readers bring acknowledged or unacknowledged definitions of femininity to their reading of Duras. Readers negotiate (confirm, condemn, or contest)

Duras the woman or Duras the writer by measuring the figure of woman they encounter against their own position. In the first instance, I consider readers who focus on Duras, the woman. In the second, I look at readers who focus on the text, the figure of woman inscribed in Duras's writings. In the third, I discuss readers who focus on the cultural construction of both the writer and the text, who consider Duras in a cross-cultural context in which a single figure of woman is contested.

Readers who read *ad feminam* tend toward ridicule or rapture. In the early fifties, some reviewers characterized Duras as a "masculine" writer, an imitator of Hemingway, who chose "hard" themes and developed steely characters. Those who maintained a conventional sense of what a "lady writer" should write condemned her; those who had a more flexible sense of the boundaries between masculine and feminine, who welcomed a strong feminine voice in fiction, praised her. Often readers who look to the woman behind the text tend to imitate her language (parodically or admiringly) in their own writing. The most striking recent example of parody is *Virginie Q.*, written by Patrick Rambaud under the pseudonym "Marguerite Duraille" after the publication of *Emily L.* in 1988.[5] The book includes not only a parody of *Emily L.* but a mock interview, an article that pastiches Duras's article in *Libération* about Christine V., and a "rewrite" of Shakespeare's *Romeo and Juliet* by "Duraille" for the stage. It is clear from the sarcastic introduction and the tone of each parody that Duras has offended Rambaud's sense of what is appropriate for a woman writer to write.

At the other end of response by readers who look primarily to Duras, the woman, is Alain Vircondelet's recent biography, which he dedicates to Duras as "a sign of my violent fidelity." His fidelity consists in defending her against what he takes to be inappropriate attributes for a woman writer. More often than not, he adopts a sort of Durassian conditional mode to speculate about Duras's life, creating a text that ultimately reflects on himself. Another recent book in which the writer falls under the spell of Duras is Danielle Bajomée's *Duras ou la douleur*.[6] Although this book is much more useful than Vircondelet's because Bajomée uses a distinct critical framework, she nevertheless writes in rich word play that attempts to engage Duras's work by echoing her style. In the introduction she acknowledges this relation between herself and the writer, her critical text and Duras's prose: "Reading Marguerite Duras here I will let myself be led by her. If it is true that art only ravishes us to the degree that it opens us up to the world, because it is the opening of a world, I will work toward seizing that very opening" (Bajomée, 7).

The second instance of negotiation I want to consider involves readers and the inscription of the figure of woman in Duras's texts. Two striking examples are Jacques Lacan and Julia Kristeva. As we have already seen in Lacan's reading of Lol V. Stein, he discovers in Duras's character a confirmation of his definition of woman and language.[7] Interestingly, Duras noted in an interview in 1981 that while Lacan's homage was enormous, it was self-referential: "It's a man's remark. . . . The reference is himself . . . it ricochets back on him."[8]

Kristeva's reading of *The Lover* provides another telling example of a reader whose understanding of "woman" is so closely aligned with the text's that she fails to see it as a position. The ideologies of reader and text are unacknowledged because they are identical; the negotiation between reader and text is one of confirmation. In *The Lover*, Duras constantly draws attention to the white, Western European character of the figure of woman as the embodiment of absence and lack. The reader is constantly reminded of the race and class status of both the white girl and her Chinese lover; we are repeatedly made aware of their different positions in the colonial system. Kristeva is not as careful as Duras in underscoring the cultural specificity of the figure of woman elaborated in the novel. In an otherwise brilliant reading of Duras, Kristeva slips toward a generalization that promotes this particular figure of woman as *the* model of feminine experience. Kristeva writes: "The Durassian woman does not represent all women. Still, she possesses some *typical features of female sexuality*. In this being of utter sadness, one tends to see the exhaustion rather than the repression of erotic drives."[9] Even though Kristeva, in the same article, recognizes that "a firm identity is a fiction" (Kristeva, 151), she fails to recognize the fiction of the feminine that she takes as a given in her study of Duras.

This blind spot is nowhere more apparent than when she considers the few, intense, potentially erotic scenes between the girl and Hélène Lagonelle. She says:

> In the space that separates two women, there is a ravished, unfulfillable dissatisfaction that could crudely be called female homosexuality. In Duras, however, this dissatisfaction involves a profoundly nostalgic quest for the same as other, for the other as same within the spectrum of narcissistic mirage or hypnosis that the narrator considers inevitable. She

recounts the psychic underground that precedes conquests of the opposite sex, that underlies the possible and perilous encounters between men and women. (Kristeva, 150–51)

Kristeva's unexamined developmental model (lesbianism as a narcissistic prelude to adult heterosexuality) privileges a male-defined heterosexual erotic. Duras also confirms this erotic in the novel. They both repress a lesbian erotic by dismissing it and cling to a singular, totalizing figure of woman. Because the figure of woman that Kristeva maintains in her own reading is congruent with "woman" as read and written in Duras's work, she perceives it to be universal rather than specific.

Both Kristeva and Duras maintain a masculine model of femininity, as Françoise Defromont has put it.[10] In my view, rather than confirm "the exhaustion . . . of erotic drives," as Kristeva asserts, the figure of woman in Duras reveals the exhaustion of a particular construction of female (hetero)sexuality. The figure of woman as absence or gap is destabilized in Duras's writing as she develops a split female subject. But even though the *position* of this figure of woman changes in Duras's texts, the *definition* is unchanged; this is the same figure of woman that has always dominated French, if not Western, discourse.

I am proposing this reading of Kristeva and Duras by exercising a third kind of negotiation, used throughout this book, that focuses on the cultural construction of both the writer and the text. The negotiation between reader and text here is one of contestation. It grows out of a "hermeneutics of suspicion" that occurs when the reader's framework is not fully aligned with the text's. Duras is a creature of her historical moment and she often draws attention to the ways her status as woman, Creole, and Communist, for example, have shaped who she is and how she is regarded. And yet, for all her awareness of cultural moment and her destabilization of the hegemonic figure of woman, when it comes to sexuality, race, Jewish and colonial identity, she exhibits a kind of fatalism that reconfirms the conservative, dominant order.

To readers informed by the cultural pluralism of American feminism and of postcolonial discourses, both the limits and the insights of her representation of "Others" become clearer. In a recent analysis of some of Duras's films, Christine Anne Holmlund, drawing on the work of Edward Said and Homi Bhabha, shows how Duras simultaneously "dissolves fixed categories of identity" and continues to promote "colonial clichés."[11] Duras inadvertently expressed the internal contradiction of her project in her 1991 television interview for "Caractères." Toward the end of that interview, she says, with great passion, that people write to avenge injustices. As I mentioned in chapter 5, Duras cites the injustice her mother suffered at the hands of colonial authorities and the suffering of the Jews in World War II as sources of her rage and writing. She adds that she knows, however, that change is impossible. She protests the instance but maintains the inevitability of the system. Finally, referring to the personal pain of her mother and the global scandal of the Holocaust, she says: "That will be my last thought before death."[12]

In the first type of negotiation I have described, readers ultimately reflect back on themselves while seeming to focus on the writer; in the second instance, the reader and text reflect and confirm each other. The third example of negotiation contests the terms that underlie the unspoken assumptions of the text and reflects back on the process of interpretation itself.

To revisit Marguerite Duras in the last decade of the twentieth century is to revisit the contradictory and impassioned feelings about women that mark Western culture. Durasophobes find her offensive because she goes too far, because she transgresses the boundaries of the feminine. Or, she doesn't go far enough, she reconfirms a masculine, masochistic, and misogynist figure of woman. Durasophiles find her fascinating because she intently explores from within the "dark continent of female sexuality" that has shaped our culture. Or, because she unsettles and remaps female subjectivity and sexuality. Durasophobes parody the incessant repetitions that mark her texts. Durasophiles are caught up in the hypnotic spell of a repetition that is never quite the same, and seem bound to reproduce it in their own texts.

There is, perhaps, no more lucid, unrelenting articulation of the figure of woman that has dominated Western literature than the Durassian woman. Through Duras's articulation of femininity we can see that the conventional figure of the homosexual, the Jew, and the colonized subject are of a piece with this particular figure of woman. They are all marked as "other" in a language in which masculine, heterosexual, white, Western, and Christian are unmarked categories, congruent with a "self" that masquerades as neutral. Duras's texts display a gendered orientalism spoken from the margins by a subjectivity that cannot imagine a space for language or desire beyond the margins. Perhaps in the long run Durasophobes and Durasophiles will draw back from their passions, from their own stakes in this figure of femininity, to recognize the power of her language and the caution of her tales.

Notes and References

Preface

1. Marguerite Duras and Xavière Gauthier, *Les Parleuses* (Paris: Les Editions de minuit, 1974), 35: "En France c'est pratiquement le black-out total. . . . Je me considère en France comme une clandestine." Published in English as *Woman to Woman*, translated by Katharine A. Jensen (Lincoln, Neb.: University of Nebraska Press, 1987): "In France it's nearly a total blackout. . . . In France I consider myself to be prohibited" (19).

2. See, for example, Marguerite Duras, "Smothered Creativity," in Elaine Marks and Isabelle de Courtivron, eds., *New French Feminisms*, translated by Virginia Hules (Amherst, Mass.: University of Massachusetts Press, 1980), 111–13; and interview with Aliette Armel in *Le Magazine littéraire* 278 (June 1990): 18.

3. See, for example, Carol J. Murphy, *Alienation and Absence in the Novels of Marguerite Duras* (Lexington, KY: French Forum Publishers, 1982); Sharon A. Willis, *Marguerite Duras: Writing on the Body* (Urbana, Ill.: University of Illinois Press, 1987); Danielle Bajomée, *Duras ou la douleur* (Brussels: De Broeck Université, 1989); and Carol Hofmann, *Forgetting and Marguerite Duras* (Niwot, Colo.: University Press of Colorado, 1991). Hereafter cited in the text.

4. See Murphy, 11–13, for one approach to periodization.

5. An interesting recent study of Duras by Trista Selous, *The Other Woman: Feminism and Femininity in the Work of Marguerite Duras* (New Haven: Yale University Press, 1988), takes a rather different, but complementary, approach to feminist theory and Duras's work. Looking at literary criticism that has been elaborated from French theory, especially French feminist theory concerning *écriture féminine*, Selous "investigates the claims made for Duras's work . . . as manifesting 'feminine' or feminist writing" (9). She concludes that Duras's writing does not represent the repressed feminine, that Duras is not a feminist and, in fact, is in many ways rather conservative. I would not refute that conclusion. Rather than consider whether Duras is a feminist, or if her writing is feminist, however, I prefer to do a feminist *reading* of Duras using North American theory, to examine the construction of gender in her work, and to consider its implications for women.

6. Edward W. Said, *Orientalism* (New York: Pantheon Books, 1978); hereafter cited in the text.

7. Pascal-Emmanuel Gallet, ed., *Marguerite Duras: Oeuvres cinématographiques, Edition vidéographique critique* (Paris: Ministère des relations extérieures-Bureau d'animation culturelle, 1984), 22; the Edition vidéographique critique of Duras's films contains videocassettes of eight films made

between 1972 and 1979 accompanied by five interviews with Dominique Noguez, made in 1984, about those films. The videocassettes were published along with the uncut written text of the interviews. Hereafter cited in the text as *EVC*; translations mine.

Introduction

1. From an interview with Susan Husserl-Kapit, in *New French Feminisms*, ed. Elaine Marks and Isabelle de Courtivron (Amherst, Mass.: University of Massachusetts Press, 1980), 175.

2. Diana Fuss, *Essentially Speaking: Feminism, Nature and Difference* (New York and London: Routledge, 1989), xi.

3. Judith Butler, *Gender Trouble: Feminism and the Subversion of Identity* (New York: Routledge, 1990), 141; hereafter cited in the text.

4. Janet Todd, *Feminist Literary History* (New York and London: Routledge, 1988), 85; hereafter cited in the text.

5. Louis Althusser, "Ideology and State Apparatuses," in *Lenin and Philosophy and Other Essays*, trans. Ben Brewster (New York: Monthly Review Press, 1971), 162.

6. See the very useful summary of definitions of ideology and other terms key to feminist theory in Catherine Belsey and Jane Moore, eds., *The Feminist Reader: Essays in Gender and the Politics of Literary Criticism* (New York: Basil Blackwell, 1989).

7. Rachel Blau DuPlessis, *Writing beyond the Ending: Narrative Strategies of Twentieth-Century Women Writers* (Bloomington, Ind.: Indiana University Press, 1985), 2; hereafter cited in the text.

8. Teresa de Lauretis, *Alice Doesn't: Feminism, Semiotics, Cinema* (Bloomington, Ind.: Indiana University Press, 1984), 5.

9. Linda Alcoff, "Cultural Feminism versus Post-Structuralism: The Identity Crisis in Feminist Theory," *SIGNS* 13, no.3 (1988): 434.

10. Jacques Lacan, "Homage to Marguerite Duras, on *Le ravissement de Lol V. Stein*," in *Duras by Duras* (San Francisco: City Lights Books, 1987), 124; first published in the *Cahiers Renaud-Barrault*, December 1965: "Marguerite Duras s'avère savoir sans moi ce que j'enseigne."

11. Marguerite Duras, *La Vie tranquille* (Paris: Librairie Gallimard, 1944), 53; hereafter cited in the text as *VT*. All translations are mine.

12. Juliet Mitchell and Jacqueline Rose, eds., *Feminine Sexuality: Jacques Lacan and the école freudienne* (New York: Pantheon Books, 1982) 30–31.

13. Kaja Silverman, *The Acoustic Mirror: The Female Voice in Psychoanalysis and Cinema* (Bloomington, Ind.: Indiana University Press, 1988), 7.

Chapter One

1. I have relied on numerous interviews Duras has given as well as on some of her own journalistic pieces for most of the biographical information

included in this chapter. Particularly useful are Michelle Porte, *Les Lieux de Marguerite Duras* (Paris: Editions de Minuit, 1977), which presents interviews done for two television programs broadcast in May 1976 on TF1; Xavière Gauthier, *Les Parleuses* (Paris: Editions de Minuit, 1974), translated as *Woman to Woman* by Katharine A. Jensen (Lincoln, Neb.: University of Nebraska, 1987); Suzanne Lamy and André Roy, *Marguerite Duras à Montréal* (Montreal: Editions Spirale, 1981), which includes several interviews and articles related to a 1981 colloquium in Montreal in which Duras participated; and a special issue of *Magazine littéraire* (June 1990), edited by Aliette Armel, that contains an excellent interview and articles by several of Duras's close friends and associates.

Alain Vircondelet's recent biography, *Duras, biographie* (Paris: Editions François Bourin, 1991), presents several problems. Although it is marred by numerous errors and a lack of scholarly apparatus (there are no footnotes and attribution of quotations is often inadequate), it nevertheless contains, intact, a few documents, like her letter of resignation from the Communist Party, that provide information about important events. All these sources are hereafter cited in the text, the translation being mine when none other is available.

2. In an interview with Bernard Pivot on "Apostrophes," on Antenne 2, 28 September 1984. This phrase was repeated, word for word, in a "Caractères" interview with Bernard Rapp, Antenne 2, 5 July 1991.

3. Marguerite Duras, *Les Yeux verts* (Paris: Cahiers du cinéma, 1987), 33–35; translated by Carol Barko as *Green Eyes* (New York: Columbia University Press, 1990), 21–23; hereafter cited in the text as *YV* and *GE* respectively. Photocopies of the letters and of the newspaper obituary are presented in the book; Barko chose not to translate them but, rather, to reproduce them as documents.

4. "Les nostalgies de l'amante Duras," an interview with Jean-Louis Ezine, *Le Nouvel observateur* 1442 (25 June-1 July 1992): 54; translation mine; hereafter cited in the text as Ezine.

5. Marguerite Duras, *La Vie matérielle* (Paris: P.O.L., 1987), 83; hereafter cited in the text as *VM*; translated by Barbara Bray as *Practicalities* (New York: Grove Weidenfeld, 1990), 73; Hereafter cited in the text as *P*.

6. Reprinted in Marguerite Duras, "L'horreur d'un pareil amour," *Outside: papiers d'un jour* (Paris: Albin Michel, 1981), 180–82. This volume, rereleased by P.O.L. in 1984, is a collection of Duras's journalistic writings from 1957 on. Hereafter cited in the text as *O*. Translated as "The Horror of Such Love," *Outside: Selected Papers* (Boston: Beacon Press, 1986), 237–40, by Arthur Goldhammer; hereafter cited in the text as *OS*. The English version does not include all the writings from the original; translations are mine except where a double reference is given.

7. Janine Ricouart, *Ecriture féminine et violence: une étude de Marguerite Duras* (Birmingham, Ala.: Summa Publications, 1991), 13; hereafter cited in the text; translation mine.

8. In 1974, in the 10/18 paperback series, and again in 1985, the

Editions de minuit published the novel along with selected book reviews published in 1958, when *Moderato Cantabile* first came out. Claude Roy's review is included among these.

9. With her usual disregard for dates, Duras correctly identifies the hospital stay as taking place in January 1980 but then says "I was seventy." She was hospitalized again in 1985, when she was seventy, but she had established contact with Andrea in 1980.

10. Three very useful articles that attempt to understand Duras's piece for *Libération* in terms of her other writing, particularly on the themes of absence, violence, transgression, and *woman*, are the two articles published together by David Amar and Pierre Yana under the title "'Sublime, forcément sublime,' A propos d'un article paru dans *Libération*," *Revue des sciences humaines* 202 (April–June 1986): 153–76, and Verena Andermatt Conley, "'L'affaire Gregory' and Duras's Textual Feminism," *L'Esprit Créateur* 30, no. 1 (Spring 1990): 69–75.

11. Marie-Pierre Fernandes, *Travailler avec Duras: La Musica Deuxième* (Paris: Editions Gallimard, 1986), 194–95; from a letter written by Duras to Fernandes from Trouville, 14 July 1985: "Les vrais écrivains n'ont pas de vie du tout. . . . Mes livres sont plus vrais que moi." My translation.

Chapter Two

1. See Elaine Marks, "Deconstructing in Women's Studies to Reconstructing the Humanities," in *Women's Place in the Academy: Transforming the Liberal Arts Curriculum*, ed. Marilyn R. Schuster and Susan R. Van Dyne (Totowa, N.J.: Rowman and Allanheld, 1985), 172–87; Domna Stanton, "Preface," in *The Female Autograph*, ed. D. Stanton (New York: New York Literary Forum, 1984), vii–xi; and Nancy K. Miller, "The Text's Heroine: A Feminist Critic and Her Fictions," *Diacritics* 12 (Summer 1982): 48–53.

2. Michèle Montrelay, *L'Ombre et le nom: sur la féminité* (Paris: Editions de Minuit, 1977), and Marcelle Marini, *Territoires du féminin avec Marguerite Duras* (Paris: Editions de Minuit, 1977), illustrate the first position, while Trista Selous, *The Other Woman: Feminism and Femininity in the World of Marguerite Duras* (New Haven: Yale University Press, 1988), illustrates the second.

3. Teresa de Lauretis, *Technologies of Gender* (Bloomington and Indianapolis: Indiana University Press, 1987), 10–11.

4. Marguerite Duras, *Un Barrage contre le Pacifique* (Paris: Editions Gallimard, 1950), 18; hereafter cited in the text as *B*; and *The Sea Wall*, translated by Herma Briffault (New York: Farrar, Strauss and Giroux, 1952; rereleased by Harper & Row in 1986 in the Perennial Library edition), 17; hereafter cited in the text as *SW*.

5. The published translation reads "Here begins the night that was the strangest in my whole life" (*SW*, 209). The French, however, uses "extraordi-

naire," and a more literal translation, I think, captures better the sense of the story he is about to recount (*B*, 228).

6. The published translation has: "it would have been a little like the *tremendous gloom* in the moving-picture theatres" (*SW*, 266). I offer "violent darkness" as a more literal translation of "obscurité violente" (*B*, 290) that is more consistent with the cinema imagery throughout the novel and the role of violence in Duras's representations of sexuality.

7. Marguerite Duras, *L'Eden Cinéma* (Paris: Mercure de France, 1977; edition "folio," 1986), 157; translation mine.

8. Marguerite Duras, *Des Journées entières dans les arbres* (Paris: Gallimard, 1954); hereafter cited in the text as *J*; and Anita Barrows, translator, *Whole Days in the Trees* (New York: Riverrun Press, 1984); hereafter cited in the text as *WD*.

9. Potentially, the maternal body could provide an alternative to the horror of Mlle Barbet's body. She thinks of her mother's body having nourished four children and the freshness of its smell. But this is a quick, undeveloped aside.

10. Jean E. Kennard, "Convention Coverage or How to Read Your Own Life," *New Literary History* 13, no. 1 (1981): 69–88, and "Ourself behind Ourself: A Theory for Lesbian Readers," in *Gender and Reading: Essays on Readers, Texts, and Contexts*, ed. Elizabeth A. Flynn and Patrocinio P. Schweickart (Baltimore: The Johns Hopkins University Press, 1986), 63–82.

11. The published translation has "individuality" instead of "personality" in this passage. However, in the French, "personnalité" is set off by quotation marks, adding emphasis both to the word and the choice of that word. Given the anthropomorphism of the image, I prefer to keep the word *personality* in the English.

12. This section is a revised version of part of my essay "Reading and Writing as a Woman: The Retold Tales of Marguerite Duras," *The French Review* 58, no. 1 (October 1984): 48–57.

13. Marguerite Duras and Xavière Gauthier, *Les Parleuses* (Paris: Editions de minuit, 1974), 67; Katharine A. Jensen, translator, *Woman to Woman* (Lincoln, Neb.: University of Nebraska Press, 1987), 44.

14. Marguerite Duras, *Le Marin du Gibraltar* (Paris: Editions Gallimard, 1952), 151; hereafter cited in the text as *MG*; and *The Sailor from Gibraltar*, translated by Barbara Bray (New York: Pantheon Books, 1966), 159; hereafter cited in the text as *SG*.

15. Judith Fetterley, *The Resisting Reader: A Feminist Approach to American Fiction* (Bloomington, Ind.: Indiana University Press, 1978).

16. The "reader" here is the reader inscribed in the text, Gerald Prince's "narratee." See Gerald Prince, "Introduction à l'étude du narrataire," *Poétique* 14 (1973): 178–96.

17. Jonathan Culler, *On Deconstruction: Theory and Criticism after*

Structuralism (Ithaca, N.Y.: Cornell University Press, 1982), 43–63; Culler borrows the term "reading as a woman" from Peggy Kamuf to define the second moment of feminist criticism. What happens to meaning in a text if we hypothesize that the reader is a woman and attempt to read in those terms?

Chapter Three

The discussion of *Moderato Cantabile* in this chapter is a revised version of part of my essay "Fiction et folie dans l'oeuvre de Marguerite Duras," *Ethique et esthétique dans la littérature française du XXᵉ siècle*, ed. Maurice Cagnon, Stanford French and Italian Series (Saratoga, Calif.: Anma Libri, 1978), 123–32; the discussion of the cycle of texts related to *L'Amante anglaise* is a revised version of part of "Reading and Writing as a Woman: The Retold Tales of Marguerite Duras," *The French Review* 58, no. 1 (October 1984): 48–57.

    1. Roland Barthes, "The Death of the Author," in *Image/Music/Text*, translated by Stephen Heath (New York: Hill and Wang, 1977); hereafter cited in the text.

    2. Nancy K. Miller, "Changing the Subject: Authorship, Writing, and the Reader," in *Subject to Change: Reading Feminist Writing* (New York: Columbia University Press, 1988), 102–121; hereafter cited in the text.

    3. Marguerite Duras, *L'Amante anglaise* (Paris: Gallimard, 1967), 9–10; hereafter cited in the text as *AA*; and *L'Amante anglaise*, translated by Barbara Bray (New York: Pantheon Books, 1968), 3; hereafter cited in the text as *AM*.

    4. Jonathan Culler, *On Deconstruction: Theory and Criticism after Structuralism* (Ithaca, N.Y.: Cornell University Press, 1982), 43–63. As I indicated in Chapter Two, Culler's formulation owes a debt to Peggy Kamuf's "Writing Like a Woman," in *Women and Language in Literature and Society*, ed. Sally McConnell-Ginet, Ruth Borker, and Nelly Furman (New York: Praeger, 1980), 284–99; and Judith Fetterley, *The Resisting Reader: A Feminist Approach to American Fiction* (Bloomington, Ind.: Indiana University Press, 1978), among others.

    5. Sharon Willis calls such characters, Jack Hold and Peter Morgan, for example, "narrated narrators" in *Marguerite Duras: Writing on the Body* (Urbana and Chicago: University of Illinois Press, 1987), 65; hereafter cited in the text.

    6. Marguerite Duras, *The Square* (Paris: Editions Gallimard, 1955), 9; hereafter cited in the text as *S*; and Marguerite Duras, *Four Novels by Marguerite Duras: The Square, Moderato Cantabile, 10:30 on a Summer Night, The Afternoon of Mr. Andesmas*, with an introduction by Germaine Brée, *The Square* translated by Sonia Pitt-Rivers and Irina Morduch, *Moderato Cantabile* by Richard Seaver, and *10:30 on a Summer Night* and *The Afternoon of Mr. Andesmas* by Anne Borchardt

(New York: Grove Press, 1965; Evergreen Edition, 1982), 3. Hereafter, the English translations of these novels are cited in the text as *FN*. The other French editions referred to are *Moderato Cantabile* (Paris: Editions de minuit, 1958), hereafter cited in the text as *MC*; and *Dix heures et demi du soir en été* (Paris: Editions Gallimard, 1960), hereafter cited in the text as *DH*. For some reason, Sonia Pitt-Rivers and Irina Morduch changed the wording of the first sentence and used "behind" or "beside" to translate "devant." I have changed the translation here to correspond more closely to the original.

7. Marguerite Duras, *Moderato Cantabile* (Englewood Cliffs, N.J.: Prentice-Hall, 1968), 9–10.

8. I have changed the translation slightly. The published translation has "a generally biased and individually noncommittal conversation builds up." I don't think this renders the style or tone of the French: "Et on débouche peu à peu sur une conversation généralement partisane et particulièrement neutre."

9. Erica M. Eisinger, "Crime and Detection in the Novels of Marguerite Duras," *Contemporary Literature* 15, no. 4 (Autumn 1974): 503–520.

10. Marcelle Marini, *Territoires du féminin avec Marguerite Duras* (Paris: Editions de minuit, 1977).

11. Carol J. Murphy, "Thematic and Textual Violence in Duras's *10:30 on a Summer Night*," *L'Esprit Créateur* 19, no. 2 (Summer 1979): 75–84.

12. The verb *devoir* is used repeatedly in this novel to qualify actions as desirable but not entirely certain. In later works, Duras will use the conditional mode in a similar way, evoking what might have been but what *is* only at the level of language.

13. The psychological urgency of the French is lost in the published English translation. The original is "Non, elle ne peut pas se passer de les voir. Elle les voit encore" (48). The translation is "No, she couldn't help seeing them. She could still see them" (138). The English suggests that it was physically impossible not to see them; the French suggests a psychological need to see them.

14. The published translation eliminates several key phrases. For "Elle voudrait *voir* se faire les choses," it has "She wanted things to happen." Also, when Duras chooses words (like *conjugaison*) that have a linguistic as well as a sexual reading, the translation chooses only the sexual connotation. Because the creation of narrative is so bound up with desire in Duras, I think it important, insofar as possible, to maintain those double connotations.

15. J. Laplanche and J.-B. Pontalis, *The Language of Psychoanalysis*, translated by Donald Nicholson-Smith (New York: W. W. Norton & Company, 1973), 318.

16. Marguerite Duras, *Le ravissement de Lol. V. Stein* (Paris: Gallimard, 1964), hereafter cited in the text as *LVS*; and *The Ravishing of Lol Stein*, translated by Richard Seaver (New York: Pantheon Books, 1966), hereafter cited in the text as *LS*. This translation is used except where indicated. Also, Marguerite Duras, *Le Vice-Consul* (Paris: Gallimard, 1966); hereafter cited in the text as

LVC; and *The Vice-Consul*, translated by Eileen Ellenbogen (New York: Pantheon Books, 1968), hereafter cited in the text as *VC*; and Marguerite Duras, *L'Amour* (Paris: Gallimard, 1971), never translated into English; hereafter cited in text as *LA*, translations mine.

17. Although Richard Seaver's translation is generally accurate and lively, some choices seem rather arbitrary and unexplained. Duras most often refers to Lol as Lol V. Stein. Seaver elimates the middle initial entirely. The town in the French is S. Tahla, which Seaver turns into South Tahla. The seaside town where the ball was held is T. Beach in the French and becomes Town Beach in the translation. These seem minor changes except that central themes of the novel include gaps in language and fragmentation of identity. The initials (and Lol instad of Lola, which is given a few times in the French) signal this obsession in a way that is lost in the English.

18. Meike Bal, in "Un Roman dans le roman: encadrement ou enchâssement? Quelques aspects du *Vice-Consul*," *Neophilologus* 58 (1974): 2–21, presents a detailed analysis of the structure of *The Vice-Consul*, relating it to *A Thousand and One Nights*. She argues that the story of the beggarwoman repeats in an extreme form every theme in the story of the Vice-Consul, becoming a *mise-en-abîme* of the primary story.

19. See especially Marcelle Marini, *Territoires du féminin avec Marguerite Duras* (Paris: Editions de minuit, 1977) and Sharon Willis's excellent discussion of Marini in *Marguerite Duras: Writing on the Body* (Urbana and Chicago: University of Illinois Press, 1987), 115–19.

Chapter Four

1. Marguerite Duras, "La Classe de la violence," interview with Dominique Noguez in *Marguerite Duras Oeuvres cinématographiques édition vidéographique critique* (Paris: Ministère des relations extérieures, 1984); hereafter cited in the text as *EVC*. All translations are mine.

2. *Détruire dit-elle* (1969), *Jaune le soleil* (1971), based on *Abahn Sabana David*, and *La Femme du Gange* (1972–73), based on *L'Amour* (1971).

3. Kaja Silverman, *The Acoustic Mirror* (Bloomington, Ind.: Indiana University Press, 1988), ix; hereafter cited in the text.

4. In her remarks on the text of *India Song*, Duras explains that the characters in *India Song* are dislodged from *The Vice-Consul* and "projected into new narrative regions." *India Song texte-théâtre-film* (Paris: Gallimard, 1973), 9.

5. Laura Mulvey, "Visual Pleasure and Narrative Cinema," in *Visual and Other Pleasures* (Bloomington, Ind.: Indiana University Press, 1989), 25; originally published in 1975. "Profilmic" refers to the images the camera records before being edited into the film itself.

6. The site of production is contrasted in film theory to the diegetic scene, that is, the fiction that is represented in the story of the film. The site of production is where the camera, filmmaker, and cinematic technology are locat-

ed, where the artifice is constructed. It is concealed from the viewer—or the viewer is shielded from it—in classic cinema in order to maintain the pleasurable illusion that the viewer is watching real or natural images, that he is in control of interpretation and is not being coerced. An unveiling of the site of production would remind him of his lack of control and disturb the pleasure of his illusion.

7. Cinematic apparatus, as Silverman notes, takes on greater importance in film theory as part of a reaction against privileging the individual voice or "auteur." The term *cinematic apparatus* refers to "the productive role of the technological [camera, recorder] and ideological apparatus." Silverman states that the camera and the recorder, identified with human vision and hearing, "make possible a certain anthropomorphism of the cinematic apparatus, its conceptualization in terms of a transcendental viewer and listener." In classic cinema this apparatus is concealed from the viewer to protect the viewer from knowledge of his exclusion from the site of production. She shows that "The absence of the site of production from the diegetic scene is as potentially disruptive of the viewer's pleasure as is the absence of the object" (Silverman, 11).

8. Marguerite Duras, *Hiroshima mon amour* (Paris: Gallimard, 1960); hereafter cited in the text as *H*; Richard Seaver, translator, *Hiroshima mon amour* (New York: Grove Press, 1961), 15; hereafter cited in the text as *HM*.

9. Deborah Glassman, "The Feminine Subject as History Writer," *Enclitic* 5, no. 1 (1981): 45–54.

10. Judith Mayne, "*Hiroshima mon amour*: Ways of Seeing, Ways of Telling," in *Annual Film Studies* (1978):50; hereafter cited in the text.

11. Catherine Portuges, "The Pleasures of *Nathalie Granger*," in *Remains to be Seen*, ed. Sanford Scribner Ames (New York: Peter Lang, 1988), 224.

12. Marguerite Duras, *Nathalie Granger suivi de la Femme du Gange* (Paris: Gallimard, 1973), 54; hereafter cited as *NG*. Translations mine.

13. Deborah Glassman, "Marguerite Duras's 'Indian Cycle,'" in *Ambiguities in Literature and Film*, ed. Hans P. Braendlin (Gainesville, Fla.: University Presses of Florida, 1988), 33–41; 36; hereafter cited in the text.

14. See Isabelle Raynauld, "Lire le film/ voir le texte," in *L'Arc*, 1990. Duras uses the term *texte-théâtre-film* for the written text of *India Song*.

15. Marie-Claire Ropars-Wuilleumier, "The Disembodied Voice: *India Song*," in *Yale French Studies* 60 (1980): 241–68; hereafter cited in the text.

16. Elisabeth Lyon, "*Woman of the Ganges* by Marguerite Duras," in *Camera Obscura* 2 (Fall 1977): 125–26.

17. Sharon Willis, *Marguerite Duras: Writing on the Body* (Urbana and Chicago: University of Illinois Press, 1987), 65; Willis uses this term for both Jack Hold in *The Ravishing of Lol Stein* and Peter Morgan in *The Vice-Consul*.

18. Marie-Claire Ropars-Wuilleumier, "La mort des miroirs: *India Song, Son nom de Venise dans Calcutta désert*," in *L'Avant-scène Cinéma* 225 (1 April 1979), gives an excellent summary and analysis of these two films and then presents a complete *découpage*, showing the relationship of the images of each film

to their common sound track. I am indebted to this article and to "The Disembodied Voice: *India Song*" in *Yale French Studies* 60 for the summary given here. A translation of the shooting script, prepared by Marguerite Duras, is available in *Duras by Duras* (San Francisco: City Lights Books, 1987), 17–66.

19. Xavière Gauthier, "Dispossessed," in *Duras by Duras* (San Francisco: City Lights Books, 1987), 81; hereafter cited in the text as *DD*. My own response.

20. The scenario was published in *Le Camion suivi de Entretien avec Michelle Porte* (Paris: Les Editions de minuit, 1977); hereafter cited in the text as *C*; translations mine.

21. Janet Maslin, "Film Festival: 'The Truck Talks and Talks but It Says Very Little,'" *New York Times*, 27 September 1977; Pauline Kael, "The Current Cinema: Contrasts," *New Yorker*, 26 September 1977, pp. 123–33; hereafter cited in the text.

22. Three exceptions are *Le Navire Night* (1979), 94 minutes long, *Agatha ou Les Lectures illimitées* (1981), 90 minutes, and *Dialogo di Roma* (1982), 62 minutes, but these are even more difficult to see than the short subjects I discuss.

23. Marguerite Duras, *Le Navire Night et autres textes* (Paris: Mercure de France, 1979; reedited 1986), 89; hereafter cited in the text as *NN*; translation mine.

Chapter Five

1. Marguerite Duras, *L'Amant* (Paris: Les Editions de minuit, 1984), 20; hereafter cited in the text as *A*. The original French is "Soudain je me vois comme une autre, comme une autre serait vue, au-dehors, mise à la disposition de tous, mise dans la circulation des villes, des routes, du désir." Translated by Barbara Bray as *The Lover* (New York: Random House, 1985), 13; hereafter cited in the text as *L*.

2. Marguerite Duras, *L'Homme assis dans le couloir* (Paris: Les Editions de minuit, 1980), hereafter cited as *HA*. This text is available in translation in Mary Lydon, "Translating Duras: 'The Seated Man in the Passage,'" *Contemporary Literature* 24 (1983): 259–75; hereafter cited as *M*. It has also been translated by Barbara Bray as *The Man Sitting in the Corridor* (New York: North Star Line, 1991). I will refer to Lydon's translation, however, because she addresses problems of translating Duras in the article that contains her translation.

3. Marguerite Duras, "L'Homme assis dans le couloir," in *Les yeux verts*, *Les Cahiers du cinéma* (Paris: Gallimard, 1980; reissued with additional essays in 1987), 60; hereafter cited in the text as *YV*. Carol Barko, translator, "L'Homme assis dans le couloir," in *Green Eyes* (New York: Columbia University Press, 1990), 42; hereafter cited in the text as *GE*.

4. Catharine A. MacKinnon, *Feminism Unmodified: Discourses on Life and Law* (Cambridge, Mass.: Harvard University Press, 1987), 50–54.

5. Marguerite Duras, *L'Homme atlantique* (Paris: Les Editions de minuit, 1982); hereafter cited in the text as *HAt*. As there is no published English translation, all translations are mine. The following discussion is based, in part, on my essay "Reading and Writing as a Woman: The Retold Tales of Marguerite Duras," *The French Review* 58 (1984): 48–57.

6. Marguerite Duras, *La Maladie de la mort* (Paris: Les Editions de minuit, 1982), 7; hereafter cited in the text as *MM*. "Vous devriez ne pas la connaitre, l'avoir trouvée partout à la fois, dans un hôtel, dans une rue, dans un train, dans un bar, dans un livre, dans un film, en vous-même, en toi, au hasard de ton sexe dressé dans la nuit qui appelle où se mettre, où se débarrasser des pleurs qui le remplissent." Translation by Barbara Bray, *The Malady of Death* (New York: Grove Weidenfeld, 1986), 1; hereafter cited in the text as *MD*. Note that the first clause, "Vous devriez ne pas la connaître, could also be translated "You should not have known her," almost an imperative that the woman be unknown, anonymous.

7. Aliette Armel, "J'ai vécu le réel comme un mythe," interview with Marguerite Duras, *Magazine littéraire* 278 (1990): 24 (my translation); hereafter cited in the text as Armel.

8. In a June 1981 interview with Suzanne Lamy in Paris, Duras discussed the essential antagonism between men and women, concluding: "We are irreconcilable, we've been trying for thousands of years to make it up between us. . . . That's what I call the fabulous richness of heterosexuality. And, on the other hand, the immeasurable misery of homosexuality. They [masculine] love themselves in loving the other. Whereas we love our reverse image." Marguerite Duras, *Marguerite Duras à Montréal*, ed. Suzanne Lamy and André Roy (Montréal: Editions Spirale, 1981), 69 (my translation).

9. Marguerite Duras, *Yeux Bleus cheveux noirs* (Paris: Les Editions de minuit, 1986), 9; hereafter cited in the text as *YB*. The French is: "Une soirée d'été, dit l'acteur, serait au coeur de l'histoire." Translated by Barbara Bray, *Blue Eyes, Black Hair* (New York: Pantheon Books, 1987); hereafter cited in the text as *BE*. I have given a literal translation rather than that proposed in the published translation because Bray's stylistic choice obscures the use of the conditional mode.

10. Marguerite Duras, *La Pute de la côte Normande* (Paris: Les Editions de minuit, 1986), 16 (my translation).

11. Philippe Lejeune, *On Autobiography*, edited by Paul John Eakin, translated by Katherine Leary (Minneapolis: University of Minnesota Press, 1989), 4; hereafter cited in the text. This edition brings together several of Lejeune's ground-breaking studies in autobiography.

12. My reading of *The Lover* is informed by the many excellent, suggestive readings that have been done by French and American scholars. I am particularly indebted to Deborah Glassman, *Marguerite Duras: Fascinating Vision and Narrative Cure* (London and Toronto: Associated University Presses, 1991), who stresses the visual character of memory in the novel; Leah D. Hewitt,

Autobiographical Tightropes: Simone de Beauvoir, Nathalie Sarraute, Marguerite Duras, Monique Wittig, and Maryse Condé (Lincoln, Neb.: University of Nebraska Press, 1990), who discusses the role of the body, anonymity, and portraits of women as well as the mingling of autobiography and fiction; and Sharon Willis, *Marguerite Duras: Writing on the Body* (Urbana and Chicago: University of Illinois Press, 1987), who discusses the woman as a figure of transgression and the novel's susceptibility to multiple readings.

13. Sidonie Smith, *A Poetics of Women's Autobiography: Marginality and the Fictions of Self-Representation* (Bloomington, Ind.: Indiana University Press, 1987), 17; hereafter cited in the text.

14. Deborah Glassman, *Marguerite Duras: Fascinating Vision and Narrative Cure*, 141. In a footnote, Glassman tells an anecdote alluded to in several of Duras's interviews: that her son, himself a photographer, asked her to comment on a family photo album that was subsequently lost. Whether this anecdote is true or part of the growing mythology about Duras is not as important as the primacy given to the image, the photograph, and particularly to the lost or nonexistent photograph, in structuring meaning in this book.

15. The original is: "C'est à ce manque d'avoir été faite qu'elle doit sa vertu, celle de représenter un absolu, d'en être justement l'auteur" (17). The translation obscures two suggestive word choices in this key passage. "Manque" is translated as "failure," which is appropriate, but the French word also means "lack," and recalls the "hole-word" of Lol V. Stein. "Auteur," which is translated as "creator," blurs the double connotation of authority and authorship in the original.

16. Elizabeth W. Bruss, "Eye for I: Making and Unmaking Autobiography in Film," in *Autobiography: Essays Theoretical and Critical*, ed. James Olney (Princeton, N.J.: Princeton University Press, 1980), 299. This essay updates her original thesis as developed in *Autobiographical Acts* (Baltimore: The Johns Hopkins Press, 1976). Hereafter cited in the text.

17. Marguerite Duras, *L'Amant de la Chine du Nord* (Paris: Gallimard, 1991), 12; hereafter cited in the text as *AC*. Leigh Hafrey, translator, *The North China Lover* (New York: The New Press, 1992), 2; hereafter cited in the text as *NL*.

18. The story of the origins of *The North China Lover* and the making of the film of *The Lover* is documented in a special issue of *Lire: Le magazine des livres* 193 (October 1991) devoted to Marguerite Duras. See, especially, Pierre Assouline, "Cinéma, cinémas," 56; and an interview with Pierre Assouline, "Mes amours, c'est à moi," 58–59.

19. Marguerite Duras, *La Douleur* (Paris: P.O.L., 1985); hereafter cited in the text as *D*. Barbara Bray, translator, *The War: A Memoir* (New York: Pantheon Books, 1986); hereafter cited in the text as *W*.

20. Marguerite Duras, "Pas mort en déportation," in *Outside: Papiers d'un jour* (Paris: Albin Michel, 1981), 288–92. This text is inexplicably omitted from the translation by Arthur Goldhammer, *Outside: Selected Writings* (Boston: Beacon Press, 1986).

21. "Dans les jardins d'Israël, il ne faisait jamais nuit," in *Les Yeux verts*, translated by Carol Barko as "In the Gardens of Israel, It was Never Night," in *Green Eyes*.

22. Marguerite Duras, "La population nocturne," in *La Vie matérielle* (Paris: P.O.L., 1987), 149; translated by Barbara Bray as "The People of the Night," in *Practicalities* (New York: Grove Weidenfeld, 1990), 135.

23. In an interview with Bernard Rapp on French television "Antenne 2," "Caractères" #41, 5 July 1991.

24. Marguerite Duras, *Emily L.* (Paris: Les Editions de minuit, 1987); hereafter cited in the text as *E*. Barbara Bray, translator, *Emily L.* (New York: Pantheon Books, 1989), 12; hereafter cited in the text as *EL*.

25. "Comme une messe de mariage," article based on an interview with Marguerite Duras and Didier Eribon, *Le Nouvel observateur* 1197 (16–22 October 1987): 61.

26. Jacques Lacan, "Homage to Marguerite Duras, on *Le ravissement de Lol V. Stein*," in *Duras by Duras*, ed. Lawrence Ferlinghetti and Nancy J. Peters (San Francisco: City Lights Books, 1987), 124; originally published in *Cahiers Renaud-Barrault*, December 1965.

27. Bice Benvenuto and Roger Kennedy, *The Works of Jacques Lacan, An Introduction* (New York: St. Martin's Press, 1986), 92; hereafter cited in the text; Jacques Lacan, "Le séminaire sur 'La Lettre volée,'" in *Ecrits I* (Paris: Editions du Seuil, 1966), 19–75.

28. Emily Dickinson, *The Complete Poems of Emily Dickinson* (Boston: Little, Brown and Company, 1960), poem number 258, probably composed in 1861, published posthumously in 1890.

29. In another Lacanian echo, the law of the father (le non du père) ensures the continuing name of the father (le nom du père).

30. American readers, especially those who know women's writing, recognized Duras's borrowing from Dickinson and saw its significance. See Marianne Hirsch, "Inside Stories," *Women's Review of Books* 8, no. 1 (October 1990): 19–20, and Vicki E. Mistacco, "Plus ça change. . .: The Critical Reception of *Emily L.*," *The French Review* 66, no. 1 (October 1992): 77–88. Mistacco reads the Dickinson reference as a commentary on a female literary tradition that unsettles canon formation. She also makes an interesting argument about gender and reception, looking at the women writers and male readers within the novel as well as at readings that were made of the novel and of Duras in 1987 when *Emily L.* was published.

31. This is the image that Duras footnotes in *L'Amant de la Chine du Nord*, 149; *The North China Lover*, 141.

32. Marguerite Duras, *La Pluie d'été* (Paris: P.O.L., 1990), hereafter cited in the text as *PE*. Barbara Bray, translator, *Summer Rain* (New York: Charles Scribner's Sons, 1992); hereafter cited in the text as *S*.

33. Marguerite Duras, *La Vie matérielle* (Paris: P.O.L., 1987), 83; translated by Barbara Bray as *Practicalities* (New York: Grove Weidenfeld, 1990), 73.

34. Marguerite Duras, *Yann Andréa Steiner* (Paris: P.O.L., 1992). As the book is not yet translated, all translations are mine. Hereafter cited in the text as *Y*.

35. "Alain Veinstein" and "The Voice in *Navire Night*" in *Practicalities*.

36. Marguerite Duras, *Outside: Papiers d'un jour* (Paris: Albin Michel, 1981), 293.

Chapter Six

1. "Floating Picnic," an unsigned review of *The Sailor from Gibraltar*, *Time*, 7 July 1967; J.W. Lambert, "'Tis a pity she's a bore," *The Sunday Times*, 28 August 1966.

2. Pierre Assouline, "La vraie vie de Marguerite Duras," *Lire: Le magazine des livres* 193 (October 1991): 49.

3. Sharon Willis, *Marguerite Duras: Writing on the Body* (Urbana and Chicago: University of Illinois Press, 1987), 2.

4. Christine Gledhill, "Pleasurable Negotiations," in *Female Spectators Looking at Film and Television*, ed. E. Deidre Pribram (London: Verso, 1988), 68; hereafter cited in the text.

5. Vicki E. Mistacco, "Plus ça change . . .: The Critical Reception of *Emily L.*," *The French Review* 66, no. 1 (October 1992): 77–88. I am indebted to Mistacco for her analysis in this article of gender and writing in reader response; she does an extensive analysis of Rambaud and others who responded "extravagantly" to the novel.

6. Danielle Bajomée, *Duras ou la douleur*, (Brussels: De Boeck-Wesmael, 1989); hereafter cited in the text; translation mine.

7. In his homage to Duras and Lol V. Stein in 1965, Lacan said "it turns out that Marguerite Duras knows, without me, what I teach." Jacques Lacan, "Homage to Marguerite Duras, on *Le ravissement de Lol. V. Stein*," in *Duras by Duras*, ed. Lawrence Ferlinghetti and Nancy J. Peters (San Francisco: City Lights Books, 1987), 124; originally published in *Cahiers Renaud-Barrault*, December 1965.

8. Marguerite Duras, *Marguerite Duras à Montréal*, ed. Suzanne Lamy and André Roy (Montreal: Editions Spirale, 1981), 61.

9. Julia Kristeva, "The Pain and Sorrow in the Modern World: The Works of Marguerite Duras," *PMLA* 2 (1987): 138–52, translated by Katherine A. Jensen; emphasis added. Hereafter cited in the text.

10. Françoise Defromont, "Faire la femme: différence sexuelle et énonciation," *Fabula* 5 (1985): 111.

11. Christine Anne Holmlund, "Displacing Limits of Difference: Gender, Race, and Colonialism in Edward Said and Homi Bhabha's Theoretical Models and Marguerite Duras's Experimental Films," *Quarterly Review of Film & Video* 13 (1991): 15.

12. "Caractères," interview with Bernard Rapp, Antenne 2, 5 July 1991; translation mine.

Selected Bibliography

PRIMARY SOURCES

Novels and Stories

Abahn, Sabana, David. Paris: Editions Gallimard, 1970.
L'Amant. Paris: Les Editions de minuit, 1984. Translated as *The Lover* by
    Barbara Bray. New York: Pantheon Books, 1985.
L'Amant de la Chine du Nord. Paris: Editions Gallimard, 1991. Translated as *The*
    North China Love by Leigh Hafrey. New York: The New Press, 1992.
L'Amante anglaise. Paris: Editions Gallimard, 1967. Translated as *L'Amante*
    Anglaise by Barbara Bray. New York: Pantheon Books, 1987. Rewrites
    the 1960 play *Les Viaducs de Seine-et-Oise*; readapted for the theater in
    1968 as *L'Amante anglaise.*
L'Amour. Paris: Editions Gallimard, 1971.
L'Après-midi de M. Andesmas. Paris: Editions Gallimard, 1962. Translated as *The*
    Afternoon of Mr. Andesmas by Anne Borchardt in *Four Novels by Marguerite*
    Duras, with an introduction by Germaine Brée. New York: Grove Press,
    1965.
Un Barrage contre le Pacifique. Paris: Editions Gallimard,1950. Translated as *The*
    Sea Wall by Herma Briffault. New York: Harper & Row, 1986.
Détruire dit-elle. Paris: Les Editions de minuit, 1969. Translated as *Destroy, She*
    Said by Barbara Bray. New York: Grove Press, 1986.
Dix Heures et demie du soir en été. Paris: Editions Gallimard, 1960. Translated as
    10:30 on a Summer Night by Anne Borchardt in *Four Novels by Marguerite*
    Duras, with an introduction by Germaine Brée. New York: Grove Press,
    1965.
La Douleur. Paris: P.O.L., 1985. Translated as *The War: A Memoir* by Barbara
    Bray. New York: Pantheon Books, 1987.
Emily L. Paris: Les Editions de minuit, 1987. Translated as *Emily L.* by Barbara
    Bray. New York: Pantheon Books, 1989.
L'Eté 80. Paris: Les Editions de minuit, 1980.
L'Homme assis dans le couloir. Paris: Les Editions de minuit, 1980. Translated as
    The Man Sitting in the Corridor by Barbara Bray. New York: North Star
    Line, 1991. Also translated as *The Seated Man in the Passage* by Mary
    Lydon in "Translating Duras: 'The Seated Man in the Passage,'"
    Contemporary Literature 24 (1983): 259–75.
L'Homme atlantique. Paris: Les Editions de minuit, 1982.
Les Impudents. Paris: Editions Plon, 1943. Rereleased by Editions Gallimard,
    "Collection Folio," 1992.

Des Journées entières dans les arbres. Paris: Editions Gallimard, 1954. Translated as
    Whole Days in the Trees by Anita Barrows. New York: Riverrun Press,
    1983.
La Maladie de la mort. Paris: Les Editions de minuit, 1982. Translated as *The*
    Malady of Death by Barbara Bray. New York: Grove Press, 1986.
Le Marin de Gibraltar. Paris: Editions Gallimard,1952. Translated as *The Sailor*
    from Gibraltar by Barbara Bray. New York: Pantheon Books, 1966.
Moderato Cantabile. Paris: Les Editions de minuit, 1958. Rereleased in the
    "Collection 10/18" series, 1973 with an essay, "L'Univers romanesque de
    Marguerite Duras," by Henri Hell, and a "dossier de presse," including
    several reviews. Translated as *Moderato Cantabile* by Richard Seaver in
    Four Novels by Marguerite Duras, with an introduction by Germaine Brée.
    New York: Grove Press, 1965.
Les Petits Chevaux de Tarquinia. Paris: Editions Gallimard, 1953. Translated as
    Little Horses of Tarquinia by Peter DuBerg. New York: Riverrun Press,
    1986.
La Pluie d'été. Paris: P.O.L., 1990. Translated as *Summer Rain* by Barbara Bray.
    New York: Charles Scribner's Sons, 1992.
Le Ravissement de Lol. V. Stein. Paris: Editions Gallimard, 1964. Translated as
    The Ravishing of Lol Stein by Richard Seaver. New York: Pantheon Books,
    1986. First published in English in 1966 by Grove Press.
Le Square. Paris: Editions Gallimard, 1955. Translated as *The Square* by Sonia
    Pitt-Rivers and Irina Morduch in *Four Novels by Marguerite Duras,* with an
    introduction by Germaine Brée. New York: Grove Press, 1965.
Le Vice-Consul. Paris: Editions Gallimard, 1965. Translated as *The Vice-Consul* by
    Eileen Ellenbogen. New York: Pantheon Books, 1987. Originally pub-
    lished in English by Hamish Hamilton, Great Britain, 1968.
La Vie tranquille. Paris: Editions Gallimard, 1944.
Yann Andréa Steiner. Paris: P.O.L., 1992.
Les Yeux bleus cheveux noirs. Paris: Les Editions de minuit, 1986. Translated as
    Blue Eyes, Black Hair by Barbara Bray. New York: Pantheon Books,
    1987.

Scenarios and Films

Marguerite Duras: Oeuvres cinématographiques, édition vidéographique critique.
    Edited by Pascal-Emmanuel Gallet, essay and interviews by Dominique
    Noguez. Paris: Ministère des relations extérieures, bureau d'animation
    culturelle, 1984. This collection contains videotapes of eight films fol-
    lowed by interviews with Marguerite Duras and Dominique Noguez. An
    accompanying booklet contains the unedited transcripts of the inter-
    views. The films and accompanying interviews are as follows: *Nathalie*
    Granger (1972) suivie de "La Classe de la violence"; *India Song* (1974) suivi
    de "La Couleur des mots"; *Son nom de Venise dans Calcutta désert* (1976)

suivi de "Le Cimetière anglais"; *Le Camion* (1977) suivi de "La Dame des Yvelines"; *Césarée* (1979), *Les Mains négatives* (1979), *Aurélia Steiner (Melbourne)* (1979), and *Aurélia Steiner (Vancouver)* (1979) suivis de "La Caverne noire" et "Work and Words."

Aurélia Steiner (Melbourne). Film, 35' color. 1979.
Aurélia Steiner (Vancouver). Film, 48' black and white. 1979.
Une aussi longue absence. Paris: Editions Gallimard, 1961. Scenario written in collaboration with Gérard Jarlot.
Le Camion. Film, 80' color. 1977.
Le Camion suivi de Entretien avec Michelle Porte. Paris: Les Editions de minuit, 1977.
Césarée. Film, 11' color. 1979.
Détruire dit-elle. Film, 90' black and white. Distribution: S.N.A., 1969.
Dialogo di Roma. Film, 62' color. 1982. Made for Italian television.
Les Enfants. Film, 90' color. 1984. Adapted as a text in *La Pluie d'été (Summer Rain)*, 1990.
La Femme du Gange. Film, 90' color. Adaptation of the novel *L'Amour*. Producers: Service de la recherche de l'O.R.T.F., 1972–73.
Hiroshima mon amour. Paris: Editions Gallimard,1960. Scenario and dialogues with a preface by Marguerite Duras. Translated as *Hiroshima mon amour* by Richard Seaver. New York: Grove Press, 1961. Film made by Alain Resnais in 1959, distributed by Zenith International Film Corporation.
L'Homme atlantique. Film, 42' color and black and white. 1981.
India Song. Film, 120' color. 1974.
Jaune le soleil. Film, 80' black and white. Adaptation of the novel *Abahn Sabana David*. Producers: Albina Productions, 1971.
Les Mains négatives. Film, 18' color. 1979.
La Musica. Film, 80' black and white. Distribution: Artistes Associés, 1966. Made with Paul Seban.
Nathalie Granger. Film, 83' black and white. 1972.
Nathalie Granger suivie de la Femme du Gange. Paris: Editions Gallimard, 1973. Texts for the two films.
Le Navire Night et autres textes. Paris: Mercure de France, 1979. Contains the texts of "Le Navire 'Night'"; "Césarée"; "Les mains négatives"; and three versions of "Aurélia Steiner," two of which were made into films.
Son nom de Venise dans Calcutta désert. Film, 120' color.1976.
Vera Baxter ou les plages de l'Atlantique. Paris: Editions Albatros, 1980. Scenario.

Theater

Agatha. Paris: Les Editions de minuit, 1981.
L'Amante anglaise. Paris: Cahiers du Théâtre National Populaire, 1968.
L'Eden Cinéma. Paris: Editions Gallimard, 1978.

La Musica deuxième. Paris: Editions Gallimard, 1985.

Savannah Bay. Paris: Les Editions de minuit, 1983.

Théâtre I: Les Eaux et forêts; Le Square; La Musica. Paris: Editions Gallimard, 1965.

Théâtre II: Suzanna Andler; Des Journées entière dans les arbres; 'Yes,' peut-être; Le Shaga; Un homme est venu me voir. Paris: Editions Gallimard, 1968.

Théâtre III: Adaptations of La bête dans la jungle; Les papiers d'Aspern; La danse de la mort. Paris: Editions Gallimard, 1984.

Les Viaducs de Seine-et-Oise. Paris: Editions Gallimard, 1960.

Essays and Interviews

Duras, Marguerite. *Outside: Papiers d'un jour.* Paris: Editions Albin Michel, 1981. Rereleased Paris: P.O.L., 1984. Translated as *Outside: Selected Writings* by Arthur Goldhammer. Boston: Beacon Press, 1986.

———. *Les Parleuses.* Paris: Les Editions de minuit,1974. Conversations with Xavière Gauthier. Translated as *Woman to Woman* by Katherine A. Jensen. Lincoln, Neb.: University of Nebraska Press, 1987.

———. *La Pute de la côte normande.* Paris: Les Editions de minuit, 1986. A twenty-page essay about the summer of 1986, focused on an effort to stage *The Malady of Death* and reflecting on her relationship with Yann Andréa.

———. *La Vie matérielle.* Paris: P.O.L., 1987. Translated as *Practicalities* by Barbara Bray. New York: Grove Weidenfeld, 1990.

———. *Les Yeux verts.* Paris: Cahiers du cinéma,1980. Reissued in 1987. Translated as *Green Eyes* by Carol Barko. New York: Columbia University Press, 1990.

Farges, Joël, ed. *Marguerite Duras.* Paris: Albatros, 1979. Translated by Nancy J. Peters and Amy Scholder as *Duras by Duras.* San Francisco: City Lights Books, 1987. The collection contains occasional pieces and working notes by Marguerite Duras as well as essays by Jacques Lacan, Maurice Blanchot, Dionys Mascolo, and others.

Lamy, Suzanne, and André Roy, eds. *Marguerite Duras à Montréal.* Montreal: Editions Spirale, 1981. This book includes several interviews and articles related to a 1981 colloquium in Montreal in which Duras participated.

Pivot, Bernard. "Apostrophes." Antenne 2, 28 September 1984.

Porte, Michelle. *Les Lieux de Marguerite Duras.* Paris: Editions de minuit, 1977. This volume presents interviews done for two television programs broadcast in May 1976 on TF1.

Rapp, Bernard. "Caractères." Antenne 2, 5 July 1991.

SECONDARY SOURCES

Books

Many excellent books and articles on Duras have appeared in recent years in both French and English. This list is very selective, representing the most useful and provocative titles. For additional titles of interest, especially articles in journals and chapters in books, see the notes.

Ames, Sanford, ed. *Remains To Be Seen: Essays on Marguerite Duras*. New York: Peter Lang, 1988. Uneven collection of articles, growing out of a 1983 conference. Of special interest: essays by Yvonne Guers-Villate on *La Maladie de la Mort*, Carol Murphy on *L'Amant*, and Catherine Portuges on *Nathalie Granger*.

Andréa, Yann. *M.D.* Paris: Editions de minuit, 1983. Vivid firsthand account of Duras's detoxification treatment at the American Hospital in Neuilly, October–November 1982.

Armel, Aliette. *Marguerite Duras et l'autobiographie*. Paris: Le Castor Astral, 1990. A journalist's effort to examine Duras's autobiographical writing as a distinctive cycle in her work.

Bajomée, Danielle. *Duras ou la douleur*. Brussels: De Boeck Université, 1989. An often sensitive study, considering pain as an organizing anthropology or philosophy of Duras's writing.

Bajomée, Danielle, and Ralph Heyndels, eds. *Ecrire, dit-elle: Imaginaires de Marguerite Duras*. Brussels: Editions de l'Université de Bruxelles, 1985. Collection of essays by leading French critics of Duras, including one by Michel de Certeau.

Bernheim, Nicole-Lise. *Marguerite Duras tourne un film*. Paris: Editions Albatros, 1974. Interviews with the cast and crew of *India Song*.

Borgomano, Madeleine. *L'écriture filmique de Marguerite Duras*. Paris: Albatros, 1985. The only book length study of Duras's filmmaking.

Glassman, Deborah. *Marguerite Duras: Fascinating Vision and Narrative Cure*. Rutherford, N.J.: Fairleigh Dickinson Press, 1991. Focuses primarily on films and texts of the Indian cycle.

Guers-Villate, Yvonne. *Continuité/Discontinuité de l'oeuvre durassienne*. Brussels: Editions de l'Université de Bruxelles, 1985. Study of thematic and discursive continuity and discontinuity in Duras.

Hewitt, Leah D. *Autobiographical Tightropes: Simone de Beauvoir, Nathalie Sarraute, Marguerite Duras, Monique Wittig and Maryse Condé*. Lincoln, Neb.: University of Nebraska Press, 1990. Excellent study of *The Lover* in the context of contemporary French and Francophone autobiographical writing by women.

Marini, Marcelle. *Territoires du féminin avec Marguerite Duras*. Paris: Editions de minuit, 1977. Often cited early effort to define "the feminine" in Duras's work.

Montrelay, Michèle. *L'Ombre et le nom: Sur la féminité*. Paris: Editions de minuit, 1977. With Marini, cited above, an important study of "the feminine" in Duras's works through the mid-1970s.

Murphy, Carol J. *Alienation and Absence in the Novels of Marguerite Duras*. Lexington, Ky.: French Forum Publishers, 1982. First major study in English; looks at Duras's major texts through *India Song*.

Papin, Liliane. *L'Autre Scène: Le Théâtre de Marguerite Duras*. Saratoga, Calif.: Anma Libri, 1988. One of the few books on Duras's theater.

Ricouart, Janine. *Ecriture féminine et violence: une étude sur Marguerite Duras*. Birmingham, Ala.: Summa Publications, 1991. A provocative study of thematic and stylistic violence toward and by women in Duras; attempts to bring together American and French theoretical perspectives.

Selous, Trista. *The Other Woman: Feminism and Femininity in the World of Marguerite Duras*. New Haven and London: Yale University Press, 1988. Beginning with a lengthy summary of Freud, Lacan, Irigaray, and other French psychoanalytic theorists of the feminine, Selous contests earlier arguments that blanks and gaps represent the "repressed feminine." Rejects the notion that Duras is a feminist writer.

Vircondelet, Alain. *Duras: biographie*. Paris: Editions François Bourin, 1991. At this writing the only biography of Duras; unfortunately marred by many errors and a lack of scholarly apparatus.

———. *Marguerite Duras ou le temps de détruire* Paris: Seghers, 1972. One of first books devoted to Duras.

Willis, Sharon A. *Marguerite Duras: Writing on the Body*. Urbana and Chicago: University of Illinois Press, 1987. Grounded in French feminist and psychoanalytic theory, this important book analyzes the body and discourse in Duras and presents her as a transgressive writer interrogating the "feminine."

Special Issues of Periodicals

L'Arc 98 (1985). Includes articles by Marini, Noguez, Borgomano, Barrault and others.

Cahiers de la Compagnie Madeleine Renaud-Jean Louis Barrault 52 (1965). Special issue on Duras in which Jacques Lacan originally published his "Hommage à Marguerite Duras"; 91 (1975) includes a discussion with Duras, Renaud, Barrault, and several actors, including Emmanuelle Riva, who played in *Hiroshima Mon Amour*; 106 (1983) includes an interview and several articles on the occasion of the production of *Savannah Bay*.

Camera Obscura: A Journal of Feminism and Film Theory 6 (1980). Contains a dossier on Duras including a translation of "Notes on *India Song*" by Duras and an important essay by Elisabeth Lyon.

L'Esprit Créateur 30:1 (Spring 1990). Most articles are in English, including an essay by Germaine Brée and several reviews of books on Duras.

Journal of Durassian Studies. A journal devoted exclusively to Duras, published by the Duras Society, George Mason University, Fairfax, Virginia 22030, Janine Ricouart, editor. Begun in fall 1989, there were three volumes as of spring 1992.

Magazine littéraire 278 (June 1990). Includes an excellent interview with Aliette Armel.

Revue des Sciences humaines 202 (April-June 1986). Includes interesting articles by David Amar and Pierre Yana on the controversial article Duras wrote for *Libération* in July 1985 about Christine Villemin ("Sublime, forcément sublime").

Index

176

Index

The Author

Marilyn R. Schuster is professor of French and women's studies at Smith College. She completed her B.A. at Mills College and her Ph.D. in French literature at Yale University. She has published articles on nineteenth- and twentieth-century French and North American literature, especially fiction written by women. She has also published articles on curriculum transformation (incorporating feminist and ethnic studies scholarship throughout the curriculum) and co-edited *Women's Place in the Academy: Transforming the Liberal Arts Curriculum* (Totowa, N.J.: Rowman & Allanheld, June 1985) with Susan R. Van Dyne.